Serialized Citizenships

Periodicals, Books, and American Boys, 1840–1911

Lorinda B. Cohoon

The Scarecrow Press, Inc.
Lanham, Maryland • Toronto • Oxford
2006

SCARECROW PRESS, INC.

Published in the United States of America
by Scarecrow Press, Inc.
A wholly owned subsidiary of
The Rowman & Littlefield Publishing Group, Inc.
4501 Forbes Boulevard, Suite 200, Lanham, Maryland 20706
www.scarecrowpress.com

PO Box 317
Oxford
OX2 9RU, UK

British Library Cataloguing in Publication Information Available

Library of Congress Cataloging-in-Publication Data

Cohoon, Lorinda B., 1968–
Serialized citizenships : periodicals, books, and American boys, 1840-1911 / Lorinda B. Cohoon.
p. cm.
Inclues bibliographical references and index.
ISBN-13: 978-0-8108-5425-3 (pbk. : alk. paper)
ISBN-10: 0-8108-5425-2 (pbk. : alk. paper)
1. Children's periodicals, American—History—19th century. 2. Children's periodicals, American—History—20th century. 3. Boys—Books and reading—United States. I. Title.
PN4878.C64 2006
051.09′034—dc22 2005033226

™The paper used in this publication meets the minimum requirements of American National Standard for Information Sciences—Permanence of Paper for Printed Library Materials, ANSI/NISO Z39.48-1992.
Manufactured in the United States of America.

For my parents and siblings

Contents

Illustrations

FIGURES

Acknowledgments

Serialized Citizenships could not have been written without the advice and support of many colleagues and friends. This project emerged from a dissertation written under the direction of Ellen Weinauer and Anne Wallace at the University of Southern Mississippi, and I thank them for their ongoing support throughout the writing of the book. The English departments at the University of Texas at El Paso and the University of Memphis have also provided significant support for this project. A University Research Institute Grant from UTEP made travel to archives possible. My chair, Stephen Tabachnick, at the University of Memphis has generously offered encouragement and support for the project. I am also grateful to many colleagues from these and other institutions, and I would especially like to thank Shelley Armitage from UTEP, Desirée Henderson from UT Arlington, and Ladrica Menson-Furr from the University of Memphis for listening to ideas and offering sage advice at crucial moments in the development of this project.

From the world of children's literature scholarship, I have received support from the Children's Literature Association. I am grateful to the ChLA for a faculty research grant, which made it possible for me to travel to archives of children's literature and complete research that was necessary to develop the project. The ChLA is an organization known for providing resources to support scholars and scholarship in the field of children's literature, and I have found this to be true. I thank all the members and especially Lynne Vallone, Anne K. Phillips, and Mark West for research support, encouragement, and advice. I would also like to thank the *Children's Literature Association Quarterly* for permission to reprint in chapter four an expanded version of "Necessary Badness: Reconstructing Postbellum American Boyhood in *Our Young Folks* and *The Story of a Bad Boy*," which first appeared in *Children's Literature Association Quarterly* 29.1/2 (Spring/Summer 2004): 5–31. I am grateful to *Dime Novel Round-Up* for permission to reprint a portion of chapter one, which was previously published as "Jacob Abbott's 'Jonas' Books and the Construction of an 1840s Middle-Class Boyhood" in *Dime Novel Round-Up* 70.2 (April 2001): 43–56.

A number of archives were used to gather materials for this study. Dee Jones, former curator of the de Grummond Collection; Gina Marie Pugliese, archivist of the de Grummond children's literature collection; and the other staff members of the McCain Library and Archives of the University of Southern Mississippi have provided valuable assistance with images and materials. Archivists from the Philadelphia Free Library, especially Joël Sartorius, and the Boston Public Library offered assistance with materials from the newspapers and periodicals of the 1840s. The Parkman Dexter Howe Collection and the Baldwin Collection of the University of Florida and the Scribner Archives of Princeton University proved useful resources for chapters on Thomas Bailey Aldrich and Frances Hodgson Burnett. Andrea Immel of Princeton University's Cotsen Collection gave early assistance and advice. I also thank librarians from the University of Illinois, Urbana and West Chester University.

For their constant support and for providing insight into twenty-first century "bad" boys, I thank my family.

Introduction

Nineteenth-Century Boyhood Citizenships in Periodical Serializations

> There is enough good literature for men and women—enough for children; but is there quite enough for the wide-awake, aspiring American boy who is just turning the corner into manhood?
>
> —William C. Sprague, *The American Boy Magazine*, 1899

When William C. Sprague noted in 1899 that boys needed good literature of their own, he signaled an awareness of the distinctions made in American culture between boyhood and manhood and a corollary connection between literature and citizenship, which is highlighted in Sprague's idea that literature is needed to help the "aspiring" boy "turn the corner" into manhood. In the United States, an awareness of boyhood citizenship arose during the nineteenth century, and with this interest came ongoing attempts to define, explain, and repair boys and their problems so that they would reach their full potential as citizens. In the first part of the nineteenth century, publishing industries for boys' periodical literature and boys' books began to be developed—writers produced and boys bought both the "good" literature Sprague mentions and other more sensational, popular texts, which were full of action, intrigue, and violence. Boys' periodical literature and series books thrived in the second half of the nineteenth century, and the success in this publishing arena continued to foster the growing cultural interest in boys and their emerging citizenships. The fascination with boyhood that emerged during the nineteenth century and the boy literature that it helped to spawn have continued to shape boyhood citizenships in the United States, so much so that profitable and widespread boyhood industries have flourished for over a century.

During the late twentieth and early twenty-first centuries, nonfiction texts about boys, and especially bad boys, sold to thousands of adult readers living and working with boys in the United States. Best-selling psychology and sociology titles include Michael Gurian's 1996 *The Wonder of Boys: What Parents, Mentors, and Educators Can Do to Shape Adolescent Boys into Exceptional Men*, William Pollack's 1998 *Real Boys: Rescuing Our Sons from the Myths of Boyhood*, and Dan Kindlon and Michael Thompson's 1999 *Raising Cain: Protecting the Emotional Life of Boys*. Using history and other textual evidence to resist theorists who argue that gender and sex are socially and culturally constructed, Gurian argues that boys are "wired differently" and need to be biologically reinstated as boys (45). Pollack writes that "[b]oys today are in serious trouble" (xix) and suggests that myths about bad boys are partially to blame: "[a] myth has been created of the young boy as the rascal and the scamp, the mischievous lad who loves to run and be loud. . . . He's tough. He breaks the rules" (xx). Critiquing the presence of women in the workplace, Pollack argues that mothers and teachers who are women do not allow boys enough time and space to express their emotions or to be what he calls "real boys": "boys are pushed to separate from their mother prematurely. . . . As early as age five or six, many boys are pushed out of the family and expected to be independent—in school, at camp, at all kinds of activities and situations they may or may not be ready to handle" (xxii).[1] Judging from the proliferation of these manuals, "naturally bad" boyhoods are one of the most prevalent late twentieth-century constructions of boyhood; the manuals struggle to place blame for cultural exacerbations of the "badness" of boys.

Literary and cultural theorists have also become interested in the treatises on boyhood and their work in the construction of masculinity. In *Making American Boys* (2004), Kenneth Kidd examines the history of the "boyology" texts that treat the "problem" of boys and explores the connections between the boyology and another form he terms the "feral tale," which uses narrative drawn partly from folktales and myths to meditate on the "wildness" of boys. Kidd argues that both the boyology and the feral tale are "implicated in larger historical narratives about human and cultural development" and that they "help mark the momentous changes by which we recognize modernity" (1). As part of his significant study, Kidd points out that the boyology form was tied more closely to American constructions of and obsessions with boyhood and finds that in the early twentieth century there was a similar proliferation of manuals that addressed, much as do their late twentieth-century and contemporary counterparts, the nature/nurture makeup of boys and the best methods of raising them.[2] Both early and later boyhood manuals suggest that literature is a significant component in society's crimes against boys, and frequently, it is the literature published for children during the nineteenth century that serves as a basis for some of the best-known narratives about boyhood.

Serialized Citizenships argues that the periodical literature of the nineteenth century, with its complex mixture of contributors, readers, and genres, offers insights into links between adult constructions of boyhood citizenships, national literary and political conversations about directions for citizenships, and literary and nonliterary responses to the constraints and requirements of adult citizenship in the United States. Adult responses to nineteenth-century literature about boys have contributed to what Lyotard would term "grand narratives" about boyhood, and these are frequently repeated in critical and popular studies on the topic. *Serialized Citizenships* seeks to challenge these totalizing narratives by closely examining the cultural context of boyhoods that are considered "representative" and also the contexts of other literary boyhoods that have been forgotten or ignored. If literature is used to explain bad boyhood, then it is important to better understand nineteenth-century periodical literature, since periodicals served as significant producers and manufacturers of culture at the time when narratives about American boyhood were being rapidly produced.

Using a cultural studies approach informed by feminist and poststructuralist theory, this book draws on portrayals of both bad and good boyhood in periodicals in order to closely investigate, challenge, and understand the boyhood citizenships constructed by texts designed specifically for children. In a discussion of the problems (and possibilities) inherent in the cultural studies approach in *The Idea of Culture* (2000), Terry Eagleton cautions that "Culture is . . . symptomatic of a division which it offers to overcome. . . . it is itself the illness to which it proposes a cure" (31). Since my project explores the cultural contexts of American boyhoods, I want to signal my awareness of the drawbacks that Eagleton notes and to complicate them. When "culture," in the form of what Eagleton describes as "questions of value, symbolism, language, tradition, belonging, or identity" (130), is used (as it is in the best-selling help-for-boys books) to describe and proliferate a problem perceived as being rooted in "literature," a homeopathic approach of culture countering culture works to simultaneously "acknowledg[e] [culture's] significance, [and] to put it back in its place" (131). Thus, while it may admittedly be symptomatic, this study of boyhood citizenships in periodical literature calls for continuing examination of the relationship between literature and local, regional, and national citizenship-shaping cultures. Lisa Lowe's persuasive arguments in *Immigrant Acts* about the role culture plays in social and political change have influenced my study of periodical and series books as repositories of both disregarded and celebrated boyhood citizenships.[3] By examining the historical and social contexts of the periodicals and their responses to regional and national politics and history, *Serialized Citizenships* suggests that periodicals and series books have influenced the construction of boyhood citizenships and shaped generations of adult responses to citizenship.

Overviews of boyhood published in studies of United States children's literature and histories of United States childhood have repeatedly defined boyhood as ahistorically stable. In the 1990s, scholars such as E. Anthony Rotundo in *American Manhood* (1993) and Dana Nelson in *National Manhood* (1998) challenged this stability with explorations of the concepts of "American" and "national" in relation to manhood and masculinity, but there have not yet been many studies of localized and particularized constructions of American boyhood.[4] Archives of children's literature provide some records of how American boyhood has been "textually" constructed, but this can sometimes be limiting in that well-known and often republished works about American boys such as Mark Twain's *Tom Sawyer* and *Huckleberry Finn* become the definitive sites for explaining American boyhood in the nineteenth and twentieth centuries. Noting this problem, Suzanne Rahn argues, "[t]he effect of focusing all serious attention on a small number of books and authors is to diminish awareness of the richness and variety of children's literature" (xv). When all (or most) attention is focused on one or two texts, another effect is the limiting of the kinds of textual boyhoods that are remembered and made part of the world of children's literature.

Within the realm of children's literature scholarship, there are discipline-related reasons for a continued focus on only a small number of texts, but this limited focus is slowly changing. Children's literature became a division of the Modern Language Association in 1980. Concerned with "serious" children's literature scholarship, members of the children's literature division explored issues of canonicity, with one resulting project a three-volume discussion of "touchstone" texts that were worthy of study.[5] Part of the concern with establishing a canon had to do with perceptions that most children's books are not sufficiently "literary" and therefore, according to scholars concerned with aesthetics, not worthy of study. Contemplating how ideas about the literary and childhood intervene in the production and definition of children's texts, Peter Hunt writes: "Because they are, in the main, marginalized by the arbiters of literary taste, children's books are thought to have certain appropriate characteristics (such as simplicity of language, limited viewpoint, or perfunctory characterization) and, consequently, many books are produced which have these characteristics" (4). Those scholars who helped to establish the field of children's literature battled disciplinary marginalization and did so by choosing to study texts that were more complicated, closer in structure, style, and characterization to adult literature.[6] While canon exploration helped to shape the discipline, it also tended to limit studies to well-known texts. The discipline of children's literature, which has shifted from focusing defensively on the canon, has begun to expand the texts studied. This shift has encouraged study of periodicals and series books, and along with this has come an awareness of how the canonical texts emerge from much larger discursive arenas, including children's periodicals, literature for adults, studies of Americanness, and manuals about boyhood. These larger arenas have influenced the literary boyhoods that are considered canonical and that are understood as representative of boyhood and also national citizenship. They have helped to define what it means to be an American boy.

While histories of childhood and the still developing discipline of children's literature have defined American boyhood, histories of American literature have also played a part in constructing American boyhood. Leslie Fiedler's thesis in *Love and Death in the American Novel* claims that in Huck Finn and Jim, Hawkeye and Chingachgook, and Ishmael and Queequeg, boyish men and their dark others proliferate versions of citizenship in which a "bad" boyhood that rebels against social norms is somehow an inherent part of Americanness. This badness manifests itself in harmless pranks against adult establishments, in restlessness, and in the breaking of laws that govern relations between white men and other citizens. Although Fiedler's theories have since been extended and complicated, the idea that American boys reach manhood by continuing to embrace boyhood as a world apart, a "light[ing] out for the Territory," is one that persists in studies of "canonical" literature and in explorations of boyhood.[7]

Although the canonical records are indubitably among the many cultural forces that constructed (and continue to construct) American boyhoods, the best-known texts were not produced in isolation from other texts. Many of the now recognized texts about American boyhoods, such as *Story of a Bad Boy* (1869) and *Huckleberry Finn* (1885), were first serialized in periodicals alongside other versions of boyhood but, until the late twentieth century, the importance of the periodical in shaping U.S. literary histories had not been extensively examined. Book histories that do take into account the significance of the periodical include Cathy N. Davidson's *Revolution and the Word* (1986) and Richard H. Brodhead's *Cultures of Letters: Scenes of Reading and Writing in Nineteenth-Century America* (1993), as well as Kenneth M. Price and Susan Belasco Smith's *Periodical Literature in Nineteenth-Century America* (1995). Aleta Feinsod Cane and Susan Alves's *"The Only Efficient Instrument": American Women Writers and the Periodical, 1837–1916* (2001) and Meredith L. McGill's *American Literature and the Culture of Reprinting, 1834–1853* (2003) also examine the connections between serializations, literary culture, and nation. These examinations of the history of the book resist the notion that the representative American books were somehow products of the solitary white male genius and that the "good" ones survive because of this. The recent attention that has been paid to book histories and to forms of production exposes the dense history of book culture in the United States, and points to ways in which this history can be expanded by further study of the periodical.[8]

During the nineteenth century, periodicals, far more than novels, were influential in shaping attitudes about citizenship in a young nation. Commenting on the cultural work of the periodical in the nineteenth century, Smith and Price suggest that the "periodical—far more than the book—was a social text, involving complex relationships among writers, readers, editors, publishers, printers, and distributors" (3). The *New York Mirror* said of the 1840s, "This is the golden age of periodicals," and I begin my study in this age partly because changes in printing technology, transportation, and education during the 1830s helped make periodicals widely available in the 1840s.[9] In the nineteenth-century United States, literacy rates rose rapidly at the same time that transportation and printing technologies changed to make reading material accessible across the states and the western territories. These changes allowed the form of the periodical and all of the social aspects of periodical culture to contribute to the construction of American boyhoods. Periodicals for children especially exploit the social aspects of the form to actively shape what Brodhead terms the "cultural identity" of the readers (6). The serialized formats of texts about and for boys record the "complex relationships" between publishers, authors, and readers that contribute to the initial textual construction of those American boyhoods that are both canonically and popularly known today.

Periodical literature and the texts that it helped to produce had enormous cultural influence on the framing and construction of both boyhood and Americanness. Boys' periodicals published between the 1840s and the 1900s contain hints of the complex construction processes behind the ongoing packaging of American boyhoods. My study, however, does not propose to construct a new metanarrative about American boyhoods in periodical literature. Rather, it examines serializations of boys' books published in periodicals and finds that the boyhoods in literary histories (*Story of a Bad Boy*, *Huckleberry Finn*) are linked, through rich histories, to other, less familiar texts (*Rollo at School*, *Jonas a Judge*, *The Boat Club*, and *Little Lord Fauntleroy*). Both the canonical and noncanonical texts concern themselves with boyhood citizenships and reveal how periodicals constructed those citizenships and reflected changes in citizenship definitions over time.[10] In the 1840s, Jacob Abbott's serializations educate middle-class boys about stable property ownership and peacemaking techniques, while magazines for working-class boys suggest that boys need to improve the quality of their citizenships through courses of controlled reading. Series books in the 1850s reflect political obsessions with tightly defined party identities as they shift from emphasizing individual property to examining the possibilities for variation of character type within boyhood clubs. Serialized boyhoods from the late 1860s emphasize the need to recall and narrate the boyhoods of the past in order to control the manhoods of the future. In the 1880s, the serialized *Little Lord Fauntleroy* shows a boy using his physical appearance and his conversational skills to export his version of American citizenship to England, while *Huckleberry Finn* constructs the American boy as someone who seeks out the wilderness in order to avoid the daily contacts of citizenship. Later serializations in the 1890s and beyond show that the *Fauntleroy* and *Huckleberry Finn* versions of boyhood continue to influence citizenships, even as the permutations respond to the specific times and contexts of production. In the regularly produced reading material of the periodical form, American customs, educational philosophies, and understandings of subjectivity are constructed in conjunction with repeated attempts to define boyhood citizenships.

Some serialized boyhoods continue to shape current cultural understandings of citizenships of boys, girls, men, and women. The cultural elevation of some text-based boyhoods and the submergence of others continue to construct boyhood citizenship. Books about boys, in their serialized and full-text productions, combined with the histories of reading evidenced in the readers' letters sent to the periodicals, provide partial records of what Pierre Bourdieu calls "particular case[s] of the possible" (xi).[11] These records fill in gaps in current understandings of the construction process of United States boyhoods, and also undermine and create fissures in the monolithic stories that have been told and retold about the American boy adventure quest. During the early nineteenth century, boys' books focus on New England boyhoods and depict them as all-white and all-male enterprises, and if only these books are read, nonwhite and non–New England versions of boyhood are fairly easily marginalized or ignored. The contextual material of the periodicals and the repetitious form of the series books, however, return repeatedly to expanded concepts of United States citizenships. This serialized repetition suggests that it is in questions of citizenship that the contradictions and impossibilities of the national, regional, and local status of African Americans, Native Americans, girls, and others emerge; significant commentary about children with citizenship potential is found in narratives about those with already conferred, government-granted citizenship privileges.[12]

My project examines citizenships and investigates their gendered nature—a gendered nature that is always filtered through race and class. Although it is beyond the scope of this book, an important future study might sift through archival material to better describe how the portable form of the periodical and the self-advertising nature of series books helped to circulate the boyhood citizenships promoted in these texts to those readers to whom the privileges of citizenship were denied. The "particular cases" of boyhood citizenship examined here reflect literary histories of children's literature, available texts and periodicals, and my own tastes and histories. The United States boyhoods that have shaped my existence, like the early periodicals and texts I explore, emerged from the rural and urban areas of New England: Keene, New Hampshire, and the Dorchester, Roxbury, and Mission Hill sections of Boston. I want to counteract what Jonathan Arac calls the "prevailing idolatry" of certain texts about American boys (*Huckleberry Finn* as first among them), while admitting (as Arac does) that the texts I choose to explore illustrate my participation in these "idolatries" as well as my own idiosyncratic idolatrous tendencies—I am as fond of Rollo and Cedric as I am of Huck (18).

Throughout *Serialized Citizenships*, I use the broad terms, what Raymond Williams would term "key words," *manhoods*, *boyhoods*, *citizenships*, and *Americanness*, to think through the periodical contexts of boyhood citizenship. One of the difficulties of investigating powerful, hegemonically controlled concepts such as manhood and boyhood is that their boundaries continue to be controlled by the disciplines that participate in these investigations.[13] Addressing this problem, R. W. Connell writes, "Gender terms are contested because the right to account for gender is claimed by conflicting discourses and systems of knowledge" (3). My study strives to avoid making broad discipline-bound generalizations about manhood and boyhood by exploring serialized texts within their local production contexts.

Manhood is, in my use, a state experienced through time and a term that designates cultural expectations: a set of cultural values/norms to be moved toward, reached, and maintained for a relatively long period of a man's life.[14] As sociological and historical explorations of masculinity suggest, conceptions of what constitutes a "man" or "boy" are, like constitutions of "woman" and "girl," always tied up with history and culture. In *Manhood in the Making*, David D. Gilmore makes this clear when he suggests that manhood is "a culturally imposed ideal to which men must conform whether or not they find it psychologically congenial. It is . . . part of public culture" (4). Definitions of manhood and manhood's boundaries, then, vary according to culture.

Related to manhood but not identical to it is the concept of masculinity. Expanding the definition that manhood involves acts of public conformity to cultural ideals or norms, Gail Bederman argues in *Manliness and Civilization* that "manhood or masculinity is the cultural process whereby concrete individuals are constituted as members of a preexisting social category—as men" (7). Masculinity is not, like manhood, related to a period of years, except in the sense that cultural definitions shift over time. As Michael Kimmel points out in *Manhood in America*, masculinity was "proved" differently in the 1850s than it was in the 1880s:

> *Manhood* had been understood to define an inner quality, the capacity for autonomy and responsibility, and had historically been seen as the opposite of *childhood*. Becoming a man was not taken for granted; at some point the grown-up boy would demonstrate that he had become a man and had put away childish things. At the turn of the century, *manhood* was replaced gradually by the term *masculinity*, which referred to a set of behavioral traits and attitudes that were

> contrasted now with a new opposite, *femininity*. Masculinity was something that had to be constantly demonstrated, the attainment of which was forever in question—lest the man be undone by a perception of being too feminine (120).

Both manhood and masculinity delimit behaviors and expectations related to the male gender, but as Kimmel helps make clear, masculinity and the ways it is proved constantly shift.[15] Interestingly, in dress, in speech, and in physical performance, masculinity is something that can be performed by women. Manhood, on the other hand, is not generally thought of as something that it is possible for women to achieve.

In relation to these definitions of manhood, boyhood might be similarly understood as both a time period (experienced in a set amount of time by individual boys) and a term to locate and contain a variety of behaviors. The time periods for defining boyhood also shift according to cultural constructions. In the late twentieth and early twenty-first centuries, some United States boyhoods last until the boys are in their late twenties. In the 1890s, upper-middle-class and middle-class boys experienced a similar kind of extended boyhood, with marriage and property ownership delayed until the boys had reached their late thirties. Even though it can vary in length, boyhood is finite, in most textual constructions of the term, and therefore somehow precious.

The "preciousness" of boyhood provides part of the impetus to write texts about boyhoods—as something lost, it is also something that can be recaptured nostalgically through texts and images. In *Being a Boy Again*, Marcia Jacobson points out that this move toward nostalgia in "boy books" was particularly strong in the late nineteenth century and that periodicals played a role in distributing this form.[16] The use of the children's periodical as a space for nostalgic texts about boys was one way in which adults actively constructed the boyhoods of the young readers. The popularity of the boys' texts during this time simultaneously permitted the reconstruction of the manhoods and womanhoods of the authors and publishers. In *Male Matters* (1996), a study of constructions of masculinity that connects gender to the physical act of writing, Calvin Thomas assesses the "social construction of masculinity, the repression of the male body that is necessary to that construction, and the way that writing—as a corporeal and material process, a way of putting the body on the line—can disturb or subvert that repression" (2). If, as Thomas contends, writing is somehow central and also anxiety-producing to bodily masculinity, then the series books and their regular, serialized production for boys represents a certain kind of anxiously embodied boyhood masculinity.

Boyhood, as it is constructed in serialized texts, is also figured as a time to shape, practice, and cultivate behaviors of manhood. Boys are the participants in boyhood, while authors of texts about boys are former boys, or observers of boys, but not usually current participants in boyhood. The textually constructed celebratory boyhoods reflect on memories of boyhood and reshape boyhood in the retelling. These texts also serve, in their subsequent canonization, to define citizenships and "Americanness" through the construction of boyhoods set in America, boyhoods defined by America, and American boyhoods juxtaposed against an English setting.

Boyishness is a corollary term to the previously discussed *masculinity*. Again, young girls (and even older ones—older boys as well) can be boyish. Texts about groups of girls often incorporate a boyish figure into the mix of characters—Jo in *Little Women* and George in the Nancy Drew series. Authors of serialized texts for boys can, with shifts in narrative perspective and with the use of pseudonyms, use "boyish" performances to convince their readers of their knowledge. In *Female Masculinity*, Judith Halberstam provides a compelling study of the complexity of masculinity and boyishness and their connections to tomboys, butch/femme subjectivities, and drag king performances. *Boyishness*, like the term *masculinity*, draws attention to what Judith Butler calls the "performative" nature of both gender and sex.

A variety of critical and theoretical investigations into gender, sexuality, power, citizenship, and serialization have shaped my exploration of boyhood citizenships in periodical literature. My reading of the function of periodicals in constructing boyhood citizenships has been influenced by Judith Butler's theories of gender, and it is helpful here to clarify the connections between her theorizing of gender and my own theories about serialization. In her groundbreaking studies, Butler argues that binary sex and gender distinctions are blurred and linked to culturally ordered performative acts.[17] Butler's *Gender Trouble* examines whether gender is "an expectation that ends up producing the very phenomenon that it anticipates" (xiv). The language of production and performance that Butler uses to explore gender intersects with my vision of how periodicals intervene in the constructions of American boy citizenships. With regular monthly or weekly publications, the serialized constructions of boyhood located in periodicals provide readers with stage directions for accurately directing their bodies to perform as American boy citizens. It is in the regularity and the widespread availability of the periodical material that I especially see connections to the availability of directions for performing gendered citizenships.

In periodicals for boys, there are connections between texts and the construction of gender. Making the connections between writing and gender even more evident, *Bodies that Matter* considers the textual in Butler's theory of the "materiality of bodies":

> If the body signified as prior to signification is an effect of signification, then the mimetic or representational status of language, which claims that signs fol-

> low bodies as their necessary mirrors, is not mimetic at all. On the contrary, it is productive, constitutive, one might even argue *performative*, inasmuch as this signifying act delimits and contours the body that it then claims to find prior to any and all signification [Butler's emphasis] (30).

In her examination here of language's ongoing construction of the gendered body, Butler emphasizes the "productive" and "performative" nature of language. My study has been informed by this proposal that the named/signified body (as boy/as boyish) itself is ambiguous, and that gender and gendered behaviors are always already produced by prior signification. The regular production of periodicals participates in proliferating the signified and textually gendered bodies. As the titles of many periodicals demonstrate, naming the bodies of the readers becomes more important toward the end of the nineteenth century. These naming moves indicate one of the ways periodical production intervenes in the performativity of the reading bodies of the subscribers.

In addition to the study of serialized texts for boys revealing how boyhood is performed, more detailed understandings of serialized boyhood citizenships can also participate in feminist goals of opening possibilities for girls. Kaja Silverman's work on "male subjectivity" suggests that studying masculinity is an important part of the feminist project, and Silverman suggests that part of the problem is that the "reality" of our "entire world" centers on the construction of "classic masculinity" and the "pivotal status of the phallus": "Since everything that passes for 'reality' within a given social formation is articulated in relation to these terms, they represent ideological stress points. . . . within our dominant fiction, the phallus/penis equation occupies absolute pride of place" (16). Part of Silverman's participation in the feminist project involves challenging the "dominant fiction" of phallic masculinity by providing a "theoretical articulation of some non-phallic masculinities"(3).[18] My project also finds it useful to ask questions about what "passes for 'reality'" and to elucidate "reality's" connection to the represented—in the case of my study, the serially represented (Silverman 21).

Although ideology does not account for all of the ways "state apparatuses" or dominant power structures can be constructed and challenged, Louis Althusser's theories about ideology provide provocative ways of understanding aspects of serialized production. For example, the letters that editors invite readers to write and the editorial addresses and prospectuses that are ever-present parts of the periodicals present interesting cases of particularly active construction and recruitment of ideologically cooperative subjects through "interpellation" or hailing of the subject.[19] In considering serialized boyhoods, both those that contribute to "classic masculinity" and those that challenge it, it becomes evident that the serialized constructions of mostly white American boyhoods point up anxieties about other subjectivities (slaves, children of color, immigrants) and their citizenship privileges in the common school classroom, in the factory, in town government, and in the "wilderness." In thinking about citizenship and serialization, I have used *citizenship* to refer to both national citizenship, which is offered fully when boys reach manhood, and also regional and local citizenships. These "smaller" citizenships are not as well defined, but are available to the young citizens in the serialized novels and to subscribers to the various periodicals. Roger M. Smith's *Civic Ideals* usefully notes that *citizenship* has always been a contradictory and shifting term in the United States, with equality as one of the central issues that constantly gestures to the entrenched inequities in the national citizenship system. Other theories of citizenship, particularly Lauren Berlant's studies of national investment in producing and maintaining what she calls "infantile citizenships," have been particularly useful in my thinking about the influence of the periodical's regularity and repetition on citizenship.[20] The multiple voices of authors, editors, publishers, and subscribers that participate in the periodical scene indicate the dominant citizenships and also register less familiar, marginalized citizenship possibilities. Even the most familiar serialized texts are surrounded by a variety of other articles and perspectives that, in their multiplicity and multivocality, reveal and resist the dominant ideologies that construct white middle-class boyhood as *the* boyhood citizenship of nineteenth-century literature.

Many of the boyhood stories that are told in the periodical literature and in series books focus on one middle-class white boy and show how he establishes his citizenship in relation to a variety of other boys and other men. These serialized productions of boyhood preoccupy themselves with the possibilities of homosocial boyhoods and in doing so hint at the ways serialized gender construction negotiates sexualities in the nineteenth century. In *Between Men*, *Tendencies*, and *Epistemology of the Closet*, Eve Kosofsky Sedgwick postulates links between the homosocial, the homoerotic, and the patriarchal, and she states that one of her purposes is to "to hypothesize the potential unbrokenness of a continuum between homosocial and homosexual—a continuum whose visibility, for men, in our society, is radically disrupted" (*Between Men* 1–2). In many of the serializations, homosocial relationships suggest that textual representations of homoerotic desire depend on local and national citizenships that are defined by education and ownership, by willingness to follow rules and to remember the past, and by physical beauty and the ability to use conversation to make positive social changes. Frequently, the productions of these homosocial relationships in periodicals and series books depend for their success on the "sameness" of their format. Within this sameness, the author–reader relationships replicate homosocial–homoerotic continuums and demonstrate how the serialized contexts of these American boyhoods contribute to gender constructions that the hegemonic cultures have subsequently embraced or buried.

The hegemonic pressures and counterpressures that shape how literature defines American boyhood come together in *The Adventures of Huckleberry Finn*, a text that has informed this study and continues to shape current constructions of boyhood.[21] Obviously, since it is a canonical and simultaneously popular text of American literature, some aspects of this text must have coincided with dominant conceptions of boyhood available at the time of publication and afterwards. Literary and cultural arbiters of taste, particularly New England readers like Louisa May Alcott, who must have, twenty-first century readers of her anonymous works speculate, privately reveled in Huck's adventures, seemed to feel it was necessary to publicly censure the book. Alcott used her familial and literary clout to denounce the book, and her criticisms forwarded debate about the book that has lasted over a century.[22] In the periodical literature of the nineteenth century, knowledge about boyhood is also debated, and these disputes seem to reveal active construction sites of boyhood (3). Many of the serialized texts claim specific or "healthier" knowledge about boys, and these claims signal that the periodicals are a self-proclaimed source of alternative knowledge to other reading material used by boys to define their boyhoods and their citizenships.

Clearly, *The Adventures of Huckleberry Finn* disrupts the status quo of boyhood at the same time that it endorses the kinds of boyhood masculinities considered safe by the dominant discourses of the culture. When American boyhood is defined by images, Huck's fishing and rafting in overalls is more safely boyish than Fauntleroy's debating politics in black velvet and lovelocks. It is my contention that both the disruption and the embrace are caused in part by the manifestation of Huck's boyhood and its connection to expressions of Americanness. Likewise, the Americanness of other serialized boyhoods also influences their subsequent submergence in the archive or their elevation in canonical status.

Some literary boyhoods are remembered because they are viewed over time as more American than others. On the other hand, some boyhoods are seen as American because they can be viewed as definitively boyish. How then is this Americanness defined? Admittedly, *Americanness* is a broad and imprecise term. I use it to suggest citizenship in the United States, but I am always uncomfortable with the term, since it appropriates all of the Americas and endows the word only with the privileges belonging to a small portion. *Americanness*, as I use it, includes those aspects of boyhood and manhood that, in their expression, put into practice and define the privileges and customs of citizenship in the United States and vice versa. That is, *Americanness* is partially defined by permutations of boyhood and manhood. During the nineteenth century, Americans took stock of their national identity by anxiously examining their literature for signs of "Americanness," while European travelers such as Alexis de Tocqueville assessed American national identity for the benefit of both European and American readers. The term then refers to practices of citizenship as they occur within the boundaries of the United States and in relation to outside nations and countries.

Americanness and *American* provide useful terms to point toward citizenship privileges that in the nineteenth century contributed to the construction of boyhood. The use of the term *Americanness* to adjectivally characterize a section (the United States) suggests a tendency to make assumptions about the boyhoods and the citizenships collected under this one heading. Americanness is a central topic in periodical literature of the nineteenth century and especially in serializations for boys. As a concept, it is one of the everyday concerns of the characters and also part of the editorial commentaries inserted into the narratives by the authors. As *Serialized Citizenship* shows, an emphasis on Americanness can be seen in Jacob Abbott's discussions of laws and properties, in George Light's recommendations for self-improvement, in William Taylor Adams's characterizations of small-town boys, in descriptions of holidays and activities that punctuate the day-to-day life of boys in Thomas Bailey Aldrich's *Story of a Bad Boy*, and in the philanthropic republicanism that Frances Hodgson Burnett exports to England in *Little Lord Fauntleroy*. The ongoing connections made between boyhood and Americanness indicate that nineteenth-century serializations were citizen-shaping projects.

In examining how serializations shape boyhood citizenships, my project extends Michael Kimmel's 1996 *Manhood in America*, which suggests that the notion of the self-made man drives current conceptions of American manhood. During the middle part of the nineteenth century, the "cult of the self-made man," which Kimmel sees as analogous to the cult of true womanhood, was distributed through numerous books cataloging how poor boys achieved success through their own hard work.[23] Some of the patterns that Kimmel traces for American manhood coincide with constructions of American boyhood in serialized texts while other serializations challenge them. For example, when the periodicals of the 1840s offer detailed instructions for training boys to make themselves, these explicit guidelines challenge the notion of the self-made man. Text-made boys, these serializations suggest, make the "self-made" men who shape the notions of Americanness Kimmel's text records. This examination of the production history of periodicals for children, then, extends current histories of American boyhood to demonstrate that there were and are multiple citizenships and multiple boyhoods.[24] The form and the content of children's serialized texts open portable and regularly constructed spaces that contain and create boyhood citizenships that diverge from and intersect with histories of Americanness and manhood that continue to be written.

During the 1840s, *The Youth's Companion* used its portable space to construct American boyhoods. In my first chapter, "Educating Boys for American Citizenship: Jacob Abbott's Contributions to *The Youth's Companion*," I examine 1840s issues of this periodical and focus on one of its most prolific contributing authors, Jacob Abbott, the producer of Rollo, a figure often used by literary histories as an example of a character who is too well-behaved to be a boy and too orderly and safety-loving to be American.[25] The sites where Abbott's serialized episodes differ from his full-length books create gaps that reveal tensions and concerns about promoting middle-class citizenship behaviors, particularly in response to American education in the 1840s.

In Abbott's texts and in the surrounding periodical matter, boys are continually taught what it means to be "properly" American and a boy—in the mixed class space of the common school, in one-on-one relationships with alternate educators (older boys and sailors), and through solitary experiments based on the purchased goods of everyday life. The New England boyhoods that I write about in this chapter participate in the shaping of national identity in part through the circulatory power of the early serializations and also through the serialization-to-series process.

Other periodicals produced in the 1840s worked to shape the citizenships of working boys. In chapter two, "Working-Class Boys and Self-Improved Citizenship: George Light's Editorials and *The Young American's Magazine of Self-Improvement*," the middle-class boyhoods constructed by *The Youth's Companion* are compared with those that the *Young American's*, a magazine designed for young machine workers, delineates. This latter periodical explores both factory life and the changes abolition will bring to emancipated slaves. It emphasizes self-improvement and education as the means to stable American citizenship, and rather than including serialized novels, this magazine serializes editorials and essays to help their readers improve. The recommended method of self-improvement is reading, and tightly controlled lists and reviews of texts make up the magazine. In this magazine, we see that while periodicals present middle-class boys with a variety of citizenship models, some of which privilege state and local identities over national ones, magazines for working-class boys encourage self-education partly in the interest of preserving peaceful industrial life and the inevitable self-improvement of the Union.

By opening up the periodical literature written for boys over several decades, we can see small shifts in treatments of boyhood and changes in the construction of citizenship. In chapter three, "Typing American Renaissance Boys: Citizenship Compromises in Oliver Optic's *The Boat Club*," I explore Oliver Optic's *The Boat Club* (1854) and the series Optic built around it as an American boys' book that has a peculiar institutionalized position in part because of Louisa May Alcott's later critique of Optic in *St. Nicholas Magazine*. As the series progresses, Optic (William Taylor Adams) moves from writing about good boys who are already rich to writing about semi-bad boys (the kind of "bad" detailed in Thomas Bailey Aldrich's more canonical text, *Story of a Bad Boy*). Optic's boys become rich not through good behavior, but through "gumption" and quick action. Optic triumphs in the world of best-selling literature for boys during the 1850s, publishing the first of his series of semi-dime novels and serializing similar series in *Oliver Optic's Magazine*, begun in the early 1860s. Apparently, these serialized stories sold very well. As a result, Optic takes what he learns from his own enterprise and his creative shifts in his representation of boyhoods and packages it into a best-selling formula for Horatio Alger.

The first book in the series, titled *The Boat Club*, categorizes boys as fixed "types" and works to define boys as good or bad by assessments of wealth and class. The "club" teaches the boy characters and readers about the intricacies of local forms and codes and promotes exclusionary and isolationist practices. I suggest that Alcott's postwar response to Optic's books is based not only on the get-rich-quick sensationalism of his novel's conclusions, but on the promotion of boyhood citizenships constructed around local rather than national concerns. This chapter examines father-centered parenting and suggests that fathers in the antebellum period fathered sons while mothers disappeared from texts written for boys. The Civil War then changes this construction so that fathers disappear and move away from house-and-town based enterprises, which leaves more room for mothers to intervene in the citizenship of both boys and girls.

In chapter four, "Necessary Badness: Reconstructing Postbellum Boyhood Citizenship in *Our Young Folks* and *The Story of a Bad Boy*," I study the serialization of Thomas Bailey Aldrich's *Story of a Bad Boy* (1869) in *Our Young Folks*. Unlike the Abbott and Optic texts, this has become a text that is representative of institutional American boyhood. Aldrich's work is often viewed as a forerunner of *Tom Sawyer* and *Huckleberry Finn*. Tom's tale begins in New Orleans, but I argue that Tom does not become a "boy" until he moves north. Throughout the book, Tom is inculcated with regional interpretations of national histories and practices until his boyhood is "Americanized" enough so that he can leave the small New England town to become a man. The production in *Our Young Folks* is a complete serialization, this re-membered and re-written American boyhood is published as a series of episodes that allow readers to reach and preserve American manhood. In this chapter, the proliferation of magazines designed specifically for boys in the 1870s (*American Boy's Magazine*, *Boys' Ledger*, *Frank Leslie's Boys of America*, *Boys of New York*) is discussed as participating in the "reconstruction of American boyhood" project that texts such as *Story of a Bad Boy* begin. With the end of the Civil War, we see an invention of a new kind of boyhood, one that insists it is separate from a world of girls' reading and interests. These magazines enlist white boy readers to succeed in a nation transformed economically and socially by postwar reconstruction.

In chapter five, "'Shall I Be Your Boy?': Conversational Citizenships in the *St. Nicholas* Serialization of *Little Lord Fauntleroy*," I discuss *Little Lord Fauntleroy* and *The Adventures of Huckleberry Finn* as texts that represent diverging views of American boyhood as they are produced in book form. I argue that illustrations and surrounding periodical matter influence the institutionalization of the depicted boyhoods. I also examine how authentic citizenship is negotiated in *Little Lord Fauntleroy* and *Huckleberry Finn* through the emphases on boundaries of nation, class, gender, and race that inflect the Americanness of boyhoods in these texts. Burnett's text, I argue, responds to the flight-from-civilization construction of American boyhood in *Huckleberry Finn* by imaging in Fauntleroy a conversational citizenship that makes use of alternate boyhood accessories (the black velvet and the lovelocks) in order to improve the citizenships of many.

In my closing, "*Beeton's Boys' Own Magazine* and *Boys' Life*: Serialized Directions for Boyhood Citizenships in the Twentieth Century," I suggest that 1890s magazines such as *Beeton's Boys' Own Magazine* use American imperialism to define Americanness against more distant "others." The repetitious productions in these periodicals of white adventures featuring adult or young adult men reveal that the sometimes-buried/denied American embrace of imperialism is inextricably tied up with the construction of American boyhood. I compare the titles in *Beeton's* to the early production history of *Boy's Life*, the magazine connected to the Boy Scout organization, and argue that isolationist moves away from imperialism in the early twentieth century curbed textual fantasies about homosocial imperial adventures. Marketed to boys facing increasing moves toward coeducation and cogendered civic and national activities, such as women's suffrage, the scouting magazine endorses a uniformed and regulated reading world that it succeeds in proliferating in a variety of forms during the twentieth century.

Throughout the nineteenth century, periodicals and series forms play important roles in publishing citizenship permutations that respond to shifting gender requirements and constructions. As this study demonstrates, the periodical form, now inflected by new technologies, continues to intervene in the gendered nature of contemporary citizenships. To understand the current influence of the periodical form, it helps to explore, if only partially, the history of periodical constructions of American boyhoods, and so this study begins by examining boy citizen education in 1840s periodicals.

NOTES

1. See also Christina Hoff Sommers' *The War against Boys*.
2. Kidd's "Boyology in the Twentieth Century" examines the antecedents of the late-twentieth-century help for boys' manuals.

3. Lowe writes that "[b]ecause culture is the contemporary repository of memory, of history, it is through culture, rather than government, that alternative forms of subjectivity, collectivity, and public life are imagined" (22). She also notes that culture can be a force for change: "This is not to argue that cultural struggles can ever be the exclusive site for practice; it is rather to argue that if the state suppresses dissent by governing subjects through rights, citizenship, and political representation, it is only through culture that we conceive and enact new subjects and practices in antagonism to the regulatory *locus* of the citizen-subject, by way of culture that we can question those modes of government" (22).

4. See also Mark C. Carnes and Clyde Griffen's collection of essays on Victorian American masculinity, *Meanings for Manhood: Constructions of Masculinity in Victorian America*. Recently, children's literature programs and scholars have begun to explore twentieth-century boys and boyhoods in children's literature. In 1999, Simmons College held a summer institute titled "Halos and Hooligans" that focused on books about boys and boyhood. See also John Stephens's *Ways of Being Male: Representing Masculinities in Children's Literature and Film*.

5. These are Nodelman's *Touchstones* texts.

6. In similar ways, early scholars of "American" literature struggled to define the literary by looking to British and Continental standards.

7. In the final lines of Mark Twain's *Adventures of Huckleberry Finn*, Huck comments on the difficulties of constructing a textual boyhood: "If I'da knowed what a trouble it was to make a book I wouldn't a tackled it and ain't agoing to no more. But I reckon I got to light out for the Territory ahead of the rest, because Aunt Sally she's going to adopt me and sivilize me and I can't stand it. I been there before" (265).

8. The study of the production histories of British novels and British periodical literature has a slightly longer "tradition" than similar studies in the United States. See J. Don Vann and Rosemary T. VanArsdel's *Victorian Periodicals: A Guide to Research* (1978), N. N. Feltes's *Modes of Production of Victorian Novels* (1986), Joanne Shattock and Michael Wolff's *The Victorian Periodical Press: Samplings and Soundings* (1982), J. Don Vann and Rosemary T. VanArsdel's collection of essays *Victorian Periodicals and Victorian Society* (1994), and David Reed's *The Popular Magazine in Britain and the United States, 1880–1960* (1997).

9. Both Susan Belasco Smith and Frank Luther Mott discuss the *New York Mirror*'s assessment of the 1840s. See Price and Smith 5 and Mott I: 341.

10. Issues of citizenship that the periodicals reflect include property, membership in civic bodies, boys' relationships to U.S. history, and changing ideas about wealth and charity in response to the Industrial Revolution.

11. Bourdieu writes: "It is, no doubt, only by using the comparative method, which treats its object as a 'particular case of the possible', that one can hope to avoid unjustifiably universalizing the particular case" (*Distinction* xi).

12. In *Playing in the Dark*, Toni Morrison discusses what she calls an "Africanist presence" in seemingly all-white texts of American literature, and following this theory, I explore how serializations that ostensibly focus solely on white middle-class boyhoods register the boyhoods, girlhoods, and citizenships of children not named in the texts (6).

13. Foucault's work on power-knowledge formulation suggests that struggles over

ownership of knowledge can hint at sites of active construction. For further discussion of how disciplinary boundaries related to the study of gender are disputed see R. W. Connell's study.

14. Time-related aspects of manhood linked to citizenship include coming of age, career, and function within a community.

15. Judith Halberstam's work in *Female Masculinity* complicates the man/woman and male/female binaries and suggests that the complex and intricate manifestations of masculinity multiply sex and gender possibilities.

16. Jacobson writes, "Some writers found outlets in the influential children's magazines of the period. Howells, who presumably would have had relatively easy access to adult magazines, published *A Boy's Town* in *Harper's Young People* (8 April to 26 August 1890)" (12).

17. In 1990, the same year Judith Butler writes *Gender Trouble*, Thomas Laqueur makes the argument in *Making Sex: Body and Gender from the Greeks to Freud* that through language and image (especially in medical discourses), sex, just as much as gender, is made: "it is explicable only within the context of battles over gender and power" (11).

18. In establishing the concept of "dominant fiction," Silverman uses Louis Althusser's discussion of "ideological representation" and its influence on the production of the "real" through combinations of "allusion" and "illusion" and "recognition" and "misrecognition" (Silverman 24).

19. I am drawing here from Althusser's "Theory, Theoretical Practice and Theoretical Formation" (29) and his exploration of interpellation in *Lenin and Philosophy* (174).

20. See *The Queen of America Goes to Washington City: Essays on Sex and Citizenship*. Berlant also explores the implications of current obsessions with "intimate" citizenships—the use of taxonomies of sexual identities and sexual acts to organize politics.

21. In *Lighting Out for the Territory*, Shelley Fisher Fishkin writes, "Mark Twain has indelibly shaped our view of who and what the United States is as a nation and who and what we might become" (7).

22. Alcott on Twain's text: "If Mr. Clemens cannot think of something better to tell our pure-minded lads and lasses, he had best stop writing for them" (qtd. in Hamlin Hill's "*Huck Finn*'s Humor Today" 297).

23. For further discussion of the cult of true womanhood see Barbara Welter's *Dimity Convictions*.

24. Alexis de Tocqueville writes in *Democracy in America* that "the entire man is . . . to be seen in the cradle of the child" (39). While scholars such as Ala Alryyes (*Original Subjects: The Child, the Novel, and the Nation*) have examined links between concepts of childhood and concepts of nation in the eighteenth century and their connections to the novel, few have explored how the form of the periodical might influence constructions of citizenship and Americanness. I suggest that since the United States, as Tocqueville notes, was known for its involvement in "associations," that the form of the periodical, which relies on associations between publishers, contributors, and subscribers, can offer insights into nineteenth-century childhood citizenships.

25. See for example, Albert E. Stone's discussion of Rollo's reputation in *The Innocent Eye* (71).

1

Educating Boys for American Citizenship: Jacob Abbott's Contributions to the *Youth's Companion*

During the 1830s and 1840s, the fiction and the advertisements in American periodicals for boys participated in the construction of American boyhoods. Throughout their production, these boyhood constructions stabilized the ways that concepts of democracy and Union were shared with young citizens of the United States. The *Youth's Companion*, a popular 1840s periodical for children, frequently responds to common boyhood experiences and connects them to future citizenship potential. The prevalent concern with boys reveals that boys were viewed as important in establishing and manipulating a nation that was relatively new but rapidly changing.

The *Youth's Companion* provides examples of the kinds of boyhood constructed by adults writing for children in the 1840s, a decade defined by reform, rapid westward expansion due in part to railroads and gold rushes, boundary negotiations with Canada and Mexico, and booming industrialization. The *Companion* "advertises" a variety of responses to these changes and through thematic content has boy characters participate in them, defining the characters' national identities and positioning the readers to define their own citizenships. The *Youth's Companion*, which devotes much of its space to material that its editors deemed educational, can be read as coming firmly out of a middle-class northeastern publishing tradition. Designed for a northern middle-class Protestant audience, the *Companion* lasted for over a hundred years (1827–1929), and by the 1840s, it had been published steadily for over a decade.[1] Histories of the *Companion* suggest that prior to 1857, when Daniel S. Ford took over for Nathaniel Willis, the content of the magazine was primarily religious, and because of this the early years of the *Companion* have not been examined as closely as the later ones.[2] While it is dominant, religion is not the only topic addressed in the early years of the magazine. Citizen-shaping and educational concerns creep into the magazine before Ford begins editorship, and the *Companion* uses educational interventions to promote both the stabilization and exploration of boyhood citizenship within the United States.

In its educational content, the *Companion* demonstrates a preoccupation with the difficulties of moving from boyhood to citizen-manhood, and it presents education as a citizen-shaping process by which the value of the self as capital can be both depreciated and appreciated. Jacob Abbott, one of the *Youth Companion*'s frequent contributors, foregrounds national anxieties about the possibilities of democratic education and the inculcation of patriotic loyalties by writing about these topics in the context of a variety of New England boyhoods. His contributions speak to frequently transmitted definitions of American boyhood and show how their periodical presentation shifts received opinions about American boyhood citizenship. The *Companion* negotiates the varieties of citizenship available in the United States through the use of educational interventions that mimic marketing strategies. In doing so, it intervenes in the standardization of education provided by the common schools by adding reading material that addresses boys and their future citizenships and by opening spaces for alternate and more portable forms of education.

The long-running *Companion* influences notions of American boyhood and citizenship through its emphasis on education and marketing education. This chapter first explores how advertising in the late 1830s and 1840s intersects with the educational content of the *Companion*. Drawing from Jacob Abbott's many serialized texts, I suggest that the *Companion*'s views of education and boyhood citizenship intersect with Abbott's. Abbott's piecemeal periodical episodes market American boyhoods that both resist and reinforce institutionalized notions of American boyhood. These boyhood citizenships are constructed partly through the complex connections between marketing, periodical production, and the multiple audiences of the periodical.

Much of the time these complex boyhood citizenships are promoted through educational rhetoric in Abbott's texts and in the surrounding periodical material. The educational situations include solitary experiments, the democratic space of the classroom, areas of play, and interactions with alternate educators. The full-text versions of Abbott's *Rollo at School*, *Marco Paul*, and *Jonas a Judge* nod to standardizations of citizenships, but these texts' periodical forms open spaces for alternate boyhoods and citizenships to be explored. While showing an anxiety for standardization (perhaps to preserve citizenships already available to white middle-class men), the *Companion* nevertheless registers the complex variety of boys, citizenships, and formative educational methods then available in the relatively new nation. The marketing discourses used to sell Abbott's texts combine with discourses of education in order to regularly promote Americanness as desirable and also to position boys to adopt stable versions of citizen manhood.

The material included in the *Companion* suggests that editors chose its content as safe and instructive for both boy and girl readers; the instructive nature is emphasized through the use of advertising strategies, especially when mischief and fiction are incorporated into a serialized text. In the early 1840s, product advertisement had not yet become a part of magazine format. Instead, authors and publishers used bylines and prefatory marks to advertise themselves and their religious or political affiliations.[3] By the mid-1840s, the *Youth's Companion* sometimes inserted illustrations of the interiors of shops, and the illustrations indirectly advertise the goods available there (see figure 1.1). These advertisements insist that readers should be interested both in the representation of the shop and in the message that the shopkeeper, as a kind of contributing author, sends. The advertisements ask young readers

Figure 1.1. *Youth's Companion* Advertisement. *Youth's Companion* 16.44 (Mar. 9, 1843): 176.

to connect the images on the pages to their lives and their parents' ability to purchase the advertised goods, and with these explicit requests, these proto-advertisements depict textual interventions in the everyday worlds of the readers. In *Advertising Fictions*, Jennifer Wicke points out that in early advertisements, there is an "active capitalization of narrative language" that creates complex connections between marketing and fiction (15). The advertisements and the fiction of the *Companion* then both construct and are constructed by nineteenth-century cultures.

American boyhood is one cultural scene shaped by the dialectic between advertisements and fiction. In the space of the periodical, boys are defined in relation to their environment, their reading material, and their education, and their responses to these changing venues situate them as able to operate as American citizens. The advertisements of the 1840s provide a means, in the absence of other texts such as subscription lists and the diaries of boys who read them, to understand how the periodical culture promoted the development of boyhood citizenship through what it deemed to be healthy and educational reading material.[4]

Although advertising plays a definite role in the periodical's construction of boyhood, the prospectus of the *Companion* reveals that early in the 1840s, advertisements were somewhat suspect. The December 6, 1839, issue of the *Companion* includes a self-advertisement that highlights its educational value while denying that the periodical uses advertisements or promotes specific denominational affiliations:

> The Youth's Companion has often been used in Sabbath Schools. The Teachers find in almost every number something suitable to be read to their scholars, which furnishes them with the groundwork for their remarks. It is also proper to be read by the scholars during the week, and circulated among them like books from the Library. *No advertisements, and nothing sectarian or controversial are admitted into the Youth's Companion—and it is adapted to the taste of all evangelical denominations* (120, emphasis original).

Although this statement denies that any advertising is used, the prospectus itself is an advertisement, and, within the periodical, contributing authors use their names and also their organizational affiliations in bylines that advertise their sects and their written products. The simultaneous denial and use of advertisement reveals that the editors and contributors recognize advertising's power. The same contradictory impulses and the anxious need to stress that the magazine is educational and has been used by real teachers for instruction suggests as well that it might have other noneducational uses.

The less-than-educational aspects of the *Companion* can best be seen when the titles of the articles belie their content. The Natural History series of articles consists mostly of adventure stories about boys or men coming into violent contact with animals. "A Story for Boys," for example, tells about one boy killing a prairie wolf and spends approximately five inches of space describing the kill. It also tells more briefly about another boy diving into an icy pond to rescue a friend. The story justifies the telling of the first adventure by asking but not answering the following question: "Now, boys, which do you think was the most noble exploit, that of the lad who perilled his life in the *killing* of a worthless wolf, or of him who ran a greater risk in the rescuing from drowning of a fellow being?" (160). An adult reader interested in ensuring that the content of the periodical is educational might focus on the Natural History section title and the "Tale for Boys" title and believe that this article will provide information about animals and their habitats; child readers, on the other hand, can enjoy a sensational story about a wolf and ignore the didactic moral at the end. Both ways of reading would potentially interest adults and children in purchasing the full-text version of the tale.

The gaps between the titles and the content reveal multiple marketing aims. These multiple aims are also manifest when the *Companion* and its serialized texts market education by including stories and editorials that discuss changing United States educational processes. Frequently, middle-class characters question and interpret educational decisions and processes. In 1837, Massachusetts passed a law that established a state board of education and made a certain amount of schooling compulsory. The law's proponents argued that it was important to train all children to be law-abiding citizens. As E. Anthony Rotundo points out, not all members of society viewed compulsory education as a boon: "The stepwise progression that sent young males upward through the grades, into college, and on to a good job did not become established until the end of the century. Given the lack of intrinsic satisfaction or ultimate reward, boys resented the time they spent at school as an arbitrary adult intrusion into their lives" (*Meanings for Manhood* 26). Parents of boys who found it more profitable for their boys to spend school hours at work also resented the education laws. Nevertheless, the Massachusetts state board of education law set a precedent that led to the establishment of public schools in other states.

As common school laws were put into effect, reading material for children began to reflect these state and national moves toward standardized education. The McGuffey Readers, first published in 1836, helped to standardize what was taught by providing a step-by-step reader system that was used throughout the United States. Even when students moved, which they did during the 1840s, partly because of improved canal travel and expanding railroad lines, the McGuffey Readers provided a measure of how far children had advanced in their educations. With their single-issue prices lower than books and their increasing portability via improved postal routes, periodicals also provided alternate sources of educational material for young students nationwide.[5] A text published in 1835 titled *New England and Her Institutions* indicates that efforts were made to obtain newspapers and periodicals even when it was inconvenient: "You can hardly find a dwelling in New England, be it a framed house or a log cabin, in which some periodical print is not taken. The newspapers of the day are scattered far beyond the route of the mails, and the region of passable roads" (25). The *Companion* was just one of the periodicals available to young readers, and as the prospectus points out, the periodical was produced in a form that could be shared by young readers and also used by teachers in a variety of contexts.

Readers of the *Companion* are invited, in part through the advertising strategies employed, to participate in the culture of periodical print and in the complex standardizing of education in the United States. Through this participation, readers learn about how to succeed in the expanding public educational systems. As Mary Louise Pratt suggests in her discussion of what she terms "contact zones," any space like the common school classroom that requires interactions between varieties of classes and genders provides dangers (the need to survive the encounter) and possibilities (opportunities for success and improvisation).[6] When periodicals offer extensive educational strategies, they recognize the power of the common school movement and provide narratives about schooling for readers in many parts of the nation. These narratives about how to behave in a classroom in effect turn periodicals into alternate and supplementary educatory spaces that investigate, endorse, and map the new learning requirements.

Many articles in the *Companion*, both those by Abbott and also those by other writers, demonstrate concerns with the educative possibilities of individual and group interactions, and the boy characters frequently work to understand institutions and laws important to loyal citizens of the United States. The popularity of these books and the number of reprints of each edition suggest that Abbott's texts' widespread appeal helped to shape the way American boyhood was defined and understood by readers during the 1840s.[7] Since Abbott serialized these books about American boys in the *Companion* as well as in other magazines of the time, periodicals have played a role in how Abbott's characters have become part of a larger record of literary American boyhood. However, opinions about Abbott's boyhoods have changed significantly during the course of the nineteenth and twentieth centuries, and his boyhoods are now assessed as didactic. Mitzi Myers argues that such dismissals ignore the historical significance of many texts: "Literary history's stodgy readings of didactic moral tales distance them not only from more recent children's literature, but even from the noisy semiotics and cultural arguments that generated them. The stories' pointed lessons about how to live at a specific historical juncture get ironed out into timeless platitudes: good youngsters do not fight, they always obey their parents, and so on. Restoring children's texts to their political and literary matrix . . . revives them as juvenile literature" (27). Tracing the context of Abbott's boyhoods and also the history of how they have been received over time can help us to better understand the complexity of literary American boyhoods.

Although Abbott's name usually appears in literary histories of American children's authors, his books are often depicted as being unrealistic portrayals of American boyhoods.[8] Abbott's characters have good natures and stable financial states and, unlike literary boys constructed in the 1860s and 1870s, they exist in comfort and have no need to dream "American dreams." "Rollo," Abbott's best-known character, has a reputation of being unfailingly kind, obedient, and possessed of an unerring sense of right and wrong. Literary boyhoods that are more typically associated with Americanness include those tied to adventures and homosocial associations with groups of boys rather than with mixtures of boys and girls (*Tom Sawyer*, *Huck Finn*), with inventive plans that sometimes involve a self-developed business (*Ragged Dick*), and with mischief played by boys on citizens and towns (*Story of a Bad Boy*). Histories of children's literature designate these boyhoods as "American" boyhoods, and often the more "American" boys find their way to some form of unexpected wealth. After the 1840s, although other children's authors imitate Abbott's production methods and some of his thematic approaches, boys with characteristics similar to Abbott's boys are not as prevalent. In series books for boys by later authors such as Oliver Optic, the gentleness and tolerance with which Rollo and other characters respond to disorderly events and people disappear, while the inquiry and experimentation and interest in property laws and possessions continue.[9] The "Americanness" that Abbott's boys display, while it might be similar to lived boyhoods, is not the kind that literary histories celebrate or recall as specifically "American."

Literary histories of children's books about American boyhood especially construct Rollo as a figure whom more canonical texts resist.[10] When Twain claims, "I have never written a book for boys; I write for grown-ups who have *been* boys. If the boys read it & like it, perhaps that is testimony that my boys are real, not artificial," he draws a distinction between his books and the "boys books" he knows (qtd. in Stone 60).[11] Twain's contemporary reviewers also look to past boyhoods like those found in Abbott's texts when they assess Twain's texts. Howells, for example, writes about *Tom Sawyer*: "It is altogether the best boy's story I ever read."[12] Rollo's reputation as not quite a "real" boy continues to be transmitted throughout the twentieth century. In a light-hearted article published in 1947 in the *Saturday Review*, John Mason Brown discusses the Rollo travel books series and sums up his opinion with the title "Prigs Is Prigs." He writes that although the travel books show a different side of Rollo, the power of Rollo's reputation "as a paragon of the seven deadly virtues" persists (20). Rollo's reputation exerts a cultural influence that intervenes in the critical influence that literary historians claim Rollo does not have, except as a character type that must be resisted in order to become a canonical boy. Abbott's characters' institutionalized reputations as being "other" than American and "other" than boys, then, come partly from writers' and critics' responses to educational interventions within the texts that construct the characters as American boys. Twenty-first century responses to the education of Abbott's characters continue to shape definitions of Americanness and boyhood.

In part, the goodness of the characters results from Abbott's educational theories. Abbott is heavily influenced by the educational philosophies of Pestalozzi, an educator whose methods also shaped the educational practices of William and Bronson Alcott.[13] In his educational experiments, Pestalozzi encouraged the use of dialogues to teach and to provide a gentle means of maintaining discipline. Following these principles, Abbott does not show his characters being physically punished. If the characters make mistakes, fathers or teachers usually correct the fault through gentle conversation.[14] Rollo is usually very quick to see his father's point of view, and he rarely makes the same mistake twice. These educational and disciplinary methods add to the too-good-to-be-an-American-boy reputations of Abbott's characters.

Within the periodical form, Abbott's characters do not come across as being so uniformly "good" as they do in their whole text form, in part because some of the episodes end without a concluding moral, creating a gap in which the reader must work to come to terms (or not) with the "right" solution. Because the complete books are marketed in bylines or in opening blurbs, the conclusions are advertised as being contained in the book form, but the episodes intervene in the didactic purposes of the whole text by allowing readers to think through what might or should happen. One such piecemeal episode from *Rollo's Experiments*, which appears in the February 28, 1840, issue of the *Companion*, depicts Rollo as neither perfect nor "bad," and thus illustrates how Rollo's reputation is not always the same when his stories are read in serial form. The episode also shows how Rollo's curiosity provides a model of an educational method being encouraged for use with middle-class boys. In this and other serialized episodes, points of address to the reader suggest how periodicals involved the reader in the production of textual boyhoods of characters like Rollo and then used the proliferation to reproduce similar behaviors in the readers.

In the seemingly unfinished episode from *Rollo's Experiments* titled "The Bee Hive," Rollo, who like the later and more "canonically" American-and-boy Tom Sawyer often concocts means of amusing himself from the material objects at hand, decides to build his own beehive by collecting bees in an upside-down flowerpot. Interestingly, the woodcut illustration that accompanies this text advertises the content to girl as well as boy readers by depicting a girl tending bees (see figure 1.2). There are no girls in this episode, and very few in the full text. The woodcut might interest girl readers in purchasing the full text, while the episode itself, which shows boys involved in the physically dangerous task of capturing bees, invites boy readers to imagine how they might participate in the same sort of pseudo-farming experiment. The teasing nature of the woodcut, which shows beehives with a girl in close proximity to them, and the advertised "droll" humor of the episode convey the idea that the readers are supposed to enjoy the story but not try the experiment. Rollo's beehive experiment is a boy-scale example of a variety of historical and cultural experiments at work in the United States in the 1830s and 1840s, and the treatments of experiments in this episode and in the whole text illustrate how experiments were used as educational methods.

During the 1840s, experiments with steam led to faster railway engines. Experiments in farming methods led to the invention of the McCormick reaper and the steel plow, both of which cut down on the amount of physical labor needed to keep a farm in order.[15] The changes brought by experiments

THE BEE HIVE.

Figure 1.2. "Bee Hive" Woodcut. *Youth's Companion* 13.2 (Feb. 28, 1840): 165.

made some older techniques obsolete at the same time that they also brought new kinds of danger to formerly safe spaces (reapers made harvesting more efficient but they could also rip off limbs). Since the United States prospered from experiments, educators began to use experiment-based strategies in their lessons; the treatment of experiments in Abbott's episode shows how changes in technology and the subsequent push to teach experimentation intersect with cultural anxieties about education methods and their influence on national identity.

In the episode, Rollo leaves the bees he collects trapped in the flowerpot overnight and finds them very weak in the morning. He then shifts the pot in a way that accidentally crushes and kills most of the bees. Jonas, the older boy who often gives Rollo advice and correction, comes by, hears the story of the beehive, and laughs, "a loud, long, and apparently uncontrollable fit of laughter" (165). He asks Rollo questions about the beehive in the manner that usually ends up with some kind of lesson or correction: "presently he succeeded in asking Rollo if he supposed that bees would make honey there" (165). Rollo answers Jonas seriously: "Certainly I do. . . . Why should they not? They don't care what shape their hive is, or what it is made of, and this flower-pot is as good as anything else" (165). Jonas asks about Rollo's plans for a queen bee and continues to laugh at the responses Rollo gives to his questions. The episode ends with the last live bee crawling out and Jonas yelling for the boys to run for fear that they will be stung. The final sentence reads, "this was the last time that Rollo ever attempted to *make up* a hive of bees" (166). Jonas, who usually gives solemn advice and takes Rollo and his friends much more seriously than the adults do, does not explain to Rollo what his beekeeping errors are. The reader, who may or may not know more about beekeeping than Rollo, is asked to laugh with Jonas at Rollo's "experiment." The title of the book, *Rollo's Experiments*, and its contents reveal that experimentation in the form of self-developed tests of the world is a pedagogical method used to enhance a boy's education outside of the common school classroom, but this piecemeal episode calls the effectiveness of experimentation into question. Jonas's response to education-via-experiment is to laugh in a chaotic way.

Like Jonas's laughter, nationwide responses to new ideas and products were often tinged with skepticism and ridicule, and these nationwide responses to the new can be connected with attitudes toward changes in education. Although he withholds information about the proper ways to trap bees, Jonas's response also indicates that he is familiar with beekeeping, a branch of farming practiced in New England to add to other supplies of sweeteners.[16] Jonas's withholding of instruction about bees suggests one possible response to boyhood invention. The lack of instruction encourages Rollo to continue experimenting—his experiments are amusing—and the lack of concern Jonas seems to have about providing Rollo with the proper information suggests that eventually, between boyhood and manhood, Rollo and his friends will come to a better understanding of bees.

Jonas's laughter about the bees is a response that most boys with some familiarity with beekeeping would join in as well, and this response is one that is linked to attitudes about changes in knowledge bases during the 1840s. If boys reading *Rollo's Experiments* were classically educated, they would be able to connect Rollo's comments about bees to Virgil's use of bees as model citizens.[17] An advice book about the proper education of boys published in 1837 laments common school changes from classical literature to "modern" languages and literature by providing a list of texts that are being read less frequently:

> Collections of letters and state-papers, and the epi-grammatic narratives of the Historian of Ferney, are to supply the place of Herodotus, Thucydides, and Livy. Ariosto, Tasso, and Boileau, are to be read in preference to Homer, Virgil, and Horace; and the works of Voltaire alone to be substituted in the place of all the poetry, all the philosophy, and all the history that has ever been written (*Boys' Manual* 48).

The article also argues that the neglect of the classical is causing boys to act less like boys and therefore interfering with their ability to become men: "nor do I know a sight more truly ridiculous than that of a boy of fourteen affecting the graces, and behaving among his superiors in age and attainments with all the disgusting ease of self-sufficiency. The same natural good sense which makes the boy act in character, will teach the man a manly behavior" (48).[18] While Rollo's beehive experiment is not the same as a curriculum of Voltaire, Jonas's "punishment" via laughter certainly makes the point that learning through experiment will not teach Rollo everything there is to know.[19] As it offers a perspective about new educational trends, Abbott's piecemeal episode about Rollo's ignorance of beekeeping methods markets another kind of knowledge to the readers, asking them to join Jonas in recognizing the ways in which Rollo's experiments indicate his lack of knowledge and point to the failure of experiments (both boyhood and national) that are made without a basic knowledge base.

There are no neat morals given in this story. It is obvious by the end that a flowerpot is not the place to "make up" a hive, but there is no lesson given about the proper way to do it. Rollo's inventive impulses are left to find means to express themselves in other ways. The whole book version in which this episode is published places the beehive episode between other experiments Rollo conducts during his leisure time. Through explicit directions and points of address to the readers, the text advertises the experiments to boy readers, with the beehive as an example readers are not meant to repeat on their own.[20] As a middle-class boy, Rollo has the free time needed to explore and sharpen the inventive entrepreneurial skills he needs to succeed in middle-class American manhood, and he is encouraged to move on if his own success comes into question. Along with readers, Rollo is encouraged to come up with his own ideas about bees and beekeeping, since Jonas's laughter and his fear of the sting prevent him from providing a lesson. Abbott's "teaching" episodes, with their theoretical grounding in Pestalozzian educational methods, resist the more formulaic reader-based curricula of the common school and foster a specific kind of inventive boyhood.

The lively, imaginative, careless Rollo in this episode of *Rollo's Experiments* is not the well-behaved, easily corrected Rollo of common reputation, and this gap between the Rollo of the periodical and the Rollo of literary history points to how periodical production can intervene in the construction of boyhood. The experiments and entrepreneurial skills used by boys in both *Tom Sawyer* and *The Adventures of Huckleberry Finn* have their textual antecedents in Rollo's "plays," although Rollo himself is the kind of good-boy character rejected by Twain. The serialized portions of Abbott's texts reveal that the didacticism existed alongside behaviors that also characterize later-nineteenth-century boys whose actions have been identified as more "American" than those of Rollo. It seems that before the Civil War, boys were textually constructed as imaginative experimenters, but subsequent evaluations of boyhood tend to erase or ignore early examples of imagination and mischief. The kinds of boyhoods prescribed by "approved" reading material found in periodicals allow for some variety in the boys they construct by creating gaps between the didactic conclusions the titles promise and the mischievous adventures they deliver. As Foucault suggests, regularity and ritual are important aspects of systematized education, but in some ways, the regularity of the *Companion*, when combined with the irregularity of 1840s serialization practices, creates a serialized space that invokes the educatory discipline of instruction and correction while allowing for other kinds of education to take place.[21] In the decade when the nationally produced McGuffey Readers standardized education around reading levels and linear movement, the regularly produced, incomplete narratives of the periodical offer spaces for readers to learn while these spaces routinely resist the standardizing forces of the national curricula and showcase boyhoods that operate inside and outside of these standards.

In addition to piecemeal episodes opening spaces of resistance to standardized education, *Companion* texts often emphasize the educational value of the printed material as a way of marketing the always-suspect fiction to adult purchasers. Marketing techniques include pre- or post-text blurbs that indicate whether the author has a religious affiliation and whether the text is educational. One example of the advertisement of a whole text about a non-middle-class boy comes from the January 10, 1840, issue of the *Companion*. The first page of this issue includes an excerpt from a new book, *Factory Boy*, published by the New England Sunday School Union. When the text is introduced, an illustration accompanies the following statement:

> The preface states that the book is substantially true. It is a very instructive narrative, and explains the advantages of piety to the young. The name of the boy about whom this book is written is Alfred Stitson. We shall make two extracts; the first, illustrative of the scene represented in this picture; and the second showing how Alfred tried to help his mother. For further particulars respecting Alfred's getting work—the death of his mother—his attending the Sabbath School—and becoming a Christian—we must refer our readers to the book.

This advertisement is followed by an episode in which Alfred, the "Factory Boy" of the title, tries to find work in a tobacco factory, but is turned away after a day's trial. It ends just as Alfred realizes that the employer, to whom he wishes to explain his family's plight, has left for the day.

The suspended, piecemeal nature of this excerpt, which, like the "Bee-Hive" article by Abbott, is not a complete "episode" with a beginning and an end, offers an incentive to buy the book. In the blurb at the beginning of this piece, the "instructive nature" of the book is noted, and the episode does instruct its potential readers about the almost inescapable cycle of poverty, and the harsh realities of child factory labor, without offering the reader the common rags-to-riches plot device of the benevolent benefactor reaching out to help the boy and his family move out of their situation. The cutoff point of this cheaper version of the story thus paints a more accurate picture of child labor than does the longer text version, while simultaneously creating in its reading consumers a desire for the longer, possibly happier, although less realistic full-text version.

The educational techniques and content that we see marketed in both "Rollo's Bee-Hive," and "The Factory Boy" are complemented by nonfiction pieces that directly address 1840s understandings of how education and gender construction intersect in the United States. The article with which "Factory Boy" shares the space of the page is titled "Learning" and has the subtitle "What Is Education? Extracts from 'Means and Ends, or Self-Training.'" Positioned prominently on the front page, this article points out that common schools in the 1840s are places where girls and the "great mass" of people receive their knowledge, but also that for young boys and men, "education" can mean an entirely different set of learning practices. In a conversation with the teacher, one of the students in a classroom of girls comments: "Mr. Smith said, at the Lyceum Lecture, that the great mass of the people received their education at the common schools; and the girls have named nearly all that we learn at the common schools [reading, writing, ciphering, grammar]." Another student adds "I often hear people say of a man that he has 'had an education,' when they mean merely that he has been through college." This discussion shows the ways in which common school democratizes some kinds of learning while it creates a need to establish other kinds of educational distinctions that maintain boundaries between those able to claim an "education" and those able merely to read and write. The article advocates "Self-Training" as the method that is democratically available to "the great mass," which includes middle-class boys, all classes of girls, and other classes of boys, such as those members of the urban working class targeted by another 1840s periodical, the *Young American's Magazine of Self-Improvement*.[22] "Self-Training" encompasses both the experimental leisure time education promoted in *Rollo's Experiments* as well as the upward mobility and stability of the Union, which are goals of self-education.

As common school curricula were implemented throughout the United States, boys who hitherto had been able to move toward manhood without any systematized education were required to submit to rules that applied to a mix of several different classes. Rotundo suggests that what he calls "boy culture," a culture centered around games of warfare and physical pastimes, flourished in the streets, orchards, and fields, but "languished in the school and in the church" (33). With the rise of the schools, boys were required to move between spheres where the codes of their separate culture operated and spheres where it did not. Sociological studies of pre–common school childhood suggest that boys spent more time with men from other generations, and the periodical material seems to support this.[23] Many articles and fiction pieces show boys participating in all-male peer groups and intergenerational groups outside the classroom, and, as demonstrated in the "What Is Education?" article, in coed groups inside the classroom. These representations offer textual models for negotiating the cultural requirements necessary to become educated young American citizens.

Some textual models include boys' responses to systematized education and also articles about self-education. A *Companion* article titled "Dull Boys," which depicts the jarring move to school as something to be grown into, mentions a scholar who became a doctor of divinity who "for two or three years after he commenced going to school, was distinguished only for quarrelling, and rude sports" (152). Significantly, these behaviors are not condemned, but given as soothing examples of the kinds of activities enjoyed by boys who finally came to terms with the educational process. The narratives about how the boys stopped participating in these antieducational activities are missing, allowing the readers to enjoy the descriptions of the wild and sometimes violent adventures and the successful careers without having to read the tale of the men's conversion to scholarly behaviors.[24] On the surface, to an adult skimming for appropriateness of content, these articles seem to focus on the transition from boy culture to school culture, while the content of articles like "Dull Boys" condones rebellion against the rigid schedule as a "natural" part of a boy's education.

During the 1840s, perhaps as a response to boisterousness in the common schools, there was debate about the purpose of public education in promoting individuality and preserving America. Both Whigs and Democrats argued for its ongoing place in American society. In *The Mind of America*, Rush Welter points out that although both parties believed education was good for the Union, "Whigs tended to see education as an institution for social betterment, Democrats tended to see the protection of individual rights" (292). The consensus about education breaks down when the two parties disagree about who should know what, with Whigs believing the right kind of education would "improve" problem areas and contain potentially revolutionary dissenters, and Democrats arguing that knowledge could be used to prevent injustices (taxes and interference with free trade, for example). By promoting self-education and institutional education within the portable form of the single issue, the *Companion* emphasizes that the self-made success that begins with reading helps the state and national governments to institutionalize education. The periodical points out that education has in many places been made available to all classes, while simultaneously distancing the governments from any responsibility for the failure of public education by constantly reminding readers that education is in the hands of the individual.

While some articles suggest that boys must take the initiative to make their education profitable, others address educational changes that make it desirable to find strategies to continue to make the "right" kind of educational choices when away from home. Abbott's piecemeal episodes that reflect on the learning and temptations that occur when boys are away from their families often conclude without resolution. In one such serialized portion of *Caleb in Town*, titled "The Contrary Boy," two cousins travel together and bicker about small details of the landscape they observe. Caleb, traveling toward his home in Boston, makes one comment about something he sees and his slightly older cousin Dwight, who is not from Boston, contradicts him:

> "It isn't any mill-dam at all," said Dwight, "I know. Is it, brother George?"
>
> The merchant had been riding then, for a few minutes in silence, thinking of his own affairs; but now he turned to Dwight and said,
>
> "What do you ask?"
>
> "Isn't that the mill-dam?" said Caleb.

> "Yes, those are the lights on the mill-dam."
>
> "There!" said Caleb. And at the same instant, "O!" said Dwight, "the *lights* on the mill-dam." They may be the lights on the mill-dam; but I knew they could not be the mill-dam itself."
>
> Caleb was about to make a sharp reply, which would have continued the dispute, when he recollected that his grandmother, Madam Rachel, had taught him that whenever he found conversation tending to a dispute, his duty was to be silent.
>
> "It takes two to make a dispute," she used to say; "and so if you can by any means keep one tongue still, the other must stop too."
>
> So Caleb just said, "Very well," and let the matter drop. (42)

The title, which suggests that contrariness will be central to the episode, never fulfills its promise since the episode ends without a specific moral about bickering and contradiction being given. Caleb's decision not to quarrel is not explicitly addressed and Caleb is not rewarded for his "goodness" or Dwight corrected for his contrariness; the child reading the periodical only receives a lively description of a verbal relationship. Dwight, as a traveling boy, uses verbal contrariness to mask his lack of knowledge, and since it is not punished, the reader might learn from this serialized episode the idea that contrariness can be a protective device when traveling in a strange place. Caleb, who follows his absent grandmother's instructions in his refusal to argue, finds that silence can be a survival strategy when interacting with older boys and possibly men.

When developing his series books, Abbott often drafted his episodes separately, and this technique has created gaps in both serialized and full-text versions that leave room for interpretation. The whole-text version, while being marketed as more complete, often contains the same narrative gaps created by the periodical episodes. The parent to whom the child might take the serialized portion in order to request the purchase of the entire book might assume based on the title that the tale will correct a behavioral "problem," when actually the episode remains unresolved in both the periodical and the book.

By not always tying up loose ends, Abbott's texts show boys operating within chaotic and unlegislated American boy society without being provided with orderly answers or explicit correction. Abbott's "Prefatory Notice" to *Caleb in Town* states "the aim is not so directly to communicate knowledge, as it is to develop the moral and intellectual powers,—to cultivate habits of discrimination and correct reasoning, and to establish sound principles of moral conduct" (5). In "A Contrary Boy," readers are called upon to think through possible responses to boyhood "contrariness" and to locate a workable response that will both preserve peace and protect individual rights.

As *Caleb in Town* and other Abbott texts illustrate, it was not uncommon in the 1840s to send boys away from home for education. Many *Companion* articles about the "proper" education of boys offer advice to both parents and boys about how to promote educated boyhoods that lead to productive citizenships. "The Only Son" tells the story of Frank Wilson and his parents. An uncle convinces the parents that Frank should be educated away from home because "[h]e is not as manly as other boys" (45). Part of the uncle's reasoning in making the claim is that Frank is too affectionate with his mother: "boys brought up by women are good for nothing" (45). The parents finally agree to send Frank away to school and there he picks up habits of reading "foolish books" and drinking (45). Frank leaves college in disgrace and dies an early death. This article demonstrates that there were differing approaches to the necessity of boys coming into contact with the temptations of the public world.[25] The mother feels it is best to protect boys; the uncle feels encounter is the best way to prepare boys for the pressures and temptations of adulthood, while the article itself reserves judgment on either of these educational approaches, warning the reader only to "shun the first advances of vice, for the descent is swift, like the swollen and headlong torrent, sweeping every landmark away" (46).[26] This detached approach to competing educational methods is one taken by Abbott himself. He describes boys studying away from home, boys learning in the home, boys at school, boys being apprenticed to older men from outside the family, and boys learning while traveling. The educational approaches are not arranged hierarchically, but are offered in their variety, with advice given for the best handling of each educational situation.

Abbott's texts frequently place younger boys in tutoring relationships with adolescents or young men. These relationships illustrate the variety of educational choices available to boys and make clear that learning behaviors have conversionary and sometimes contagious properties.[27] The periodic interventions of the adolescent cousins and young men have the power to redefine or reorganize the boyhood of the younger boys. One of Abbott's non-Rollo texts, *Marco Paul*, shows that the lines between healthy and unhealthy forms of education are not always clearly drawn. In this text, Marco travels away from home, and Marco's cousin Forester plans a course of study for Marco. Not quite as active but more studious than the younger Marco, Forester is a kind of feminized boy, who enjoys stillness and study more than travel and adventure. Claudia Nelson suggests in her study of British boys' fiction, *Boys Will Be Girls*, that in British fiction for boys, "the ideals of womanliness were presented to Victorian boys as the ideals of manliness" (5). Abbott's treatment of "the ideals of womanliness" complicates Nelson's argument since his episodes show womanly and boyish attributes being exchanged between characters. Forester, who portrays some of the characteristics of womanly manliness promoted in British fiction, increases Marco's ability to learn while sitting still, but Forester also becomes more active to accommodate Marco's desires to learn out-of-doors. The exchange indicates that in Abbott's model of boyhood citizenship, boys can successfully educate each other and expand each other's citizenship capabilities.

By using older adolescent boys and other nonparental educators, Abbott's books show how schooling in American citizenship occurs in the space between conversion and rebellion, between well-behaved, more American boyhoods and bad boyhoods, which Abbot constructs as also American, but unregulated, dangerous. In *Marco Paul*, Forester might be read as an older boy who has been thoroughly converted to a manly/feminized boyhood. However, Forester's plans for Marco's curriculum eventually make compromises that accommodate Marco's tastes. Marco's efforts to teach a crew to row move Forester from spectator to participant, because he sees participating as a way to teach Marco a lesson about leadership. In an outdoors lesson, the rowing commands become a text and the boat a classroom. Forester must move from inert scholar to teaching boy in order to teach the concepts of boyhood rowing.

Forester's bookishness and his successful approach to rowing also teach Marco an 1840s version of Americanness, a version of national identity avoids the revolutions that occurred throughout Europe during the later part of the decade. Anarchy will not work, this episode says—everyone in the boat (or in the nation) must follow the same kinds of rules and must understand the same kind of language. Thus, when Forester demonstrates that in order for rowing to work, the leader must first explain clearly the language of the commands to all those rowing with him, he is simultaneously showing Marco that one model for American citizenship depends on all citizens of the nation agreeing to abide by the same rules.[28] He also steps in to show Marco that good leadership in part relies on good teaching, a concept that seems to reflect the quickly spreading state-based public education laws. Training the miniature nation of the law-abiding crew to know a system of language, or the laws of disciplined boating, prevents anarchic upsets of the boat.[29]

As seen in *Marco Paul*, younger boys and older boys could sometimes develop educational influences on each other. In nineteenth-century periodicals, class was also seen as a contagious influence. The presence of middle-class children in periodical literature provides what R. Gordon Kelly terms "the gentry ideal" for children to follow. *Rollo in School*, the Abbott book that establishes Rollo's long-lasting good boy reputation, provides an example of this contagion at work. In the incomplete serialized episodes, however, we see that badness can be as contagious as gentry behavior.

In this text, Dovey, a girl who manifests "bad boy" characteristics, indulges in classroom behaviors designed to disrupt the order of the schoolroom space, which, in this text, resembles a kind of small-scale democratic nation with a woman leader. Dovey is trained in school citizenship by Miss Mary, and her "conversion" to good student is slow and makes itself plain not in behavior reform, but in sincere penitence. Throughout the text, Dovey continues to misbehave, but she is genuinely sorry afterwards. The readers have the fun of reading about and perhaps buying the published book because of Dovey's naughtiness, while the consciences of the parent buyer and the publisher are salved by the nominal conversion from wild girl to docile school citizen. The episodic breaks, which sometimes end before reform or punishment occurs, provide a textual space for unconverted boyhood to be (re)produced outside the text.

In *Rollo at School*, planning the course of education for middle-class boys is an important issue, as it is in *Marco Paul*. In this text, Miss Mary, a schoolteacher and a woman (not, as in *Marco Paul*, an adolescent boy cousin) tells Rollo that he must clarify with his father what his course of study should be. This deference to the father or to the family does not occur when Dovey arrives. Miss Mary accepts Dovey into the school and effectively takes control of her course of study. Rollo's father has more power over Rollo's education—possibly because of his middle-class status, while Dovey's father is absent from the text. Jonas, in this text, serves as a kind of Forester-like figure by offering advice about going to school. Unlike Forester, however, Jonas is active and does not seem to have any say about the content of Rollo's course of study. Abbott's move from treating home-based education to discussing formal schooling seems to mark the national shift toward public schools as the dominant sources of educational content. Instead of planning curricula and offering lessons, adolescent boys serve as peripheral educators.

At the beginning of the book, Rollo has had no experience with formal education. Rollo's position as a privileged boy—he is properly dressed for school, prepared for school's demands, and well fed—makes him somewhat more cooperative than other students such as Dovey and Julius. A description of Rollo's desk illustrates this privilege: "Rollo's was in beautiful order; but it was partly because his mother had told him exactly how to keep things in order" (59). Dovey's desk is described as having a "number of rude marks and drawings on the lid inside. The books were all tumbled in in confusion, and crumbs of gingerbread were scattered about the bottom of the desk. In one corner was a paper box, which she had made; there were flies buzzing in it, which she had caught and imprisoned there" (57). Dovey is almost totally unaware of the conventions of classroom decorum, she is given a certain amount of leeway as she learns to follow the rules.

At one point, Rollo, who seems to have an aptitude for school conventions and for a version of "manliness" similar to Forester's in *Marco Paul*, displays this aptitude by discouraging another student from fighting with Dovey. When she wants the drinking dipper, she grabs for it, and Rollo convinces another student to give it up without physical violence. The children ask the teacher to banish Dovey from the school, but the teacher is convinced that she can change Dovey and that the children can learn beneficial lessons from her. The teacher then proceeds to point out examples of Doveyism throughout the classroom. She explains, in a monologue that draws attention to the ways in which Dovey's behaviors are similar to those often attributed to boys, that those guilty of Doveyism "upset their inkstands, they cut their fingers, they tear their clothes by climbing, or get into the mud by running along and not minding where they are going, they scratch the furniture, and bring mud into the house, and break glass, and hurt themselves and one another" (62). Miss Mary calls on Rollo to help her tame Dovey. Rollo's "manly" behavior is used to help Dovey become womanly, while Rollo's "masculinity" is increased through his association with the active and daring Dovey.

The education at the school, which is open both to the financially privileged Rollo and the destitute Dovey, works to democratize their behavior by teaching them the same standards. Dovey's lack of knowledge allows her to disrupt the rules without being severely punished for not following them. As a girl who plays extensively with and acts like the worst of the boys, she is not punished as severely as boys who refuse to follow the rules. Although Rollo does not always understand the rules of the school, his loyalty, or, reading the school as a model nation, his patriotism, allows him to follow the rules and to save questions for later. He often puts his questions to his father and to Jonas, so that his understanding of the cultures in which he is able to practice his middle-class northeastern boyhood successfully extends from the local to the national. Jonas, who lives liminally between boyhood and adulthood, gives Rollo advice about how best to follow school rules and offers him advice about actual national laws and then applies them to boyhood. Rollo seems able to reap the benefits of a democratic world where young men and women from different classes and backgrounds come together, but he approaches the institution of school in a doubled way. He works within the system when there is mixed company, and he questions and considers the system itself when he is with older and younger members of his own gender and class.

Common school classrooms, as they are represented in periodicals, use white northeastern middle-class boys to train disruptive working-class tomboys to follow and be loyal to the rules of an institution. I would suggest that these narratives of common school coeducation pave the way for women to participate in the United States' government via suffrage, because they show how men and women might work together within a larger institutional framework. In these texts, young men are constructed as trainers of disruptive young women in the school and in the schoolyard. In the years leading up to the 1848 Declaration of Sentiments at Seneca Falls, the coeducational space of the classroom prepared boys to adhere to the rules of order in order to "manage" vocal and physically disruptive girls. In Massachusetts, these girls found livelihoods in the Lowell mills, where they combined their own disorderliness with that of others to make trouble for the managing men.[30] Within the periodical, middle-class boys' responses to disruptive girls become textual testing grounds for larger issues of participation in the government and the workplace. Rollo's cautious interactions with Dovey show that sometimes even the best of managers cannot combat the changes brought by those with entirely new ideas about what is acceptable participation in the common space. As Rollo's compromising response to Dovey's insistent grab for the dipper demonstrates, "good" American boys like Rollo must sometimes avoid a separate fraternity and bend nonviolently to the will of the "other" in order to maintain peace and order.

Particularly in the Abbott texts, but also in other articles and stories, readers learn repeatedly that one of the main characters will pursue a behavior that will need to be corrected by either an adult or an older adolescent. The action-question-discussion-instruction-correction format then gives both the middle-class boy character as well as the implied middle-class reader purchase on how educational forms work. The readers are then offered models for controlling their own behaviors and the behaviors of others around them. In her reading of the Rollo books, Jani L. Berry suggests that discipline was important to middle-class Americans during the 1840s because of a variety of disorders in the American world around them: "rapid increases in population, immigration, industrialization, and urbanization were transforming the nature of American life and causing significant civil unrest. Many Americans, especially of the middle- and upper-classes, feared the downfall of American civilization" (100–1).[31] Berry argues that the emphasis on order in the Rollo books has to do with the kind of American patriotism the books seek to promote—a patriotism of stability rather than of change: "Order not only prevents violence but also provides for steady economic progress" (100).[32] Although the Rollo books do discuss obedience to authority and the importance of leadership, the main message from the piecemeal periodical material seems to be that obedience to a leader is best, but there will always be instances of disorder, revolt, and revolution that can be survived. Rather than writing disorder and revolution out of existence, Abbott's texts grant them space to exist, sometimes to be resolved by a complicated discussion of laws and customs, but other times to flourish.

Access to laws and existing bodies of knowledge were not just relevant to children's periodical publishers in the nineteenth century, but were also linked to the establishment of aunifiednational identity. In *National Manhood*, Dana Nelson argues that earlier in the century, narratives of exploration and quests for scientific knowledge had been used to solidify concepts of capitalist citizenship as linked to a powerful white national fraternity.[33] Schoolroom knowledge in Abbott's texts operates in similar ways, except that inside the schoolroom, an advanced model of cogendered community is in effect. Unlike the worlds of government and law into which the Rollos and Calebs of Abbott's texts enter as adults, the schoolroom world of boyhood is a space that must be shared in an orderly way with sometimes-disorderly girls. Abbott's texts show how boys come to terms with this cogendered space both in and out of the classroom. In order to make sense of the space of the classroom, they often turn to a fraternal network of information outside of it. If the capitalist citizenships about which Nelson writes are put into place through the constructions of fraternities, then capitalist boy would-be citizens find that before reaching these fraternal orders they must work through the nonfraternal civic space of the common school classroom. Rollo's experiences in the classroom direct him to gaps in his knowledge about the rules followed by boys and the laws followed by adults. These gaps provide the episodic material for sharing Rollo's methods of learning with a nation of young reading citizens.

Abbott's *Jonas a Judge* focuses on "legal education." This text relates American justice to boyhood by asking readers to think through a variety of broken laws and legal disputes. Jonas is studying to become a lawyer and he uses the field of boyhood as his courtroom, connecting boyhood arguments to regional and national laws. The preface of the book indicates that the disagreements Jonas settles for Rollo are meant to be taken to heart by boy readers:

> In settling the questions and disputes which arise between Rollo and his companions, Jonas lays down general principles, which are equally applicable to cases occurring among other boys; and thus it is hoped that this little book may be the means of ending or preventing contention among many little circles of brothers and cousins.

This preface suggests that both parents and boy readers might be influenced to actively apply the general rules that are discussed. When Jonas bases his judgments of boyhood disagreements on U.S. law, he schools boys in law, and boys are constructed as peaceful citizens.

Jonas demonstrates how, in America, law works to maintain peace and to prevent violence. He applies rules of citizen manhood to boyhood, all the while acknowledging that boys do not often follow any sort of property laws and this is why their disputes end in violence. As the text details the boys' increasing knowledge of national property laws, the disputes become more complex, but the arguments, which Jonas sees as characteristic of boyhood, do not cease.

Jonas's distance from boyhood and his understanding of and discussion of written laws versus the boyhood laws of the street, field, and barnyard illustrate the connections between boy laws and the laws of democracy. When he shows how adult laws encourage work rather than play and fixed purchases rather than loose trades, Jonas demonstrates the slow processes by which boys moved in the 1840s from boyhood to adulthood.[34] As an adolescent educatory figure who remembers boyhood and is learning about the laws of manhood, Jonas provides middle-class readers with valuable information about the inevitable transition from boyhood to manhood.

Jonas a Judge revolves around boyhood property and boundary disputes. In this text (as well as in other Abbott texts), one of Rollo's never-punished faults is that he likes to give orders to his younger sibling Nathan as well as his friends. In "Requests and Demands," Rollo's commands are discussed as a legal issue when Rollo asks his cousin Lucy to return to the house for a dipper he has forgotten. Lucy refuses and they take the point to Jonas. The focus of the discussion is not on the politeness of the requests, which might seem to have been the logical issue for a didactic digression, but rather, the question of whether Rollo has any claim over Lucy that would make her legally obligated to return to the house. Jonas decides in Lucy's favor:

> When we *request* anything, we do not pretend that we have any right to require it to be done. We leave it to the persons whom we ask, to decide; and if they decide not to do it, we acquiesce. But when we *demand* any thing, then we can properly insist upon it, and show the persons that we have a claim upon them, and that they ought to comply; and we are displeased if they do not comply. That's the mistake that boys are always making. They demand when they only have a right to request, and so get into a quarrel (95, emphasis in original).

In its treatment of demands and forced labor, this chapter resonates with references to national political and social issues, particularly slavery and women's rights. The argument Jonas makes about claims and the right to make claims on other persons could be easily extended to apply to the injustices that boys and men of the 1840s inflicted on slaves, all women, and other oppressed groups by making demands when they should have made requests.

Rules of order and lines of possession are clearly drawn in middle-class and working-class children's periodical literature, and this emphasis suggests an anxiety about property lines and boundaries at work in the larger world of adult literature as well as in United States legislation and expansion. The

1840s was a decade obsessed with boundaries and ownership, partly because the United States was still trying to define itself and its relationship to other nations. It was during this decade that John O'Sullivan coined the term *Manifest Destiny* to describe the objectives of the United States. The United States expanded its territories and rearranged boundaries in the Pacific Northwest and in what became California and Texas. In the 1830s, the Indian Removal Acts taught the American people that property rules and boundary lines could be redrawn through legislation. The members of the United States government took away the properties of the Native Americans east of the Mississippi, so why might they not at some later date remove properties from the hands and households of white citizens if that became their desire? In works of literature written in the post-Jackson era, serialized stories, humorous anecdotes, and editorial commentary emphasize and express anxiety about the rules and laws governing boyhood possession of property.

A final example from *Jonas a Judge* reveals that laws of property, which were important at the national level in the 1840s, also emerge in Abbott's constructions of boyhood. In an episode titled "Possession," the topic of property comes up when Nathan and Rollo argue about ownership of an apple.[35] They had been given two apples a few days before, but the apples had been forgotten and separated until one of them is found in Nathan's basket of belongings. Rollo's main claim to ownership is that the apple looks like his apple, while Nathan claims he remembers that he put his apple in his basket. The boys take the argument to Jonas, who says that all signs of entitlement are Nathan's since the apple was with his own belongings: "Nathan is entitled to the apple. We find it in his possession; and nobody has a right to disturb any one in the possession of property, unless they can show superior title to it" (168). Rollo does not seem to have any other claim to the apple.[36] Here, Jonas creates title to property through a person's proximity to the object in dispute. This interestingly seems to establish a precedent or possibility that boys' possessions do not necessarily have to be purchased. The serialized episodes from *Jonas a Judge* demonstrate that the power to hold and to transmit property, which is a power that marks citizens in the United States, is a power about which periodical literature schooled boys as it returned regularly to various permutations of the subject. Rollo learns that citizenship and its control are language-based enterprises that need to be mastered in boyhood. Boys who master the textual ins and outs of property can also expect to manipulate, maintain, and protect their rights as citizens.

Rapid changes in national boundaries, transportation, and educational practices were some of the reasons it became important in the 1840s to provide boys with textual models of boyhood citizenship. Although Abbott's boys have come to be understood as unrealistically obedient, serializations of his texts in periodicals show that his boys frequently explore multiple responses to the cultural situations in which they find themselves, and their responses are not always closed, obedient, and correct. We see this in the disputes they have about the laws of property and capital dispersal, and, in the *Companion*, education about property joins other educatory content and boys are constructed as citizens within families, schools, towns, and nations. As we have seen, the partially serialized stories in middle-class periodicals contribute to this citizenship-shaping process. The serialized texts construct boys as capitalist consumers when they employ advertising formats designed to encourage individual ownership of the full-text versions, but regular readers know that the piecemeal texts can be read with pleasure and shared with multiple "owners" or borrowers of the paper. Educationally, both serialized and full-text forms teach children to skillfully interpret narratives, and thereby encourage the kind of entrepreneurial skills required for success in many middle-class American enterprises. The serial nature of the developing common school curricula is reflected in the episodes of Abbott's texts, and many strategies for surviving in the common school are given. Abbott's episodes also show how education can be gained from other boys and older men and how it can occur in multiple places, indoors and out, at home and abroad. Although Rollo himself is less industrious and curious than the middle-class boys produced by an American educational system that endorsed periodicals as supplementary reading material, nonetheless, his character, in its various forms of production, seems to encourage the curiosity and consumption that mark both later boys and their grown-up forms—inventive middle-class capitalists who become the industrialists of the 1870s and 1880s.

The cooperative boy citizenships endorsed by Abbott and the *Companion* adhere to rules and written laws and constitutions, while demonstrating an anxiety about disruptions to this order. In the later 1840s, in *The Young American's Magazine of Self-Improvement*, the kinds of language-based enterprises around which Abbott constructs property-owning citizenships turn inward to focus on improving the property and citizenship-potential of the self. Dana Nelson points out that during the late 1700s and early 1800s, there was an emphasis on whiteness and masculinity that was used to stabilize the concept of nation. The periodical literature for boys shows that in part these fraternizations based on whiteness, membership, and respect toward the government worked in similar ways in texts for boys, but there are places where boyhood and Americanness construct themselves in "fraternal" orders that ignore whiteness or even boy-ness in their emphasis on citizenship through order and citizenship through internal improvement.

This lack of a tightly similar connection between "national manhood" as Nelson defines it and educated American boyhood as it is constructed in periodicals suggests that American boyhood was defined more loosely than American manhood was. It seems that boyhood citizenship, as it is constructed in serialized texts about boys being educated at home, at school, and at play, is created and revised against American laws and codes, especially American laws and codes for men. Education and interaction with those who have had experience with the worlds of both manhood, especially public manhood, and boyhood, move boys from noncitizen boyhood, without regulation, form, or order, to boyhood that is based closely on regulations and forms. This emphasis on orderly boyhood, which is both constructed and challenged in the piecemeal Abbott texts serialized in the *Companion*, becomes much more fixed and closed in periodicals designed for young working-class readers. In the *Young American's Magazine of Self-Improvement*, the language of men's public institutions is used to establish a code of boyhood citizenship practices, a code that becomes somewhat less flexible and more capital- and class-conscious in middle-class boys' texts of the 1850s.

NOTES

1. See David L. Greene's history in Kelly's *Children's Periodicals of the United States*. See also Frank Luther Mott's discussions in *A History of American Magazines* 2:266 and 4:17 and Betty L. Lyon's history in "A History of Children's Secular Magazines Published in the United States from 1789–1899" (70).

2. Nathaniel Parker Willis's son and daughter both entered the magazine world, and the son like his father tried to control the content of the magazines with which he associated himself. The Willis of *The Youth's Companion* is Fanny Fern's (Sara Willis Parton) father. Fern's brother, who worried about what her personal reputation (she was a divorcée) would bring to the *Home Journal*, rejected her contributions. See Mott's discussion of the disagreement and Fern's subsequent rise to fame (II: 352).

3. For example, the byline of an 1841 article titled "Piety in a Wife" is *Presbyterian*. The *Companion*'s heading always declares it as being published by the offices of the *Boston Recorder* (Nathaniel Willis founded the *Recorder* and Sidney E. Morse edited it), which suggests that the *Companion* is in line with the Whig-leaning political aims and the combined Presbyterian and Congregationalist affiliations of that newspaper.

4. It was not until the mid-1850s that extensive subscription and circulation records were kept and published in the United States. David Reed's *The Popular Magazine in Britain and the United States 1880–1960* lists *The Newspaper Record* (1856) and the *American Newspaper Directory* (1869) as two of the projects that organized circulation and subscription rate information about early newspapers and magazines (13).

5. See Andie Tucher (*Froth and Scum*) and Cathy N. Davidson (*Revolution and the Word*) for further discussions of how transportation of texts had an influence on the kinds of material read. For an interesting discussion of how the gold rush of 1849 influenced constructions of manhood see Michael Kimmel's *Manhood in America* (60–62).

6. See Mary Louise Pratt's *Imperial Eyes: Travel Writing and Transculturation* (6–7).

7. Because of their frequent republication, Abbott's books are relatively easy to find now. Some of the full-text versions of the Jonas series include those published by T. Allman in 1840 (the miniature forty-eightmo editions), by Ticknor in 1844 (brown cloth binding, woodcut illustrations), by Clark and Maynard in 1864 (red cloth, embossed with diamond pattern), and by T. Y. Crowell in 1885 (green cloth binding).

8. See Alice Jordan's *From Rollo to Tom Sawyer* for an example of how Abbott's books are often used as an example to set off how far American children's books have come.

9. I will discuss Optic's *The Boat Club: A Tale for Boys* at length in chapter three.

10. In *American Childhood*, Anne Scott MacLeod remarks on the distance between Rollo and characters of the later nineteenth century: "Except that their creators approved of them, Jacob Abbott's Rollo and Burnett's Little Lord Fauntleroy had almost nothing in common" (155). Interestingly, she places Fauntleroy alongside Ragged Dick in a chapter titled "Good Democrats."

11. Stone also discusses Henry James's relationship with Abbott's texts. See 25–26.

12. *Mark Twain–Howells Letters* I: 110.

13. See Betty L. Lyon's discussion in "A History of Children's Secular Magazines Published in the United States from 1789–1899."

14. See MacLeod's discussion of discipline in *American Childhood* 104–5.

15. The first steam locomotive was used in 1830, the reaper in 1831. John Deere patented the steel plow in 1837. Other inventions include the Colt revolver in 1836 and Goodyear's vulcanized rubber in 1839. Later inventions of the 1840s include the telegraph in 1844 and the rotary printing press in 1847.

16. *Jonas on a Farm in Summer* is roughly contemporary with *Rollo's Experiments*. Abbott scatters Rollo and Jonas episodes throughout the late 1830s and early 1840s issues of the *Youth's Companion*.

17. See Virgil's *The Georgics, or the Art of Husbandry* for a comparison of bees and hives to individuals and communities.

18. See "Classical Learning Vindicated." *The Boys' Manual: Comprising a Summary View of the Studies, Accomplishments, and Principles of Conduct Best Suited for Promoting Respectability and Success in Life*.

19. Jonas's laughter might be read as a punishment, since it invites the readers to laugh as well, and thereby places Rollo and his beehive experiment on a sort of Foucauldian public scaffold and ensures that he will not use the same beekeeping methods again.

20. See Ronald J. Zboray and Mary Saracino Zboray's "Books, Reading, and the

World of Goods in Antebellum New England" for a discussion of how texts were often linked to other kinds of goods. See also Zboray's *A Fictive People* for an extended discussion of antebellum economics of reading.

21. See Foucault's discussion of "serial space" in the "Docile Bodies" section of *Discipline and Punish* (147).

22. This magazine is discussed in more detail in chapter two.

23. Philipe Ariès discusses how changes in education practices changed understandings of childhood.

24. For other narratives, see "The Boy Who Could Govern His Thoughts" and "The Bad Scholar Who Made Himself a Good One."

25. "The Young Man Away from Home" also discusses the dangers of what boys might learn when apart from their families. See also "The Proud Boy."

26. "The Only Son" indicates that the respectability of parents in no way guarantees that their sons will be properly brought up to contribute to the family and community in a positive way. This redefinition of each generation's place within American society seems to be a peculiarly American aspect of the education of boys.

27. Patricia Caldwell's *The Puritan Conversion Narrative: The Beginnings of American Expression* suggests that the language of conversion continues to work its way into the literature of the United States.

28. Between 1804 (Amendment XII—presidential elections) and 1865 (Amendment XIII—abolition of slavery), the Constitution and the amendments to it remained unchanged. For boys being educated about American government during the 1830s and 1840s, this meant there had been a relatively fixed body of knowledge and set of "rights" that dictated the workings of the Union and their place within that Union.

29. See chapter three for a more extensive treatment of boating.

30. The mill workers used their newspapers as organizational tools. In May 1846, the *Voices of Industry* resolved to print the name of any woman who did not abide by a petition against operating four looms instead of the regular three: "any one giving her name, and violating this pledge, shall be published . . . as a traitor, and receive the scorn and reproach of her associates" (*Factory Girls* 104). This use of the newspaper was successful in keeping the number of looms at three.

31. Also see Marvin Meyers, *The Jacksonian Persuasion: Politics and Belief* (Stanford, CA: Stanford University Press, 1957), and Michael Feldberg, *The Turbulent Era: Riot and Disorder in Jacksonian America* (New York: Oxford University Press, 1980).

32. Here, Berry is specifically thinking of *Rollo at Work*.

33. See Nelson's discussion of Lewis and Clark (65).

34. Rotundo argues that the shift from boy culture to manhood happens suddenly, without rite of passage or warning, in the early part of the nineteenth century (55).

35. The *Companion* version of this chapter is published in the December 4, 1840, edition and is titled "Possessions."

36. Jonas argues, in an interesting discussion of identity, that Rollo cannot prove the apple is his. Rollo asks what identity is and Jonas answers: "Identity is *sameness* . . . I mean that your recollection is not sufficient proof that this apple is the very same one which the man gave you, and not the one which he gave Nathan. Possession

is nine points of the law. You can't disturb it without better proof than that" (169). This example is just one of the multiple instances in which periodicals and series books teach boys how to possess themselves and the materials around them in ways that are legally binding.

2

Working-Class Boys and Self-Improved Citizenship: George Light's Editorials in the *Young American's Magazine of Self-Improvement*

One of the many alternatives to the *Youth's Companion* during the 1840s was the *Young American's Magazine of Self-Improvement*, a magazine designed for urban working-class boys. The audience of *Young American's Magazine of Self-Improvement* includes, according to its prospectus, all classes of "young Americans." Many of the articles, however, target working-class audiences by focusing on labor unions and lives of workers. As it addresses literate young working-class men, the magazine encourages specific kinds of self-education designed to normalize new citizens and to stabilize understandings of democracy by drawing connections to the unions of working-class citizens and to the Union of the United States.

Like the *Companion*, the *Young American's Magazine of Self-Improvement* discusses the importance of property, but it mainly addresses the property of the self, which it posits as a piece of capital that can, like land, be "improved."[1] *The Young American's Magazine of Self-Improvement* encourages a respect for the property of the self, first and foremost. The "improvement" that is at the heart of the magazine's content goes along with the origins of the word *improvement* (which are property based), and the notion that in order for a title to property to exist there must be use of that property. Thus, the young men addressed in this magazine are encouraged to become "owners" of themselves by active intellectual "improvement." The magazine ties self-awareness and self-improvements to conceptions of work and union. For the skilled workers addressed in magazines like the *Young*

American's Magazine of Self-Improvement, a growing understanding of participation in an anxiously precarious national union mirrors the sometimes tenuous solidarity of the labor union itself. Many notices within the periodical describe the various kinds of unions available to apprentices associated with trades—the Mechanics Union, for example. Mechanics became important members of the working classes during the 1840s and the 1850s. At this time, the United States began mining iron domestically, and consequently, iron became a major factor in developing sophisticated tools that improved the speed of labor and "mechanized" agriculture. While the mechanics may not have been the workers inventing these new tools, or the ones paying for their production and implementation, their familiarity with these new technologies gave them a kind of intimacy with and control over the seamless production of mechanical goods in the United States.

In its celebrations of the intelligence necessary to run machinery and to contribute to the organization of labor, the magazine especially targets skilled workers. The magazine's discussions of union and urban industrialization in this periodical are then extended to a discussion of slavery and the rights of free workers versus the rights of working slaves. The magazine grapples with whether or not freedom and equality, which are celebrated as aspects of Americanness, can exist for working-class young men (women are absent from such discussions) and across color lines. By the end of 1848, the magazine, which, with its beginning in 1847, contemplates the stability and future of America and the condition of America's young citizens, takes a more open abolitionist stance and calls on its young readers to do the same. Many of the articles by the editor are dedicated to the topics of "self-knowledge" and "self-improvement," which coordinate with the title. The reason for the extended coverage of these topics seems to be that the publishers believed that improvement in the working conditions of young Americans who are members of the working class would not come about until there was some discovery of selfhood among the members. The articles published suggest that the discovery of selfhood on the part of the workers would help to maintain the economic prosperity that the Young American Party felt to be an important part of America's future. The self-aware workers would make the factories better places to work and would continue to work there, loyal to the project of building the nation and loyal to the nation itself.

As demonstrated in chapter one, the *Youth's Companion* and Jacob Abbott's contributions to it reveal that publicly and privately owned property and the proper management of both are prominent concerns of middle-class American men during the 1840s. The middle-class boys work through these conventions of ownership and trade on their way to manhood. Dana Nelson suggests usefully that property, defined either by "personalty" or "realty," works to define masculine identity as part of an intricate mix of discourses about citizenship (3).[2] The term *personalty* applies to slavery and slave-trading, with slaves viewed as personal (moveable) property, but the self-knowledge and self-awareness advocated by the *Young American's Magazine* also qualify as attributes of a different kind of "personalty": that is, the magazine suggests that the "self" as opposed to the body can be a saleable and improvable commodity that can influence "destiny" and "citizenship." Throughout its production, the magazine urges its audience of young Americans to find ways to own themselves in order to become fully American. In the late 1840s and early 1850s, property was seen as important to the ongoing establishment of the nation, and Homesteading Acts signed land over to men as long as they were able to live on and improve it. Representative Charles Skelton of New Jersey argued, "Let each man have a plat of ground to live upon and a house to dwell in. Then you will have built up there a population of intelligent and independent freemen, who will defend our country in the day of need and the hour of danger" (qtd. in Welter 300).[3] Like the men encouraged to take advantage of land grants in the West, working-class boys without access to land were urged to stake claims in themselves. In the terms of the magazine, this stake means "improvement" of the self via guided reading; in this way, reading for intellectual improvement becomes a kind of self-homesteading project. At the same time, the magazine publishers and editors work in government-fashion to provide the rules for the claim. Mirroring the government's rewriting of ownership in the Homesteading Acts, in this periodical, outsiders in the form of adult editors still decide what constitutes ownership/improvement.

In thinking through what it means to ask young factory workers to stake a claim in themselves, it is helpful to understand how "self-improvement" connects to the process of being a "Young American." During the 1840s, politicians and writers frequently explored the concept of "Young America." Ralph Waldo Emerson used the term in a speech he delivered on February 7, 1844, to the members of the Mercantile Library Association, an association made up of an audience similar to the skilled worker audience of the magazine.[4] The term *Young America* was then used by politicians to refer to the youthfulness of America as a nation and to those young citizens whose bodily presence and voting power were required to shape and expand the nation. The political tendencies of the Young America movement shaped a party that situated its politics somewhere between the Whigs and the Democrats. The Young Americans were not Jeffersonians or Jacksonians, but instead embraced the changes that technology and industry brought to the nation. They were characterized as eager young men at work in both cities and in the western territories; they were men who wanted the United States government to work for their own prosperity and growth. The term Young America is closely tied to 1840s political and industrial movements in New York, particularly New York City. The Young Americans were interested not just in how America defined itself territorially, but also in having a hands-on, self-aware relationship with nation building. Many members of the party from New York were writers and magazine editors, and the early Young American's work was accomplished in part through literary interventions in the party's project of "nation building."

When the *Young American's Magazine* associates itself with the "Young America" movement, it separates itself from Philadelphia's Sunday school pamphlet publishing industries and Boston's elite/transcendental intellectual movements. The political connotations of the title indicate that the magazine attempts to shape the needs and desires of the Young American selves struggling in the "here and now" of the factory life of the 1840s. Although some members of the Young America movement were supporting what Spiller summarizes as "capitalistic progress and romantic individualism," workers who decided to define themselves as "Young Americans" by buying the magazine and by joining unions and associations that encouraged education had more complicated motives that were tied in part to purchasing, via improvement, citizenships that permitted their participation not just in labor unions but in the larger Union of the states.[5]

The Young America movement flourished in part because periodical culture in the 1840s was flourishing, and also because the movement harnessed the culture's growing interest in reading and connected it to issues of young masculinity and citizenship. Edward L. Widmer's *Young America* focuses on the *Democratic Review*, a periodical that attempted to combine literature and politics and shaped the Young America movement. The cover of Widmer's book depicts a newspaper boy on a curb in front of a wall plastered with signs about pills, exhibitions, and riots, an illustration that suggests the inextricably linked issues of boyhood, periodical literature, class, and Americanness. The *Young American's Magazine*, with its emphasis on texts, citizenship, and improvement, attempts to carry the project of the *Democratic Review* to younger readers. The *Democratic Review* and the *Young American's Magazine* join other literary and political movements that celebrated youth in ways that worked to redefine Americanness and democracy.[6] The emphasis on youth provides a means of resisting the goals and politics of the parent generation while allowing for the embrace of the objectives and reputations of their political grandparents. The *Young American's Magazine of Self-Improvement* focuses on young learners and promotes the idea that intellectual and political pursuits should be harnessed and privileged during youth.

While the *Young American's Magazine* is not directly connected to Duyckinck's *Democratic Review* coterie, the issues of region, generation, and improvement addressed by the Young American Party shed light on how boyhood and young adulthood were connected to issues of urgent nation building and citizenship shaping through textual production.[7] One of the goals of the Young America movement was to use culture, particularly literary culture, to shape American identity. As it formed its goals, the Young America movement borrowed from European intellectually and politically motivated youth movements, but it attempted to develop an original vision of Americanness.

As members of an emerging political party, Young Americans promoted youth by becoming proponents of classlessness and by adopting optimistic policies toward change. The early Young America movement wanted to foster aspects of Americanness that privileged a new kind of thinking tied not to old, wealthy intellectuals and to specific regions, but thinking that was somehow larger and connected to a broad spectrum of people and places. In part to rescue themselves from the shame that might, in the United States, be associated with lack of money or goods, the Young Americans embrace learning but reject economic snobbery. This move to separate intellectual status from economic status permeates the *Young American's Magazine* as it calls on young men to improve themselves with education but at the same time to remain content in their positions as workers rather than owners.

The American writers associated with the Young America movement occupied privileged but somewhat unstable class positions, as did the mechanics that the *Young American's Magazine* addresses. Mechanics were viewed differently from other factory workers, and it is useful to explore why this particular audience was targeted for self-improvement. The mechanics, able to understand, build, repair, and also dismantle the machines that were run by workers being trained and paid for their alienated labor, occupy a higher-class position than do the workers who work with but do not understand the operations of the machinery. In the United States, mechanical abilities continue to be celebrated throughout the nineteenth century. In the December 1885 issue of *St. Nicholas*, George Kringle discusses steam engines and decides: "It takes a head as well as hands to put a steam-engine together" (121). In the May 1886 article of the same magazine, J. Abdon Donnegan reports on "The Handiwork of Some Clever School-Boys" displayed at the Fair of the American Institute and writes:

> Many educators maintain that manual training of a pleasant character, adapted to the age of the pupils, should form an essential element in the education of boys and girls, and should be placed on a par with the regular studies. There is no doubt that such instruction stimulates ambition and tends to develop taste, skill, and natural invention. At the same time an insight into mechanical occupations, with some practical experience in the handling of tools, may assist a boy in choosing a calling suited to his taste, and better prepare him to enter some practical industry, if his choice should incline toward such an occupation (551).

The mechanical occupations were seen as providing boys with a means of combining the physical and the intellectual; this powerful combination could help boys to prosper and could transform the growing United States.

Throughout the nineteenth century, boys were encouraged to gain the ability to use their hands to promote individual welfare and relative prosperity, and their achievements were often noted in later periodicals for boys. In 1886, Charles Barnard praises the "manly spirit" of the boys with the "broken bod[ies]" who have used their hands to form the "Crippled Boys' Brush Factory" (924) and J. Abdon Donnegan depicts "The Handiwork of Some Clever School Boys" in his drawings of "Simple Mechanical Apparatus Made by Boys under 14 Years of Age" (see figures 2.1 and 2.2). An editorial in *Beeton's Boy's Own Magazine* in 1890 compares the class status of clerks with that of mechanics: "There is nothing derogatory about labour. It is labour that has made the world what it is. The rise from the rank of what is called unskilled labour to that of the artisan or the mechanic—is indeed a very great one" (c203).[8] Like these later assessments of labor, the *Young American's Magazine* also tries to rescue manual labor from snobbery by associating it with a stabilizing kind of self-improvement: "Let it be settled . . . that a stated portion of each day shall be devoted to the acquisition of skills in some department of industry—to manual labor, for the sake of the strength it imparts, the disorder it baffles, the comfort it creates, the inde-

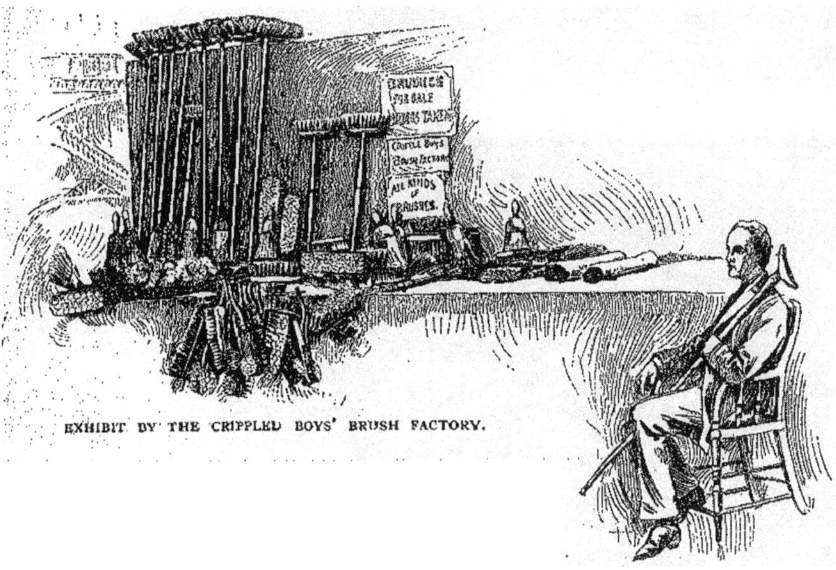

Figure 2.1. Crippled Boys' Brush Factory. Charles Barnard. "The Children's Exhibition." *St. Nicholas* 13 (Oct. 1886): 922.

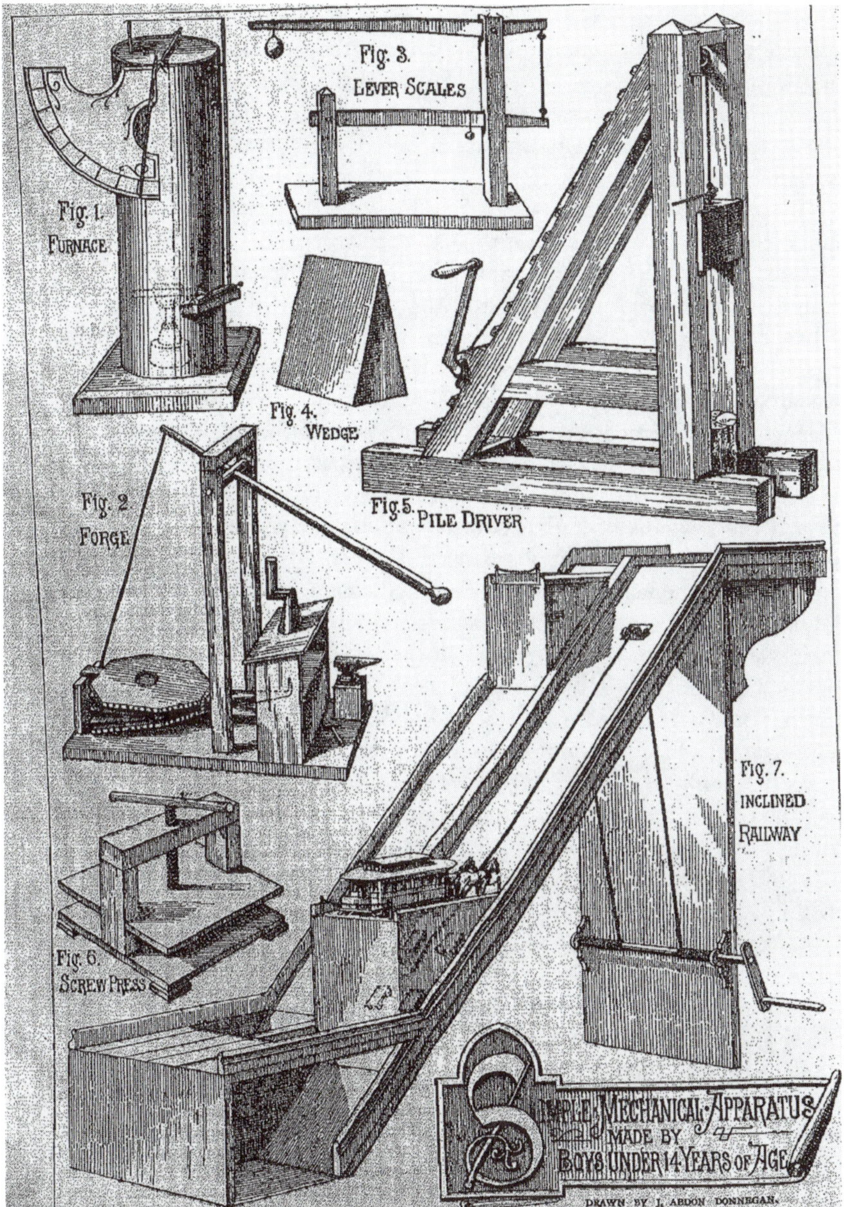

Figure 2.2. "Mechanical Apparatuses." J. Abdon Donnegan. "The Handiwork of Some Clever School Boys." *St. Nicholas* 13 (May 1886): 548.

pendence it secures" (154). These ongoing, half-century-long attempts to elevate the status of mechanical expertise in the face of other kinds of assumptions about class suggest that there was a need to reassure the mechanical workers of their importance in order to prevent them from having access to other pursuits and/or to control their attitudes if they happened to gain access.

In its messages to working-class boys, the magazine encourages the embrace of factory work if not the embrace of working conditions. The prospectus declares that the magazine will "repudiate the notion that true elevation of condition requires the quitting of any useful employment; and do what it can to break down the foolish, not to mention wicked prejudice against Labor, which still so extensively prevails, as well as to check the overweening veneration for Professional life, so common among all classes" (9). In part, this statement critiques views of work linked to more tightly controlled European class systems that equated leisure with superior humanity. It also alludes to the increasing professionalization brought about by more formalized systems of higher education. The declaration places the kind of self-education system that the magazine promotes on the same level as the education of the leisured and professional classes, and it does the same with work. Here, the class snobbery of Boston, which the Young Americans and their New York–based movement worked to avoid, continues to be carried out in George Light's insistence that self-improvement via education need not be totally separated from labor.[9] Labor in this system is something to be appreciated, and it does not necessarily preclude self-improvement.

As the *Young American Magazine* celebrates labor, it encourages laborers to train their minds as well as their bodies. The magazine's idea that the right kind of literature would enhance understandings of nation and contribute to a stabilizing patriotism is one that older Americans who had been involved in politics looked on with skepticism. This resistance can be seen in John Quincy Adams's response to the *Democratic Review*: "literature [i]s, and its nature must always be, aristocratic; . . . democracy of numbers and literature [are] self-contradictory" (qtd. in Widmer 37). Not only did it seem implausible that literature could be something produced by and for the common "man," it also seemed implausible to Adams (and to others) that literature could be used to promote democracy. Asking young workers to use literature to improve themselves as Americans claims to do just that, however.

As the *Young American's Magazine* and the Young America Party redefine literature and its uses, there are also moves to rethink the meaning of Americanness by contemplating the significance of industrialization and the expansion of United States' borders. These moves relate significantly to the Young America Party's obsessions with progress and with expansion, which enter into their writings about South America, Canada, and the West. The young workers in the New York factories were, for the constructors of Americanness, one of the main ingredients of the future, both in terms of their relationship to the West and in terms of what their daily experiences provided for literature.[10] In *Country Boys and Merchant Princes*, Allan Stanley Horlick explains that as the older apprenticeship system fell out of use in the 1840s, merchants began to comment on the process of social mobility, which the apprenticeship system had allowed them to control: "Not only did merchants and the writers who shared their point of view *describe* more explicitly the way young men moved in society. Increasingly, they employed their efforts to *prescribe* the way young men should move in society" [Horlick's emphasis] (15). The workers whose workplace mobility the merchants "prescribe" were also seen as an audience that needed to be guided toward a similarly prescribed vision of Americanness. Amy Kaplan argues in "Manifest Domesticity" that the project of Manifest Destiny applies the language of home to the project of bringing America beyond its borders, and that domesticity applies the language of empire to its project of foregrounding the home. We can see this process in the Young America movement when the members of the party employ the languages of both empire building and domesticity in their arguments for a Young Americanized New York literary scene that colonizes the intellectual and physical lives of the workers in the interest of constructing a new American. The *Young American's Magazine* turns its young working-class readers into its "mission" as it seeks to civilize them with politics, reading lists, and the rhetoric of patriotism and loyalty.

The prospectus of the *Young American's Magazine* connects politics and literature to citizenship, but it somewhat anxiously declares the necessity of education and self-improvement. These are also connected to citizenship, and editor George W. Light presents the connections as necessary to the upkeep and spread of "liberty":

> Taking its stand upon those two grand principles of American Institutions, the Right of the People to Self-Government in the State, and to Private Judgement in Religion, it will show that these principles may not be put aside as mere rhetorical flourish. They not only mean but *command* something. They involve the doctrine that all classes of the community (when in a condition to exert their powers) are [capable of fitting themselves to judge wisely upon the high affairs of state and the deep things of religion]. This is true—let temporal and spiritual despots sneer at it as they will: and no one can neglect the responsibility this truth fastens upon him, without proving false to his country and to the Kingdom of God. The life of liberty depends upon acknowledging and living up to it (10, emphasis original).

This passage insists that all classes of Americans, not just the financially or genealogically elite, have the ability to participate and think clearly about "affairs of the state." The magazine calls on workers to bring themselves into the "condition" of being able to do this and simultaneously challenges those who would exclude the members of the working classes from this kind of participation to be working counter to the "life of liberty."

Many of George W. Light's other editorials in the *Young American's Magazine of Self-Improvement* urgently emphasize the need to educate all members of the union. The above statement from the prospectus, which through Light's use of uppercase letters has the effect of a speech, challenges some of the tenets of American law and its practice by pointing out that, while the law insists that citizens have freedom of religion and the ability to participate in self-government, many of those with power are not allowing those without power to have either of these two things. The magazine contends that it is the duty of those who hold these powers to help others to gain them. The magazine then claims that it is actively intervening in this process.

The magazine does encourage readers to learn about the citizenships available in the United States, but of course, it works to help others gain only the privileges that it deems sound, wholesome, and conducive to the political interests of the rest of the members of the magazine. During this time, magazine publishers and editors have power, and seem sincerely interested in offering power to others, but the magazine shapes its offerings in a way that is skewed to the political interests of the publishers and editors. By recognizing and citing the revolutionary potential of selfhood and by simultaneously containing the revolution through texts, which are intriguingly made up of less fiction and more exhortation, the selves that come to be known by the readers are the selves created textually by the publishers of the periodical.

The call for the improvement of the "condition" of working-class boys reveals how periodical interventions in factory conditions and in the citizenships of working boys participate in gender constructions that are tied to Americanness. As Susan Jeffords notes in *The Remasculinization of America*, class connects to gender in patriarchal institutions such as factories: "[b]y emphasizing masculinity as a mechanism for the installation of patriarchal structure, it is possible to see the ways in which, through the structural relations of gender, men of color or of the working class or of other groups oppressed via defined categories of difference can be treated as women—'feminized'—and made subject to domination" (xii). If working-class men, then, are somehow feminized by the existing patriarchal structures, political moves to include young working-class boys in future state relations also push toward including women in state relations. If Jeffords's formulation works for this 1840s magazine, the urgent need for "improvement" reflects concern about not just a lack of education, but also about a lack of masculinity. The magazine's guidelines for using education to masculinize the feminized (powerless, oppressed) young workers suggest a way for women to move toward participation in the affairs of the government. It is interesting that Light's argument for improvement of young working-class men is made at the same time that the explosion in the numbers of magazines changed women's literacies at a rapid rate. Perhaps the "patriarchs" of the literary and political worlds found working-class boys to be a less threatening form of the feminine, especially if they could be properly educated. Again, the missions of Manifest Destiny and domesticity merge in the way that Kaplan argues they do, except that the *Young American's* strategy is to domesticate/civilize the factory workers, in order to maintain a kind of control "back east" during the expansion west. The control that the program of self-improvement establishes seeks to relocate and shift power from the hands of better-educated middle-class women into the hands of young men who are skilled workers.

In his editorials, Light participates in the "civilizing" of the workers by advocating a carefully disciplined system of self-improvement. Light ties success in education to the discipline necessary for labor, and he compares the publishing houses that are patronized by the magazine to other kinds of industries more familiar to the readers. Light writes that:

> The presses of the American Publishers are kept so continually active, and throw off so many books of value and interest, that we have thought a paper giving a short account of the operations of a few of our eminent booksellers, in addition to some special notices would not be without interest to our readers. We hope to be able to devote our attention to all the leading publishing houses as we proceed (69).

This section sketches a kind of solidarity between the diligent workers involved in the "operations" of the publishing industry and the workers who are also young readers. Americanness, as it is defined by hard work, productivity, and activity, is tied both to reading and, by its declared interest value, to the worker-readers themselves. The editorial accounts of the reasons for including reviews that celebrate the offerings—the hard work—of the leading publishing industries do not necessarily reveal what other accounts show to be true about the way successful magazines related to the publishing houses. The editors of magazines often maintained their powerful positions because of the space they gave to reviews, and accounts suggest that these reviews were, to an extent, "purchased" by the publishers. In his biography, *My Own Story*, John Townsend Trowbridge, an editor and frequent contributor to magazines published in both Boston and New York, recounts how the review system worked for the editor: "It gave me free access to concert halls and theatres, and I was surprised and flattered when some of the great publishing houses began to send me their books for notice, and to quote the *Yankee Nation* as authority in advertising them" (151). This anecdote suggests that the positive reviews in Light's magazine not only reflect the disciplined work of the publishing industry but also indicate that publishers were willing to exchange editorial favors for the boons that provide editorial comforts.

Not only do the needs of the editors play a part in the kinds of texts that magazines review, but changes in the regional power centers of publishing during the 1840s also influence choices about the kinds of texts that are suggested for the readers. During the *Young American's Magazine*'s publishing run, publishing technologies were rapidly expanding, and New York, rather than Philadelphia or Boston, became the center of this expansion. The movement of publishing technologies to New York hints at the number of workers—skilled workers—needed in order to put these publishing industries into place, and this clue suggests one reason why certain kinds of workers were targeted with educational materials. Although New York outstripped Boston in publishing technologies, Boston continued to produce and publish. It was definitely a center for children's periodicals, and the kinds of young workers targeted in New York could also be found in Boston. The *Young American's Magazine* then had potential readers in all of the urban centers where skilled factory workers are employed.

While the magazine suggests solidarity between the publishers and the urban workers of the east, in the books it reviews, it also turns its attention to the west and south. In many ways, the political texts recommended by the magazine coincide with the vision of the future that John O'Sullivan forwarded when he coined the term Manifest Destiny, a phrase used not only by the Young America Party, but by numerous generations of Americans to define their country's mission and actions. O'Sullivan was associated with the Young America movement and promoted working-class suffrage, particularly in Rhode Island. By the late 1840s, spurred on by O'Sullivan's vision of Manifest Destiny, endorsement of expansion regardless of policies on slavery characterizes the Young America movement. On the other hand, *The Young American's Magazine* establishes itself as focused on workers' rights and on abolition instead of expansionism. Throughout the publication of the magazine, the editors take an abolitionist stance that aligns the plights of workers with the plights of slaves in America. Light writes in the prospectus about the magazine's stance on African Americans and their position in the United States: "Recognizing the cardinal Christian doctrine of Human Brotherhood, its whole spirit will be opposed to the Opposition and Depression in all their forms, whether their victims be of any caste or of any color. It will show that sound policy, no less than duty, calls sternly upon the more prosperous classes to take the most generous interest in the elevation of every branch of Society" (9). This proclamation of liberatory purposes seems at odds with the disciplinary and stabilizing motivations behind the advocacy of fixed reading practices and carefully controlled programs of self-improvement.

One way of understanding the combination of liberty and controlled education is through the concept of Union that the magazine promotes. The subtitle of the magazine indicates how it mixes education and liberatory patriotism in order to improve the citizen selves of its young readers: "Combining Literary Entertainment and Instruction with an Effort to promote the Union through Self-Improvement with Every Department of Industry." This emphasis on Union underscores prevalent anxieties about the stability of the Union in the late 1840s when Jackson's long presidency had promoted national needs over states' desires, and had caused some of the southern states to begin to discuss dismantling the Union. Revolutions in Germany, France, Russia, and England had demonstrated to America that factories could produce not just capital but unruly workers who had the ability to demand change. As the editor, Light aligns himself with workers, and draws a comparison between unions of workers and the Union of the states. Light writes: "The progress of society consists in nothing more than in bringing out the Individual, in giving him a consciousness of his own being, and in quickening him to strengthen and elevate his own mind" (8). In repeated editorials and articles, Light argues that the only way for strong workers' unions to emerge and a stable and improved national Union to exist is for the young workers to improve themselves through education.

The reasons for the need for workers to improve their citizenships becomes clear in an article that addresses the question of whether disunion is a necessary part of improvement. In "Abolition Reasons for Disunion," Phillips suggests that even though disunion will disrupt the lives of the workers, it probably is inevitable. Phillips explains the history of the moves to disband: "The youngest of us can remember the time when it was thought an offence next door to treason, to *calculate* the *value* of the Union. Of late years, there are many who not only calculate its value, but openly declare that they would rather part with it than sanction the evil it upholds. Foremost among these are Abolitionists" (113, emphasis mine). In pointing to the "value" of the Union and to the fact that some profits are not worth the ethical cost, Phillips indirectly offers the workers reading the magazine a way to assess the state of their own working environments and the efficacy of their labor unions. His strongest statement draws his readers' attention to the need to be careful with the language of contracts: "We curse the Constitution of 1789, because it is a cunning device to evade the laws of God; a policy of insurance which the North gave her Southern sisters when they started on this mutual slave voyage" (118). As this magazine encourages its readers to improve by expanding their reading, it also suggests, especially in this commentary on how writing coerces a person or a nation into following inhumane policies, that they should improve their reading so that they, like the abolitionists, can detect the "cunning device[s]" that operate on them (118). When Phillips writes, "[t]he abolitionist is not opposed to the government, but to this government, *based upon and acting for slavery*," he struggles to explain the need for disunion in order to regain true union of the states. At some levels, he respects the power and the idea of the Union, but he rejects the nation that remains unified while profiting from slavery.

As they negotiated and proclaimed political positions about workers' rights and abolition, the editors at work behind the production of magazines were attributed great power by book-related industries. John Townsend Trowbridge, an editor and a frequent contributor to magazines published in both Boston and New York, demonstrates that notice was taken by the public and by publishing houses of political commentaries in the magazines. This is vividly demonstrated when Trowbridge is not allowed to remain in the editorial chair at the *Yankee Nation* because he publishes an editorial that is construed as abolitionist.[11] In Trowbridge's account, the power of a single editorial effectively puts the *Yankee Nation* out of business. For a magazine like the *Young American's Magazine* to take an openly abolitionist stance is to invite adversity in the area of publishing success. The abolitionist stance, so unpopular that it could run an established magazine out of existence, probably shortens the life of the *Young American's Magazine*. Certainly, the stance is at odds with the declared position of some of the most prominent members, O'Sullivan among them, of the Young America Party. While the magazine lasts, it repeatedly negotiates the problem of existing as a "self" in a nation where some selves are legally prevented from participating in the kinds of text-based improvement activities that are central to the magazine's project.

In the *Young American's Magazine*, the ongoing stability of the nation is tied to the ability of young Americans to first become aware of the "self" and then to actively seek to improve it through a course of recommended reading. This need for awareness of "self" perhaps relates to the presence in factories of rising numbers of adolescent men with unformed citizenship loyalties and potentially dangerous access to revolutionary ideas. During the late 1840s and early 1850s, factories that had been primarily staffed by women and small children began to hire more young men as numbers of immigrants to the United States increased and machines replaced artisan jobs. As a result of these changes, the young men sometimes are given greater numbers of opportunities to learn how the machines worked and how to repair them, and some are educated in the process of machine manufacture. The reading lists serve as citizen shaping measures for these young men, who if not immigrants themselves, might have access to immigrants with revolutionary backgrounds and information.

The drive to shape the young men in the factories relates to the youth movements that influenced the European revolutions of the 1840s. As it responds to these youth movements and attempts to develop an American version that harnesses their power, the Young America Party embraces the rebellions as reflecting the revolutionary spirit that had swept America and then France fifty or so years before. When the *Young American's Magazine of Self-Improvement* recommends Carlyle's *History of the French Revolution*, it both celebrates and attempts to contain the revolution through textual explanation and evaluation. The literature of revolution that the magazine recommends for working-class boys reveals how these young men's Americanness was constructed by the political milieu at work at the time of publication.[12] They also suggest that the periodical itself promotes certain kinds of revolutionary acts in the interest of self-construction while advocating loyalty to the right kind of self-improved Union. Biographies of heroes of the American Revolution are also recommended. These heroes, who changed the destiny of their nation, indicate to those "young Americans" searching for self-improvement that one way the self can be improved is through struggle for the nation, a struggle that the magazine constructs as inevitable and imminent.

As the factories hire more young men, there emerge, in the larger public, fears and suspicions about the changes recent influxes of immigrants escaping revolutionary chaos elsewhere might bring to the United States.[13] The *Young American's Magazine* both addresses these new workers and also strives to contain and avert the kinds of fears excited by changes in factories and changes in population, especially the fears related to the future of Americanness. Some accounts of factory life illustrate that rather than being docile and adapting easily to United States cultures, young factory workers are discontented and manifest cultural resistance in the forms of lateness, absenteeism, and drunkenness.[14] While books for middle-class readers such as *Factory Boy* depict young boys working in factories as loyal, quiet, and diligent, the *Young American's Magazine* explores these workers' interests in revolution with texts that note and then also contain the described rebellions. One way this happens is when essays encourage workers to direct their energies toward solitary reflection and invention rather than organization. William Ellery Channing emphasizes invention when he writes to the readers that "great ideas come to us no less from outward, direct, laborious teaching than from indirect influences, and from the native working out of our own mind" (101). The reading strategies promoted by this working-class magazine, then, assist in the development of new ideas, the kinds of ideas that might improve both the workplace and the state of the nation.

While the Abbott-authored periodical literature published in the middle-class *Youth's Companion* parses the reasons for following an established order, without necessarily aiming at "progress," the *Young American's Magazine*'s aim is to aid society's progress by constructing individuals. In Abbott's books, change is often brought about by establishing order, as it is for example when Jonas begins to work for a lawyer and slowly effects change by cleaning the inkpots and neatening his and the lawyer's work areas.[15] Jonas's changes seem restorative rather than progressive and tend to make work more efficient rather than "fairer." This kind of change may, however, be similar to the progress advocated by Light's magazine in that Jonas quietly and peacefully changes his working conditions. In the *Young American's Magazine of Self-Improvement,* Thomas Dick writes about the need for shorter hours of labor, and a short piece that follows this commentary on business hours points to the need to use every spare moment for improvement: "It is hardly credible what acquisitions in knowledge one may make, by carefully husbanding and properly applying every spare moment" (Burgh 126). In part, then, better working conditions were one of the aims of the unions, and in this way a similarity might be drawn between Abbott's "change" and Light's "progress." One of the ways Light's magazine's content works for progress is to encourage the young workers to read more and to read the books the magazine reviews, especially the ones that adhere to its specific political and social goals.

When the magazine claims that self-knowledge and self-improvement are available to all classes and colors of people, it is making a revolutionary claim. On the other hand, the absence of articles about women and girls at a time when many young women are working in factories suggests that improved selfhood and increased self-knowledge are enhancements made available more easily to boys and men of all classes and colors. The *Young American's* subscription rate is relatively high—$1.00 per year, which is the same price as the *Companion*. However, the *Young American's* is longer and more elaborate than other periodicals produced during this time, and this length seems to indicate that rather than being designed to be bought individually, it is meant to be purchased by union leaders and organizers or by more powerful men who might distribute the magazine among the young workers, possibly at the "ragged" or union schools established at some factories and workplaces.

Rather than promoting a revolutionary selfhood, the content and price suggest that the magazine encourages the production of a selfhood remarkably similar to those produced and recommended in periodicals designed for another class of boy readers. The poets who are included in the recommendations are also often the same ones quoted in magazines that R. Gordon Kelly would argue are aimed at the gentry class.[16] In 1844, Hugh Murray, a Scottish observer of America, writes that poetry in America served political as well as aesthetic purposes: "The newspapers, which with us rarely contain any Parnassian effusions, and those mostly of the lowest class, are here the main vehicle. They are expected to gratify the imaginative as well as the political propensities of their readers" (131). The presence of poetry in working-class newspapers and the frequency of poetry recommendations in the *Young American's Magazine* suggest the ways in which texts read by several classes might be used to promote political change as well as to provide entertainment, depending on the audience and venue.

Like the *Companion*, this magazine also focuses on education, but it exhorts its readers to maintain individual-, rather than sect- or school-motivated goals of self-improvement. It makes the readers aware of selfhood and its status as the only "true" possession, while at the same time advocating solidarity with the group. The term *improvement* brings together the emphasis on property previously noted in the discussion of the *Youth's Companion* and the awareness of self as a way of displaying good American citizenship. The *Oxford English Dictionary* places a capital-related definition first in its classification of the word *improvement*: 1.a.: "The turning of a thing to profit or good account; profitable management or use; making the most of a thing for one's own profit: realization of the profits of anything" (750). The second definition points more specifically to land than to other forms of property or capital: 2.a.: "The turning of land to better account, the reclamation of waste or unoccupied land by inclosing and bringing it into cultivation" (751). The magazine continually returns to language that highlights the importance of improving the capital and the "territory" of the self, and it ties this need for improvement to larger national issues.

Light writes that the price of the magazine is designed to encourage a wide readership: "one dollar a volume in the hope of a wide circulation" (8). The prospectus targets not only the readers but also those members of the middle classes who are willing to promote the magazine's vision of "progress" and "union." It also claims to be looking for friends of a "sound popular literature for continued encouragement in the enterprize [sic]" (8). The use of "popular" in the magazine's objectives indicates that it means for its readership to include the many rather than be limited to the few. The term *sound*, often used in an organic context (an apple can be sound), suggests that literature can work like food to contribute either to growth or to withering. The "rotten" forms of popular literature, probably the penny newspapers, which flourish in the industrial cities at this time, lead in Light's formulation, not to sound progress, but toward rottenness and stagnation.[17] Following the organic meaning of *sound*, the rotten can often lead to fertilization (think of a compost heap) and also to combustion. Literature, and particularly the regularly produced, cheaper periodical forms, then, were seen as having both the potential to be sound and the potential to be dangerously, combustibly rotten.

In writing about the parameters of the magazine, Light appeals to the promoters of the "sound popular literature" and reveals that his interests are not just in the young "unschooled" workers, but in the established merchants and mechanics, perhaps those who own some of the industrial capital but also have an understanding of the workers' needs and political interests: "We consider ourselves already laid under special obligations to the merchants and mechanics of Boston, for the liberality with which they have favored our undertaking. We are also gratified by the generous treatment which the work has received from the most intelligent conductors of the

Press, in all parts of the country where it had been circulated" (8). In one issue, the "Mechanic Apprentices Library Association" is described in particularly appreciative terms because of members' ability to use organization to gain self-improvement: "This well-known useful Association, which numbers about 300 members, presents the interesting phenomenon of an institution entirely composed of and conducted by minors—young mechanics—with no other motive than self-improvement, and a desire to raise their fellow apprentices to a true estimate of the dignity of Labor in the Mechanic Arts" (136). Light's celebration of these groups demonstrates that the "progress" and "self-improvement" the magazine purportedly offers to give its working-class readers are forms approved of and encouraged by American men who are separated economically and industrially from the cultural situation of the young American readers.

The main aim of this magazine, although focused on progress and the situation of the workers, seems to be preservation: the articles that predict disunion of the states look ahead and work to stabilize citizenships that will be shaken by the upcoming chaos. Other Union-promoting pieces focus on the possibilities for inventing solutions for the nation with the help of the self-improved workers. The union of workers must be kept "sound" and this, in turn, will provide a soundness for the Union. Light proclaims the preservation-oriented purpose in the following way:

> The leading purpose of this Magazine is to awaken a more general interest in Self-Improvement—Physical, Moral, Intellectual, Industrial and Prudential, and to meet the wants of those who are more or less engaged in that noble work. But while it will aim to embody in its pages—by means of original contributions, and carefree selections and compilations from able writers—a good share of the best self-educational spirit and talent of the age, no effort will be wanting to make an entertaining and useful MISCELLANY OF PROSE AND POETRY for the general reader (9).

While the poetry and prose mentioned in this section of the prospectus suggest that portions of the magazine will not be aimed specifically at young workers, the rest of the magazine is meant to help readers to become "self-educated."

As articles and book recommendations demonstrate, the practical skills of the workers and the numbers of readers who are immigrants shape the rhetoric of self-education that is included in the magazine. Light elaborates at length on the self-education of the intended audience: "It will seek to impress deeply upon the minds of all persons engaged in the practical pursuits of life, the importance, the duty, and the practicability, of [educating themselves], in a manner worthy of being created in the image of God and provided with illimitable means of improvement" (9). In this section of the prospectus, the laboring/mechanical class audience is indicated in the phrase "engaged in the practical pursuits of life." The next section extends the discussion of the practical: "It will endeavor to disseminate correct views of the *kind* of education best suited to Republican citizens in general, and to each of the Practical classes of Society in particular; and to point out the best course to be pursued in its acquirement" (9, emphasis original). As in Henry Ward Beecher's emphasis on learning and self-improvement in his *Lectures to Young Men*, a text recommended by the *Young American's Magazine*, during the late 1840s, there is an increased drive to convert young men to Americanness through the means of education. At this time, the face of the American working class changed to become largely a class of immigrants from Ireland, Germany, and Italy. So, when *The Young American's Magazine of Self-Improvement* insists that it can point to the "best course" of education, a course that will lead to republican rather than other kinds of citizenship, it does so anxiously, in part because it witnesses the kinds of changes being made to the face of the American working class.

Later nineteenth-century educational texts echo this magazine's early obsession with education. The 1879 version of the *McGuffey's Sixth Eclectic Reader* illustrates this, with its inclusion of Lyman Beecher's "Necessity of Education" lecture: "We must educate! We must educate! or we must perish by our own prosperity. If we do not, short will be our race from the cradle to the grave" (99).[18] Similarly, in promoting the preserving qualities of education, Light discusses the need for members of the "Practical classes" to pursue education and his magazine's ability to meet those needs: "We believe it will be able to demonstrate that the Useful Avocations of Life, instead of constituting any obstacle to the best kind of Self-Education, may and should be so regulated as to contribute eminently—as Providence doubtless designed they should—to the highest Intellectual and Moral, as well as Physical, interests of those engaged in them" (9). This magazine then diligently regulates the self-education of the members of the practical classes. It is designed to produce a "sound" self-education, rather than one that might easily be obtained by reading other, slightly cheaper, but more widely available penny newspapers.

The magazine devotes much of its space to book lists and book recommendations, and the amount of space devoted to book suggestions reveals how powerful the editors felt books could be in shaping citizenships that would contribute to the stability of the Union. The books reviewed and suggested in the section of the magazine titled Literary Notices indicate the directions Light wants the education of the practical classes to take:

> Leigh Hunt's *Stories from the Italian Poets*, *Autobiography of Goethe*, Carlyle's *Heroes and the Heroic in History*, *Sartor Resartus*, *French Revolution*, Mrs. Somerville's *Connection of the Physical Sciences*, Schiller's *Thirty Years' War*,

> Spurzheim's *Phrenology*, Mahan's *Intellectual Philosophy*, Emerson's *Poems*, H. W. Beecher's *Lectures to Young Men*, Hague's *Christianity and Slavery* (17).

These books emphasize points in history when disruption or change occurred. Even Hunt's *Stories from the Italian Poets* focuses on stories about Italian heroes like Aeneas, who begins a new nation based on the best parts of the old, but leaves the past behind. The recommendation of *Sartor Resartus*, which translates as "tailor remade/retailored," has interesting implications in the context of the magazine's advocacy of self-improvement. The title invokes work done for others and also suggests how defining the self in terms of the occupation might also leave room for refashioning or shaping of the self. Carlyle himself takes a position in relation to revolution and rebellion that seems to intersect with the magazine's positions. Obviously, he is fascinated by it, but he also distances himself from it and carefully analyzes it. By recommending histories of the revolution to industrial workers, especially relatively conservative histories as opposed to current calls for revolution, the list carnivalesquely opens a space for consideration of the possibilities of revolution while simultaneously providing only the title of a history that acknowledges it as past and gone rather than present.[19]

Other texts that the magazine reviews provide a sense of the magazine's attitudes toward class. Spurzheim's *Phrenology* presents a view of the human condition that ties class and occupation to biology. Phrenology argues that the body itself provides a coded but decipherable framework that reveals each individual's capabilities. By decoding the phrenology of any given person, the workers (as well as the owners) would be able to read whether or not a certain type of "self" could be improved. Spurzheim's *Phrenology* and its science of understanding and describing types connects to the rhetoric of whiteness and manhood that Dana Nelson claims is repeatedly linked to nation and citizen building in the early federal period. Readings of "types" and "characteristics" encouraged in Spurzheim were part of extensions of phrenology that worked to read race, foreignness, and belonging as well. The recommendation in the *Young American's Magazine* reads as follows:

> Spurzheim's work on "Phrenology," has passed into the hands of the Harpers, and they have issued it, at a comparatively low price, in one handsome octavo volume, with illustrative engravings. This is probably the best treatise on phrenology extant. To a believer in the science it is an invaluable storehouse of facts and arguments; while its clearness of style, and its fine exposition of the nature and operation of the human propensities, sentiments, and faculties, make it interesting to those who are skeptical in regard to the organs (71).

I would suggest that part of the implication here is that the selves so ardently in need of improvement could actively separate their inherent (genetic, phrenological) weaknesses from their improvable weaknesses and also actively participate through phrenological study in associating with other "selves." While the magazine ultimately recommends developing capabilities to the utmost possible degree, it also promotes titles that suggest that self-improvement can only go so far. To be a young American, it seems, is to be a self that can be improved—a self with some already inherently improvable characteristics.

Readers of the *Young American's Magazine* are encouraged by this positive review of the book to consider phrenology as a "storehouse" of information about "human propensities." Although the review leaves some room for doubt about the validity of phrenology, overall it seems to indicate that this kind of study can only help to identify areas for improvement, and as a corollary, areas or persons where improvement is impossible.[20] Knowing how to judge character by physiological characteristics would also allow readers to judge membership, and establish belonging to the "union" of the nation.

All of the titles, including Emerson's poems and H. W. Beecher's lectures, seem to presuppose that the young American worker will already have reached a fairly advanced literacy level. The texts are not simple, and are all quite lengthy. Beecher's *Lectures*, which was written in 1844 and republished several times, contains direct addresses to the reader that indicate levels of assumptions about the literacy of readers and their agency. Beecher dedicates the 1893 edition of his volume to his father Lyman, who was, as noted earlier, a proponent of educating for the sake of Americanness. In the preface to the 1845 volume, Beecher writes about the fact that he wants his readers to be companions with the ability to think on their own:

> I ask every YOUNG MAN who may read this book not to submit his judgement to mine, not to hate because I denounce, nor blindly to follow me; but to weigh my reasons, that he may form his own judgment. I only claim the place of a companion; and that I may gain his ear, I have sought to present truth in those forms which best please the young; and though I am not without hope of satisfying the aged and the wise, my whole thought has been to *carry with me the intelligent sympathy of* YOUNG MEN (n. pag., emphasis original).[21]

Several aspects of this preface are worth noting. First, Beecher aligns himself with his readers by claiming the readers are his companions. He constructs them as readers with agency, and because of this construction, they are rhetorically positioned to agree with his ideas. For the proponents of a "sound popular literature" writing reviews in the *Young American's Magazine*, this would be a rhetorical move that would encourage the "right" kinds of self-improvement. By enlisting the "intelligent sympathy" of young men, Beecher negotiates an awareness of the self that allows only for those views that are in line with his own. Second, Beecher claims twice that he writes expressly for young men as opposed to young women or the young in general. These lectures, then, can give insight into views of young men held by older, literate, Protestant New Englanders at the time the piece was written. Third, Beecher goes out of his way to point to his form. He chooses a form he claims will appeal to the young men for whom he is writing. Part of the form he is discussing may be his short and somewhat titillating lecture titles which include: "Industry and Idleness, Twelve Causes of Dishonesty, Six Warnings, Portrait Gallery, Gamblers and Gambling, The Strange Woman, Popular Amusements, Practical Hints, Profane Swearing, Vulgarity, Happiness, and Temperance." What young man would not want to be enlightened about the "Strange Woman"? The topics he chooses for his lectures promote self-improvement strategies that relate to potential problems faced by workers both in and out of the urban factories.

Beecher's preface to the second edition comments on the regional needs for the lecture topics in response to what seem to be claims of exaggeration or outlandishness:

> It is proper to remark, that many of the statements in these Lectures, which may seem severe or overdrawn in New England, are literally true in the West. Insensibility to public indebtedness, gambling among the members of the bar, the ignoble arts of politicians,—I know not if such things are found at the East; but within one year past an edition of three thousand copies of these Lectures has been distributed through the West, and it has been generally noticed in these papers, and I have never heard objections from any quarter that the canvas has been too strongly colored.

Written in 1846, Beecher's "Preface" describes the West as a place full of exaggerated dangers for young men, a place where text-based guidance can fill an American need to promote certain citizenships as well as fill an economic demand that is profitable for the author accused in New England of strongly coloring the canvas. The West serves in this text as a place where behaviors that are given in the East because of regularized education are behaviors that need to be prescribed. Negative behaviors also must be addressed, because the proper responses to them need to be explored in detail.

In order for his text not to disrupt the sensibilities of the East, Beecher needs to paint the young men's temptations as realities in the West. Beecher emphasizes the reality of his examples in part to sell his text to eastern boys who might be called upon by economic necessity as well as American rites of passage to live and work in the West. Beecher's defense of his lectures' content in his preface then provides anxious eastern readers with a reason to buy his lectures. Young boys are provided with a script for defending their choice of reading material to their mothers or to anyone who might choose to question the content. Beecher's preface markets the work by noting its use of exaggeration and by accounting for it. To the young working-class readers directed to this work by the *Young American's Magazine*, these descriptions of the difference between needs in the East and needs in the West would provide a map of cultural values by which they could locate their own brand of Americanness.

If reviews of books like *Phrenology* and *Lectures to Young Men* can be read as advertisements that promote "self-improvement," then they advertise aspects of Americanness important to the publishers. The reviews provide lists of materials that, if available in the households of the workers, would convince the younger members who read them to proceed to either accept their place as workers or move up into relatively "safe" positions as loyal, nonrebellious citizens. If this "advertising" campaign is successful, the owners of the factories are provided with educated workers who will work loyally since they believe they have selves in the process of being improved. Early advertisements focused on selling texts; in this periodical, the "advertisements" are designed to sell books that would promote "soundness" and improve the selves of young workers. Thus, the record that the lists of books leave for scholars now is one that helps to trace what privileged but sympathetic middle-class reformers deemed to be sound alternatives to other kinds of reading material.

The middle-class magazines of the 1840s and the subsequent books based on the serialized stories in the magazines provide texts that are chosen for content that reduces "selfishness" and thoughtless behavior. This rule applies except in those cases where selfish behavior is necessary to reinforce the established rules of society, as when Jonas discusses property and possession. The books recommended in the *Young American's Magazine* are written by diverse authors and seem to encourage individual choice in reading matter rather than, as in the middle-class magazines, promoting the purchase of the same authors again and again based on their religious affiliations and their ability to keep their name and their characters' names in the public eye. The titles of the books in the *Young American's* lists, though, are designed to fill in specific gaps in the knowledge of the skilled laborers. Fiction is not recommended. Neither are particularly religious or "true" stories that border on fiction because of the narrative techniques with which they are told. Fiction seems to be withheld from these magazines as a way of preventing "unsound" addictions. The recommended histories encourage selves to become stable participants in the project of preserving the Union and furthering its aims. According to the recommendations, the workers should think through histories of the past in order to move toward new histories that would advance progress in the present.

The *Young American's Magazine of Self-Improvement*, with its desire to inform, uses a repetitive technique in its series articles, especially in the series that have to do with self-improvement. The gaps in knowledge that are filled and the gaps that are specifically left open replicate the new methods of line manufacture that were part of nineteenth-century industrial factories. The reading workers are instructed to focus on one aspect of education (self-improvement) and to learn it thoroughly without really getting a sense of any larger picture. The repetitive urging of self-improvement works in tandem with the lists of books and reviews. These lists, the magazine insists, if followed, will lead to self-improvement. If the workers adhere to the guidelines of the magazine, the lists and the editorial rhetoric of selfhood produce more self-aware workers, but because the listed texts are chosen for their closeness to the political aims of the publishers, they also tend to nurture group subjectivities rather than individual ones. Magazines for working-class boys urge the idea that the self is the only sure possession. The self is the one piece of capital that can be increased in value through the use of portable texts without fear of inflation, speculation, or collapse; the obsession with self-improvement points to anxieties about other kinds of possessions, including ownership, stakes in unions, and citizenships in the larger Union of the United States.

The self-owned and self-improved citizenships promoted by the *Young American's Magazine* eventually veer away from the aims of the Young America politicians. By the 1850s, the Young America movement has changed its parameters and the nation's understanding of it shifts as well. By this time, Widmer notes, "Young America" became a "slangy nickname for the spirit of restless expansionism and ugly greed that characterized the decade" (19). The belief that controlled reading would improve the characters and the selves of the readers also changes in the 1850s to coincide more directly with the idea that money rather than self-aware labor marks citizenship success. During this time, the "greed" of expansionism makes its way into boys' books; many series books begin to display an overwhelming respect for the wealthiest citizens. William Taylor Adams (Oliver Optic), a prolific writer of boys' books during the 1850s, places a heavy emphasis on large monetary rewards that, in his texts, reveal the true character and citizenship potential of the boys. In these books, the best boys have money and the most American boys know how to invest the money to the greatest advantage. As it turns out, in these texts, boys without some kind of economic sponsor have almost no chance of gaining citizenship through self-improvement.

NOTES

1. The Young America movement is separate, but related to the magazine discussed here.
2. See Nelson's *National Manhood*.

3. See Welter's *Mind of America.*

4. See *The Collected Works of Ralph Waldo Emerson*, Vol. 1, 217–21.

5. See Spiller's discussion of the Young America movement in *Collected Works of Ralph Waldo Emerson* (221).

6. For an expanded discussion of the turn to youth in the post-Jackson era, see Widmer, 4.

7. The coterie included Hawthorne and Melville, among others.

8. See my discussion of *Beeton's* in the concluding chapter.

9. See Widmer's discussion of the Young America movement's suspicions of Harvard and the intellectual trends in Boston (12).

10. Walt Whitman mines the sights and sounds of industrialization and urbanization for material. See "Song of Myself." Herman Melville does the same in "Paradise of Bachelors and the Tartarus of Maids."

11. He himself became more of an abolitionist later in his life, but was always a cool, reticent one.

12. In *A People's History of the United States*, Howard Zinn discusses the class struggles that occurred during the 1840s in the cities and at sites of expansion and terms these struggles "The Other Civil War," 206–46.

13. By 1860, over 60 percent of the factory workforces were made up of immigrants. See immigration numbers in Ira Leonard and Robert Parmet's *American Nativism, 1830–1860*, 32–33. See Wilentz's *Chants Democratic* for discussions of the workforce in New York City, 110. Michael Denning's *Mechanic Accents: Dime Novels and Working-Class Culture in America* focuses on popular texts and working-class reading cultures.

14. Others were more organized, as when the Lowell mill workers refused to be given more work with fewer machines for lower wages after managers tried to recoup losses after the Panic of 1837. See discussion in *Women at Work*, 109. A fascinating study of women's roles in later (1870) textile mill resistance can be found in Mary H. Blewett's "Manhood and the Market: The Politics of Gender and Class among the Textile Workers of Fall River, Massachusetts, 1870–1880." See also Sean Wilentz's *Chants Democratic: New York City and the Rise of the American Working Class, 1788 –1850.*

15. See my discussion of *Jonas a Judge* in chapter one.

16. See *Mother Was a Lady.*

17. Andie Tucher's *Froth and Scum* points out that the penny newspapers revealed discrepancies in reporting and encouraged working-class readers to participate in meaning-making and truth-making processes.

18. From Elliott J. Gorn's *The McGuffey Readers: Selections from the 1879 Edition.*

19. Although Marx's *Communist Manifesto* was not immediately translated into English, some of the factory workers who were immigrants would have been able to read the original.

20. Interestingly, in the 1840s, phrenology's insights began to be replaced by the "science" of mesmerism, a science to which not everyone had access. See "Mesmerism Challenges Phrenology as America's Favorite Science" in *The Mad Forties* (91–101).

21. Reprinted in the 1893 version.

3

Typing American Renaissance Boys: Citizenship Compromises in Oliver Optic's *The Boat Club*

> [H]is stories were only slightly better than [dime novels], and towards the end of the 19th century, were sometimes banned from [libraries] because of their sensationalism.
>
> —*Oxford Companion to Children's Literature* on Oliver Optic's work

The literature published during the 1850s by Nathaniel Hawthorne, Herman Melville, and Walt Whitman influenced F. O. Matthiessen to such an extent that he dubbed the decade the "American Renaissance." This decade also saw Susan Warner's *The Wide, Wide World* and Harriet Beecher Stowe's *Uncle Tom's Cabin* reach bestseller status.[1] Although many children's books and periodicals were published during this decade, American children's literature has never been assessed as having a concurrent flourishing.[2] In its catalogue of "landmark" children's literature texts, Peter Hunt's *Children's Literature: An Illustrated History* mentions only William Taylor Adams's (better known as Oliver Optic) *The Boat Club* as a representative American text from this decade (354). While any list of "important" books is of course shaped by the tastes of the list maker, Optic's presence as the only American writer seems significant. How did the flowering of American literature intersect with the content and reception of Optic's texts? How do his texts relate to other stories that American literary history and histories of children's literature tell themselves about the 1850s? Oliver Optic, in part because of the prolific number of books and magazine articles associated with his authorship, has come to be known as a dime novelist, and that reputation brings all of the negative connotations of cheaply produced, sensational literature. Far from being "sensational" in the conventional sense, *The Boat Club* is sometimes more didactic and religiously exacting than the Jacob Abbott books of the previous decade and much more order-oriented than the regulated reading worlds established by the *Young American's Magazine of Self-Improvement. The Boat Club* and the other texts in the series challenge current theories about 1850s children's literature that claim that books for children were at this time either sensational or didactic. Optic's texts use the series form to compromise between these two "types" of children's literature and to negotiate other compromises related to citizenship faced by boys moving toward manhood in the 1850s.

The history of the reputation of Optic's texts provides insight into how the boyhoods constructed in this series intersect with later more "canonical" American boyhoods such as *Story of a Bad Boy*. The often misread content of *The Boat Club* also calls into question notions about this text's intervention in the construction of later more canonically "American" boyhoods. Among these constructions is the one that suggests that *Huckleberry Finn* emerges out of nowhere in direct resistance to boys' stories that depict boys as angelic orphans or dependent Mama's boys. One of the theories about "popular" children's literature posited by Zohar Shavit in a discussion of canonical children's literature is that in order for literature to be popular, it must create a "*portrayal of a children's world in which adults hardly exist at all*" (95, emphasis original). *The Boat Club* problematizes this formulation since its perceived sensationalism makes it more "popular" than canonical, and also, since instead of portraying a world without adults, it is full of instances of parental guidance and control.

While Oliver Optic's books are listed as significant by histories of children's literature, his texts are now "misread" or altogether unread because of their reputation. Because of the received opinion that Optic's texts are merely sensational dime novels, *The Boat Club*'s content has been ignored, and much more critical study has been given to boyhood texts from the late 1860s, the beginning of the "Golden Age" of children's literature, an age in which texts for children supposedly veer away from overt didacticism and "cheap" sensationalism to less formulaic presentations complete with more complicated characters and story lines.[3] Anne Scott MacLeod writes in "Children's Literature in America" that "[b]y the end of the 1870s mainstream writing for children . . . was more sophisticated, more varied, and more important to the publishing business than ever before" (129). Optic's texts complicate the dichotomies between sensational and didactic that critical studies of children's literature have used to determine what is worthy of study and what is not. The evaluations of Optic's texts that circulated during his most prolific period as a writer have also contributed to the ongoing misreadings of his series and the boyhoods they construct.

Optic's texts have remained unexamined in part because of the ways his reputation for writing sensational rags-to-riches stories was circulated during his career. *The Boat Club*, which explores the founding of a club for the "best" boys in a small New England town, extends the middle-class boyhoods constructed in Abbott's Rollo series. Optic's boys are more like the conceptions of Rollo that exist in discussions of Abbott's reputation rather than being similar to the textual Rollo. While Abbott's characters will work with members of society who break rules in order to share their rights and privileges as well as to educate them, Optic's characters exclude, shame, and ban outsiders and rule breakers. Some of his "good" boys are actually much more docile and submissive than any of the Abbott characters. Richard L. Darling notes that the book review industry participated in giving Optic his sensational reputation by reviewing Optic's texts in magazines for adults. A review in the *Nation* states, "If we could have our way the sale of them would stop immediately and entirely" and the *Penn Monthly* characterizes the texts as the "sensational, flashy 'Oliver Optic' books" (qtd. in Darling, 25). Optic responds to charges of easy sensationalism by comparing his texts to other leisure time pleasures:

> Boys don't skate for the development of their systems as a general rule; they skate for the fun of it. . . . many books . . . are exciting, interesting, or amusing, with no immoral or dangerous tendency in them. Boys may read for amusement, and will derive as much benefit, mentally, from the study of language as the bodily frame does from manly sport (qtd. in Darling, 25).

Here, Optic suggests that when it comes to reading material, sometimes compromising between entertaining and instructive reading can be productive in teaching language and maintaining a healthy mind; he also connects this compromise to sports that contribute to "manliness."

The attacks on Optic have proven to be more powerful than Optic's responses that suggest that boys need some "manly" fun in their reading material. During the 1870s, Optic's sensational reputation is even more firmly established by Louisa May Alcott, who, in her serialized text *Eight Cousins*, inserts a covert description and criticism of Optic's work. In this text, Alcott has Mrs. Jessie, an angelic mother, proclaim that she does not quite like some of the books the boys have been reading because of the information and morals they contain. Mrs. Jessie remarks: "The writers of these popular stories intend to do good, I have no doubt, but it seems to me they fail because their motto is, 'Be smart, and you will be rich,' instead of 'Be honest, and you will be happy'" (199). Mrs. Jessie also reacts negatively to the use of slang:

> But my boys are neither bootblacks nor newsboys, and I object to hearing them use such words as "screamer," "bully," and "buster." In fact, I fail to see the

> advantage of writing books about such people unless it is done in a very different way. I cannot think they will help refine the ragamuffins, if they read them, and I'm sure they can do no good to the better class of boys, who through these books are introduced to police courts, counterfeiters' dens, gambling houses, drinking saloons, and all sorts of low life. . . . I am not satisfied with these *optical* delusions. . . . Even if the hero is merely an honest boy trying to get his living, he is not permitted to do so in a natural way, by hard work and years of patient effort, but is suddenly adopted by a millionaire whose pocketbook he has returned; or a rich uncle appears from the sea, just in the nick of time (200, emphasis mine).

Alcott's text, then, forwards the idea that the citizenships Optic's texts offer to the "right" kind of boys are gained too easily without enough hard work and struggle. Mrs. Jessie's comments also convey that Optic's representations of members of the working class are dangerous both for working-class and middle-class readers, because of the contagious nature of their slang-based language and the messages they offer about becoming wealthy.

Optic responds to these charges in his September 1875 issue of *Oliver Optic's Magazine*, and he defends himself with Alcott's own success: "Even the author of 'Dick Dauntless' and 'Sam Soaker,' whoever he may be, would not dare to write up a heroine who rose so rapidly from poverty and obscurity to riches and fame as you did" (qtd. in Darling, 27). Optic drives home his point by urging Alcott to take her own advice in regards to the content of his books: "we must ask you to adopt the motto you recommend for others—'Be honest and you will be happy,' instead of the one you seem to have chosen: 'Be smart and you will be rich'" (qtd. in Darling, 27).[4] In fact, as we will see, Alcott's charges about Optic's texts making citizenship too easy for the poor are not quite "honest," especially in regard to the content of *The Boat Club*, which is a text that sets rules for boys' memberships in clubs along lines of class and wealth.

Alcott's assessments of Optic seem to have contributed to Optic's works' near disappearance from the nineteenth-century texts currently investigated by critical and cultural studies. The *Oxford Companion to Children's Literature* includes only a brief three-inch entry on Oliver Optic, and it repeats, without critiquing, the analysis of Optic's work made by the *Nation* and by Alcott. The lack of current critical examination is driven home by the fact that although Optic's name is always listed in surveys of nineteenth-century American children's literature, the online *MLA Bibliography* records very few Optic citations.[5] While not a critical success, during the 1850s, Optic's texts were very popular, and his series sold quite well. This sales success lasted for more than a decade. Darling notes that "in popularity and in remuneration, Adams must have been one of the most successful authors of the time. *Old and New*, reporting in 1870 the most popular works of the previous three months at the Boston Public Library, declared that the novels of

Oliver Optic and of Horatio Alger, Jr., were the most popular boys' books" (25). The success of the series—Optic produced six titles under the "Boat Club" heading and capitalized afterward on the series concept when he produced more series and helped Alger to do the same—indicates that these books were read by many boys and provide insight into which textual boyhoods resonated with readers.

The boyhoods presented in Optic's texts reflect 1850s concerns about training boys to define citizenship and to "compromise" for the good of the nation. While Abbott's boys strive to make democratic and common spaces peaceful by attempting to understand the laws of private ownership, Optic's boys make common spaces private by waging war on those boys who do not follow the forms and codes they have established within their privately owned groups. This exclusivity mimics national moves to tighten borders and citizenship boundaries and to prevent waves of European immigration from increasing uncontrolled. Similar in nature to the nativist impulses of the Know-Nothing Party of the 1850s, this text's club admits "worthy" American boys who follow codes that create and maintain boundaries of participation and belonging. As I will argue, this text's exploration of the compromising nature of establishing belonging offers a way to read literary history's participation in the quasi-marginalization of Optic's brand of textual boyhood citizenship.[6] With critical studies more interested in Alcott, or in Optic's protégé, Alger, or in the forerunner of *Huckleberry Finn*, *Story of a Bad Boy*, histories of children's literature and members of the children's literature discipline have also compromised on Optic's status. His name is always mentioned, often as a way of beginning discussions of other figures, but the boyhoods of his texts, boyhoods that brought him a profitable career as a series writer, and boyhoods that were read by boys themselves, have been seriously neglected. This chapter argues that both the proliferation of Optic's reputation and the boyhoods Optic constructs can be better understood by examining the ramifications of compromise. Literary historians and other canon makers have repeatedly attempted to let Optic belong without taking him seriously. The boyhoods that belong in the end to the Boat Club of the series title reveal how certain boyhood citizenships are elevated while others are forgotten.

After his publication successes in the 1850s, Optic employs his knowledge of series books to actively "father" the construction of the rags-to-riches mythology of Americanness by serializing Alger's *Ragged Dick* in the 1860s.[7] Just as the Know-Nothing Party of the 1850s uses a formulaic calculation of nativism to establish party citizenship, Optic makes use of his knowledge of formulaic series to establish his position in the publishing world and to offer a similar position to Alger.[8] Anne Scott MacLeod compares the two writers in "Children's Literature in America": "Operating on a scale well within the comprehension of his young working-class readers, boys less privileged than Adams's [Oliver Optic] readers, Alger married the American dream of social and economic advancement to the rules of a newly industrializing mass society" (121).[9] Like Optic's characters, Alger's boys are always rewarded when they display a particular kind of good-heartedness, perhaps not with riches, but with stable middle-class clerkships offered to them by the rewarder. This good-heartedness signals the ability to belong, and simultaneously suggests that new customs will not be brought in to challenge the existing systems of power.

Optic's speedy production of sequels to *The Boat Club*, and the subsequent series he was able to produce as a result of his first series success contribute, I would argue, to the "dime novel"/"get rich quick" reputation of his work.[10] Other titles in the "Boat Club" series include *All Aboard*, *Now or Never; or, The Adventures of Bobby Bright*, *Poor and Proud; or, The Fortunes of Katy Redburn*, and *Little by Little; or, The Cruise of the Flyaway.* Although the first text in Optic's series offers material rewards to the boys who follow the rules, *The Boat Club* does not emphasize unequivocally the capitalist values of the new rising middle class. Other values promoted by *The Boat Club* suggest that character and motivation matter far more than monetary reward as a sign of right living. Throughout this text, Optic types boys in order to tell the story of their rewards and punishments, and the strategy of typing boys provides Optic with a successful formula built on the reproduction of similar texts. Optic's series books capitalize on a design guaranteed to deliver the same reading experience each time. With this design, Optic manufactures a syndicated success based on the similarities between texts in the series. Although Optic's series are popular with readers, they come under criticism from the library review panels and lists of literature for children, which are put into place at the end of the nineteenth century. The response of library gatekeepers to these texts as ones to be kept out of archives of "real literature" suggests parallels between the gatekeeping at work in the Know-Nothing Party, the boat club of Optic's text, and the literature review processes. Each is concerned with establishing rules for belonging and admittance.

These gatekeeping projects also converge in interesting ways around the centrality of father figures. Peter Hunt points to the centrality of the "father" in the review process when he reads aesthetic evaluations of literature as patriarchal: "children's books do not fit easily into the patriarchal world of literary/cultural values. . . . uncanonical works are the more likely to be of and for childhood, and less likely to conform to adult social and literary norms" (6).[11] The successful sameness of Optic's series and the emphasis on fatherly assessments of character type that we see in *The Boat Club* suggest that while pushing against adult literary "norms," Optic's texts conform to social norms of the 1850s. Even though his texts have not been considered substantial contributors to constructions of American boyhood,

Optic's regularized and formulaic productions of texts about and for boys ensure their presence in library collections now, while other texts with equally interesting treatments of boys and boyhood have not had the same expansive staying power.

During the 1850s, then, Optic's boyhoods gain publishing power, but subsequent reviews squelch the power these boyhoods once held. So, in what ways have the boyhoods he created contributed to understandings of American boyhood? I see the boat club itself and the clubs of reputation makers bringing together hegemonic and counter-hegemonic critical crosscurrents about the textual construction of American boyhood.[12] The reputation makers compromise on Optic's boyhoods by always noting and then qualifying certain boyhoods as too sensational and too bad or too didactic and too good. *The Boat Club* reinforces myths of the American "rags-to-riches" dream, but instead of granting it in the city or in the wilderness, the dream comes true in the context of small-town boyhoods. This reinforcement coincides with a concomitant suggestion that orderly compromise can allay anxieties about class disruption, caused by immigration and westward expansion, within stable northeastern communities. The noncanonical canonical status that this text has now and the anxious reception of this text in the 1850s indicate that Optic's texts engage tensions existing in dominant textual constructions of boyhood, both those that were part of the popular literature of the time and those that continue to be celebrated in the canonical "clubs" of literary history makers.[13] The compromises of *The Boat Club* along the lines of didacticism and sensation and good and bad citizenship help explain the peculiar status of Optic's boyhoods. This same urgency to compromise shapes the citizenships of the consensus-seeking 1850s. The compromises on boyhood influence the subsequent rejection in the late nineteenth century of these compromised/compromising citizenships.

In Optic's vision of American boyhood, one boy resolves that money spent on celebrations can be better used to mark and reward other signs of American independence like respectable poverty; other boys decode and come to terms with the politics and infighting that is sometimes covered by the orderliness of the local town meeting. When modeling adult civic bodies on their own, boys practice and perfect behaviors that best work to gain popular power and popular vote. Other boys learn to detect and punish violators of local and national codes, while protecting "citizens," in this case, club members, in good standing. Others discover that financial transformation can reveal how seemingly equal relationships based on democratic models function only by maintaining inequalities.

During the early 1850s, as the United States reassured itself of its national identity in the aftermath of the U.S.-Mexican War by arguing that, since Mexico had been paid for the territory acquired by the United States, no conquest had occurred, political thinkers looked to the past, to the politics of their fathers, to find purposes and solutions for the future.[14] The new territories heightened anxieties about which states would be slave states, and Henry Clay's Missouri Compromise of 1820 was revisited in a compromise proposal that alleviated sectional tensions by making use of small revisions that would reinforce party loyalties over sectional ones. Among other compromises made by thinking through historical decisions, California became a free state in return for stricter enforcement of the Fugitive Slave Law in the north, while popular sovereignty over the issue of slavery was granted to the Utah and New Mexico territories. In the elections of 1852, when Democrats endorsed the compromise and Whigs did not condemn it, a brief period of consensus based on party loyalties was reached. This consensus made it difficult to distinguish between parties, and caused the parties to look for ways to make their differences from the other parties explicit. When Stephen A. Douglas proposed to make the territories west of Missouri and Iowa (areas where the Missouri Compromise had banned slavery) into states, he also suggested that the states be given the same popular sovereignty that the Compromise of 1850 had granted New Mexico and Utah. This act, termed the Kansas-Nebraska Act, disrupted the consensus brought by compromise, and in order to avoid losing votes based on sectionalism, politicians looked for new ways to define themselves against the other parties. One of the issues that brought voters together was the issue of nativism—a "Know Nothing" party issue that avoided the sectional tensions surrounding the slavery issue by turning the focus on immigrants and their citizenship status. The "Know Nothings" formed a third, powerfully disruptive, and strangely conservative party that reached the height of its popularity at the time of *The Boat Club*'s publication. In *A History of American Immigration*, George M. Stephenson notes that the Know-Nothing Party began as "an oath-bound secret fraternity composed of a national council, with state and local councils. Members were admitted only after a searching examination and an elaborate ritual. A candidate had to be descended from at least two generations of American ancestors" (111). In its elevation of the citizenships of those whose fathers and grandfathers had also been citizens, the "Know-Nothing" Party embraced the past—the father—by quietly rejecting classlessness and working to regulate America's boundaries against the rapid influx of immigrants while continuing to desire expansion and the prosperity it would bring.[15]

In Massachusetts, a state with many Conscience Whigs, or Whigs opposed to slavery, the Compromise of 1850 and the consensus of 1852 caused political activists to rethink their allegiances to their parties.[16] The Conscience Whigs were often citizens with investments in the commercial endeavors of the state, and from a commercial perspective, these citizens were worried about the economic changes that would be brought to their state by influxes of immigrants and by the low prices of land in the western territories, which drove in-state property prices down. With the slavery issue at temporary rest, the Know-Nothing platform was attractive to many of these former Whigs. In 1854, in Massachusetts, almost every legislative seat in the state went to the Know-Nothings and a Know-Nothing governor was elected. Other states that turned over governorships to the Know-Nothings in the 1850s included Rhode Island, New Hampshire, Connecticut, California, and Kentucky.[17] The sudden rise of the "Know Nothing" Party in Massachusetts during the election year when the introduction of the Kansas-Nebraska Act had caused the expansion of slavery issue to split up the Whig Party suggests that turning the discussion of citizenship privileges to immigrants allowed those who were ostensibly abolitionist but privately anxious about changes abolition might bring to displace these anxieties onto the "foreign" other rather than the native one. One of the main aims of the party was to elect only "native" citizens to local and national government. This party gained popularity by inflating the importance of a citizenship history and by arguing that those who were true "Americans" could make the best legislative decisions. The politicians of the 1850s, then, look to their political fathers when they find consensus by returning to slavery compromises of the past, and they use family citizenships and nativism to establish a political cause for the present. Written in New England during Massachusetts's occupation with fugitive slaves and abolitionism, Optic's text's focuses on the admission of "worthy" American boys to a club; in its emphasis on creating codes and forms to police the boundaries of worthiness and belonging, the *Boat Club* suggests ways that "Know-Nothingism" worked out anxieties of New Englanders, who, while behind abolition in theory, had trouble imagining their world as one that could be shared with freed blacks.

Like the 1852 consensus politicians and the members ofthe Know-Nothing Party, the boys in *The Boat Club* depend on their fathers for guidance about the shape their club will take. One of the arguments that has been made by Claudia Nelson in *Invisible Men*, about children's literature produced between 1840 and 1900 is that the texts show children encountering the world without the presence of their fathers and sometimes without the guidance of parents at all. Nelson addresses the importance of mothers and the ambivalent role of fathers as they are portrayed in British periodicals: "writers on domesticity presented fathers as ineffectual and uninvolved. . . . educators and theorists saw the mother, not the father, as providing the best blueprint for child rearing and cultural engineering. However competent they might have been thought to be in the outside world, men appeared in the great majority of periodical nonfiction as mere amateurs in the home" (202). Current histories of social relations and histories of popular nineteenth-century children's literature both attest to the importance of the mother in socializing children during the nineteenth century. Further sex-gender construction studies contend that mothering more than fathering has contributed to the production of Western capitalist male-dominated patriarchal society. Histories insist on the importance of mothers during the 1850s, and evidence of the presence of mothers and women in the child-rearing process can be found in women's writing in periodicals and in popular literature.[18] In contrast to the received opinion about children's literature and absent parents, *The Boat Club* emphasizes father figures and their involvement in their son's lives. This can be seen especially when the boat club establishes itself under the direction of Captain Sedley, a wealthy, retired sea captain and the father of Frank, the best-behaved boy in Rippleton. Captain Sedley buys his son a boat and tells him: "you must form a society, a club, as they do in the city. You must have thirteen boys; twelve to row and one to steer. . . . But, boys, you must be careful whom you invite to join the club. We do not want any bad boys—especially none of the Bunkers" (68). *The Boat Club* and its sequel *All Aboard* do not portray a world devoid of adults, and Optic's texts, unlike the "cult of the true woman" texts and magazine images that sold well at the same time as Optic's first series, do not create the worlds with omnipresent and engaged mothers who work to bring up sons who will continue to reinforce the patriarchal value systems of their middle-class worlds.[19] In *The Boat Club*, Mrs. Sedley, Frank's mother, and the Widow Weston are present, but are not as central as the father figures. In Optic's text, Captain Sedley establishes the club in order to assiduously "parent" his son and the other members. He controls the boys through firm codes of conduct and through a system of material rewards for good behavior, and in doing so shapes them to become citizens prepared to promote the stability of local and national adult organizations.[20]

The presence of Captain Sedley and other father figures in this text suggests that fathers as well as mothers play a role in the construction of boyhoods that conform to a party or national line. The centrality of Captain Sedley seems at odds with *The Boat Club*'s position as a representative American children's literature text of the 1850s, since the later and more dominant construction of American boyhoods involves the story that the boys head to the "territories" to get away from overbearing aunts and mothers. Although most of the boys in *The Boat Club* stay in their small town, this text establishes the possibility that rather than providing escape from the mother, the later adventure quest responds to father-generated rules and ideas that in the end just do not work. The Know-Nothing Party, similarly, after its meteoric rise, meets its demise when legislators who win seats with their Know-Nothing father-based affiliations subsequently use their legislative powers to grapple with the slavery question and to forward their private Free-Soil agendas in the newly organized territories.[21]

In his early directions about the boat club, Captain Sedley recommends that his boy use what "they do in the city" as a model for his own club society. Significantly, cities were also among the contested spaces that the members of the Know-Nothing Party sought to control as they saw more and more immigrants coming in to take jobs and cast votes.[22] The party admitted members who held the same views as they did about giving "outsiders" the citizenship privileges of land and votes, and they instructed the members to claim that they "knew nothing" when outsiders asked about the organization. When the Bunkers learn about the club, like immigrants seeking naturalization, they begin to attempt to gain favor in order to obtain a ride on the boat, but the rules of the club help to keep them out. The need to row the boat with one single trained group without taking turns allows Frank to directly refuse to include the Bunkers without having to comment on their poverty and their mischief. As the father of his son, and the "founding" father of the club, Captain Sedley dictates who will have the chance to join his son's club based on preconceived judgments about "good" and "bad" boys, and he gives his son rules that secure the stable identity of the club.

Captain Sedley fathers the club by ordering his son to choose members who are relatively similar to each other and who have reliable histories of being good members of the town. Throughout the texts in the "Boat Club" series, characters continue to be evaluated based on behavior. Good boys are "typed" as always good and as future contributors to the community. Bad boys are typed in similar ways—and their "badness" is usually a result of environmental and hereditary factors. In Optic's texts, a few boys resist "typing" and vacillate between states of goodness and badness, between being productive and destructive members of the community. The textual compromises about these figures suggest the instability of the larger compromises at work in the nation during the 1850s.

In the world of Rippleton, fathers and other adults use surveillance and citizenship histories to type the boys. An active proponent of this surveillance, Captain Sedley can only be sufficiently happy if his son Frank is good. Near the beginning of the book, Captain Sedley eavesdrops on a conversation Frank has with his friend Charley about taking a raft over to the Widow Weston's house. Frank refuses to take the raft, because his father has told him that it is wrong, while Charley argues that it will be fun. Frank's father chimes in after eavesdropping for a while and gives an example of an experienced swimmer who falls in and drowns because of the surprise of the situation. Charley decides to forgo the raft ride, not because he is persuaded by this example, but because he realizes that rafting is impossible since Frank's father, like the most domineering of managers of one of the mills and factories springing up throughout New England, has happened upon the scene at the moment Charley is about to revolt against Frank. When Captain Sedley gives the boys the boat, he explains that his decision to purchase it was based on his observations:

> Two months ago, when the Bunkers first began to amuse themselves with the raft, the idea of procuring it occurred to me. I saw that you and Charles both had a great desire to join in their sport. For obvious reasons, I could not permit Frank to do so; but I immediately resolved that you should have the means of enjoying yourselves in safety and comfort, and I ordered this boat to be built (65–66).

This reward for the boys' obedience about not using the raft is based on silent observations made without the boys knowing exactly what was at stake. Like evaluations of citizenship based on arbitrary assessments of true "Americanness," Captain Sedley's assessments of goodness seem capricious and arbitrary; it is difficult for the boys to know when and where they will be rewarded or punished.

The gift of the boat is so generous that it allows Captain Sedley to actively participate in his son's world. Optic's text mentions the cost of the boat ($400.00) in a scene when Frank cautions another boat club member to be careful with the property; this price is shockingly expensive even more than a century and a half later. This figure gives Sedley almost complete control over the boat club's rules. He orders his son: "You must have no profanity, no lying, no vulgar language; and no boy must be permitted to neglect his school, or his duties at home, on account of the boat" (70). Frank's knowledge of the price and his divulging of the price to Charley seems important—his father has allowed him to understand that his goodness has a monetary worth and his reward must therefore be respected. That this amount was spent on a gift for boys illustrates the extent of generosity and the lengths to which Captain Sedley goes to purchase his son's loyalty.

This hands-on parenting of boys differs from the kinds of parenting described by historians of nineteenth-century boyhood. In *American Manhood*, E. Anthony Rotundo argues that from the mid-nineteenth century on, boys spent several years in a "free nation," a same-sex peer group world that had activities and rules entirely separate from the world of the father, the work world, or the world of the mother, the home (31). He argues, in contrast to the evidence of *The Boat Club*, that fatherless clubs were an important means of exclusion and inclusion in the realm of boy culture:

> Loyalty also laid the basis for one of the great passions of nineteenth-century boys—the formation of clubs. Meeting in attics and cellars, these clubs ranged from a small-town cabal that specialized in melon theft to a natural history "museum" established by Theodore Roosevelt. Two common purposes of these boys' clubs were nurture and athletics. Fellow members raided local orchards and gardens, then they cooked and ate their booty together. Boys formed athletic groups that organized extensive competitions among members (39).

Optic's text, while constructing a club for boys, inserts fathers and other adult male mentors, such as Uncle Ben, Captain Sedley's loyal first mate, regularly into the text, and thereby demonstrates that boy-governed institutions in the small-town world of Rippleton are realized only through the power of the father's wealth and the father's laws.

Optic participates in the textual fantasy of the possibility of a father-controlled boy-governed world when, in his introduction, he claims to be a kind of boy himself. The subtitle, *The Bunkers of Rippleton: A Tale for Boys*, and the preface emphasize the text's use of boys as a necessary element in the profit of the father:

> The author of the following story pleads guilty of being more than half a boy himself; and in writing a book to meet the wants and tastes of "Young America," he has had no difficulty in stepping back over the weary waste of years that separates youth from maturity, and entering fully into the spirit of the scenes he describes. He has endeavored to combine healthy moral lessons with a sufficient amount of exciting interest to render the story attractive to the young; and he hopes he has not mingled these elements of a good juvenile book in disproportionate quantities (5–6).

In this preface, Optic claims knowledge of boyhood based on his (less than) half manhood. In adulthood, he refuses to admit his distance from boyhood and claims that, once having been a boy, he is able to easily to step back over the boundary of years. He also points out that he has written a book that consciously conforms to the wants and tastes of "Young America," an emphasis that is especially intriguing in light of the ongoing presence and importance of Captain Sedley, the father, in the text.

As Edward L. Widmer points out in *Young America*, the political group that called themselves "young Americans" rejected their fathers' politics with a "disdain for the past" and embraced economic optimism and westward expansion along with "youth, liberty, and classlessness" (66, 85).[23] In this text, then, Optic claims to write to the young Americans, who tended to publicly acknowledge the citizenship potential of the working class and to endorse westward expansion. The content of the text, with its emphasis on "types" of characters and its policing of membership boundaries, seems rather to covertly align itself with the aims and missions of the "Know-Nothing" Party. Partly in line with "Know-Nothing" politics, Optic's text does fixate on regulations and on keeping careful track of who is in and out of the club. In some ways, however, it seems that Optic's text compromises between these two party models as his text connects proper, nativist responses to "American" events like the Fourth of July and town meeting to the Young Americans' beliefs in the American mythologies of rags-to-riches and the economic bounty of the West. In its treatment of scenes of Americanness, the text displays a range of possible boyhood responses to these spheres of American manhood that are part of Captain Sedley's world and usually in his control. The text then manipulates the responses of the readers by fantastically rewarding characters whose responses to these encounters are good in the way that Captain Sedley defines good.

In order to maintain control over "native" Rippleton goodness, Captain Sedley lavishes the club with gifts and creates an elaborate system of rewards for good behavior and punishments for "foul" language and fighting. He builds and furnishes the boathouse, and he also provides uniforms for the club members so that it is easy to distinguish members and nonmembers. This way, even when the boat is at a distance, Captain Sedley can regulate to some extent the company his son keeps.

The club also allows Captain Sedley to parent his son in his outdoor and indoor activities. Even the reading material is controlled, and intriguingly, in the text's description of its selection, the almost always absent Mrs. Sedley makes an appearance: "The library cases were filled with books, which had been selected with great care by Mr. and Mrs. Sedley. On the table were placed various pamphlets and periodicals, and when the club assembled, Uncle Ben was there, seated in the coxswain's arm chair, poring over the pages of the Sailors' Magazine" (133). These literary furnishings provide for the leisure time when the boys are not physically involved in rowing the boat. Optic, himself a magazine editor and a writer of series books/dime novels at a time when popular writing was dominated by women, constructs a reading space for his characters and points to his own concern for "good" reading material by having the Sedley parents demonstrate their care with its selection. The literary furnishing of the boathouse, an all-boy space, suggests that reading, which Cathy Davidson in *Revolution and the Word* argues caused anxieties about the social control of women, caused similar worries about reading boys.[24] One possible way to read the intrusion of Mrs. Sedley into the selection of reading material is by thinking about how reading and writing might mark gender boundaries. These connections are fleshed out when Calvin Thomas, in *Male Matters*, argues that "Because it is both act and appearance, both process and visible, material result, writing can be thought as a scene of gender ambiguity, and thus a cause of anxiety, for any author invested in preserving the boundaries, institutional or otherwise, of gendered identity and ego coherence" (3). Optic, who in this text writes about boyhood citizenships because he is "more than half a boy himself," gestures to the ambiguity and fragility of these gender and type-based, tightly controlled citizenships by writing a woman into his reading selection scene. Her presence indicates both the impossibility of writing "other" kinds of citizenships out merely by selecting members based on club rules and also the text's inability to imagine entirely homosocial boy citizenships. Mrs. Sedley's involvement with the reading material and her choice of technical rather than fictional material contrast with Optic's endorsement of popular fiction as a kind of pleasurable exercise for the reading boy's mind. The reading selections hint that in the leisure hours, with bodies at rest, fictional reading material that even smacked slightly of the sensational might eroticize the semiprivate space of the clubhouse. Mrs. Sedley's nonfiction choices counteract the potentially "sensational" presence of other kinds of reading material, and her choices help to regulate the indoor pursuits of the club members.

When winter sets in and the members of the club are no longer able to relieve their restlessness with physical exercise, language-based activities take up the club members' time. Leisure time becomes formally structured, rather than open-ended, and therefore potentially dangerous, . Fred Harper proposes a debating club, and his proposal is put into effect: "the members derived a great deal of pleasure, and obtained an excellent mental discipline, from their discussions" (251). The members of the club also invite older adults to lecture on topics of interest: "George Weston gave them a number of familiar lectures on 'California;' Captain Sedley on 'Life on the Ocean;' and Mr. Hyde, the schoolmaster, on 'Natural Philosophy and Chemistry'" (251). With this regulated leisure time, disagreements among the members of the club are kept to a minimum, just as the "Know-Nothing" Party avoided divisive issues of slavery and territorial expansion by focusing on immigrants and Americanness.

As the club takes shape, detailed descriptions of club life continue to reveal attitudes toward the political body of America and the construction of "good" citizens. These descriptions shape the responses of readers. In exploring poverty and wealth in the lives of small-town boys, Optic's texts demonstrate a nervousness about philanthropy that reflects attitudes held by New England transcendentalists. For Ralph Waldo Emerson, philanthropy does the poverty-stricken person a disservice by making goods available too easily and by not teaching self-sufficiency.[25] Philanthropy in this construction is reward without work. At the same time, goodness and striving to work, even without succeeding, are behaviors which, when recognized in the poverty-stricken person, can be rewarded in a financial way. These anxieties about philanthropy and citizenship can be seen in *The Boat Club* when Frank wants to give the Widow Weston money he has been saving for the Fourth of July, and he convinces his friend Charley to do the same. On the one hand, the text constructs this as a good deed, the kind that should be recognized and rewarded or at least praised by adults. However, the text makes it very clear that there is some shame attached to being on the receiving end of philanthropy. The boys know better than to give the money to the Widow Weston's young son, who would reject it because of this shame. Rather, they offer it to her in private. In its description of philanthropy and Tony's response to it, the text positions boy readers to give to the poor but to avoid receiving charity.

This philanthropic gift to a charity-dependent widow is curiously tied to Independence Day. With Tony, the widow's son, Frank and Charley talk about the "glorious fourth" and are careful not to mention that they have given up their means to participate in the celebration. That the two sons choose to celebrate their nation's independence with an act of independent generosity not guided by parents and a simultaneous display of masculine financial power is significant in terms of the way Americanness is marked and celebrated in this text. One of the messages seems to be that there is something a little unruly and perhaps dangerous in displays of military power (the grassroots militia that worked for independence in '76) and in anniversaries of that independence. Good middle-class boys in *The Boat Club* give up their spending power and stay at home, and display their power by giving their money away in the name of charity. Independence, in good boys like Frank, is better to be marked by masochistically giving up the pleasure of gingerbread and firecrackers for the good of a destitute woman.[26]

Optic's text establishes its version of American boyhood amid a combination of contradictory cultural pressures that shape boyhood and Americanness at this time. On the one hand, the book insists through Frank's sacrifice in giving up his Independence Day celebration that American rituals are an important educational force in the task of establishing citizenship at the regional and local levels. During the 1850s, many political parties (including the Know-Nothings) desired to celebrate those aspects of independence and liberty in developing their responses to immigration, the parties vacillated between wanting to maintain the comforts of liberty and denying others the same rights and privileges. Frank's sacrifice of the independence celebration for a morally healthier alternative—philanthropy—suggests that anniversaries of independence as they are marked during the early 1850s are more dangerous than other leisure-time pursuits. Frank establishes his good citizenship when he makes his ritual act of generosity "American" by arranging for it to be an independent act, one conceived and carried out without his father's knowledge.

In the descriptions of this Fourth of July incident and elsewhere, *The Boat Club* explores how boys compromise on ethical dilemmas in order to showcase exemplary citizenships and to "type" as good or bad the various Rippleton boys who play roles in the club. In *Disorderly Conduct*, Carroll Smith-Rosenberg notes that rapid changes in American society triggered attempts to order and type the world and the people in it as a way of "impos[ing] order upon the chaos of the nonsexual world"; she goes on to suggest that this happens especially in treatments of adolescents in American literature (91).[27] *The Boat Club* demonstrates in its ambivalence about the independent act of philanthropy and the independence celebration how fragmented American boyhood citizenships of the 1850s textually construct and reinforce some of the problems faced by the American political body.

Some of the types of available citizenships that *The Boat Club* records are depicted in the celebration that occurs in lieu of the Independence Day trip to Boston. The text offers another "type" of citizenship model in its description of Uncle Ben's participation in the boys' Fourth of July activities. Uncle Ben is a sailor and Captain Sedley's right-hand man.[28] Sailing, not as captain, but as second mate, is a career choice that seems to allow for ongoing boyhood or a liminal subjectivity situated somewhere between boyhood and adulthood, possibly because ownership and the adulthood that comes as part of ownership are not issues and neither is responsibility for possessions and goods. Sailors, like boys, are outfitted with the goods they need; they do not own property or produce goods. Although Captain Sedley does not give the boys their money back when he finds out about the philanthropy, he does ask Uncle Ben to take Frank, Charley, and the widow's son Tony out, not on a raft, but in the safer rowboat. To add to the celebration, Ben gives the boys firecrackers. Ben seems to enjoy indulging the boys, perhaps reaching back to his own boyhood beginnings and expressing his ongoing unstable citizenship status as "second mate" by allowing the boys some explosive fun.

After Ben donates the firecrackers, and demonstrates his near-boyhood citizenship status, another set of boy citizenship types is explored. Charley's character is compared with Frank's when he uses the firecrackers quickly. Charley's logic in doing so is that he sees the Bunkers, a group of troublemakers, coming and he wants to use them before they will demand them from him. However, the lack of firecrackers only serves to enrage the Bunkers. They begin to fight with Frank, presumably because he is the wealthiest boy and therefore the boy most likely the one to be controlling the supply of firecrackers. Frank refuses to fight, and Tony Weston, who, as the son of a poor widow, is characterized as having a less regulated temper, physically defends Frank, and Charley, not to be outdone by Tony, joins in.

The fight is brought on by Charley's earlier determination to use the firecrackers so as not to be coerced into giving them to the Bunkers. Frank indicates in his explanation about the fireworks that if he had any, he would have been willing to give them away. Charley's conspicuous consumption of the firecrackers seems in line with American views of display and enjoyment of private property; in America, in Charley's view, one is not compelled to share one's property. Frank's indicated wishes to share suggest that he approaches American notions of property and consumption with nonviolence and considers avoiding bodily harm as more important than preservation of property. Frank's nonviolent response to property challenges can be compared to the way that Know-Nothing members veer away from physical violence and revolution by focusing instead on written rules. In the aftermath of the U.S.-Mexican War, with fears rising about sectional violence, the Know-Nothings sought to control their world with regulations rather than with physical violence, although their anti-immigrant rhetoric was certainly verbally damaging.

Another typing of boy citizens can be seen in *The Boat Club*'s treatment of the Bunkers, who are less economically privileged than Frank and more prone to rule-breaking than Tony. The Bunkers' name and actions are connotatively reminiscent of American approaches to independence. Like the early grassroots militia troops who rebelled against British occupation and taxation, the Bunkers, who are not at the upper social and economic levels of their community, seek to seize by force what they desire. They do this in the fight on the Fourth of July, and also when Tim Bunker, the leader of the Bunkers, steals a wallet so that he can buy a boat, and then frames Tony Weston. The Bunker name, with ties to the Battle of Bunker Hill, hints that in some ways their "charge ahead and grab what can be grabbed" behavior echoes the late-eighteenth-century moves toward independence. Frank's nonviolent response and his avoidance of what he comes to recognize as a decadent rather than a solemn celebration suggest that some levels of American society have moved far past the need to physically rebel in order to enjoy liberty. However, the presence of the Bunkers and their physical power attest to an underlying anxiety about the number and kinds of people in America and their potential for rebellion if they are not taught to follow the upper middle classes' notions of how Americanness and independence should be expressed. The Bunkers' dialects also suggest that in the postrevolutionary antebellum northeast, waves of immigrants from what were seen as the less stable countries of Ireland and Germany create the potential in America for violent rebellion against those with property and different privileges, privileges that allow for the luxuries of refusing to fight and being charitable. In Optic's texts, only a very few boys demonstrate through their actions that peaceful nonviolent behavior is an option. In most cases, the text locates a compromise between nonviolent surrender and violent physical defense of property and reputation. The celebration of independence here becomes a complicated multiclass scene of contention over the method and means of celebration.

As members of the club from opposite ends of the economic spectrum, Frank and Tony seem to be constructed as more "American" than Charley, in part because of the ways they demonstrate their initiative. Frank earns his money and plans his investment, not in gingerbread, but in Widow Weston's well-being. This is a plan he invents himself, a plan not designed overtly to give Frank's father reassurance about the nature of his son, but one that does so nevertheless. Tony, although without the spending power of Frank, and therefore lacking the capital to fulfill his own plans in the same effortless way, uses his physical power to defend Frank. He demonstrates his independence/Americanness by throwing himself wholeheartedly into the fray without consulting anyone. Both boys make independent decisions about what do with their economic and physical capital and demonstrate control of that capital by using it without asking for permission.

Charley's generosity differs from Frank's, and the text uses Charley's motives for his generosity to discuss the "type" of boy and citizen he will become. On the morning of the Fourth, Charley finds Frank's father worshipping the "Supreme Being" and giving thanks for the Sedley family's nativist citizenship: "the sounds of the booming cannon and the pealing of the bells, which the westerly breeze bore up the lake, reminded him of the gratitude he owed to God for the political, social, and religious privileges which had been bequeathed to the country by the father of the revolution" (36). During this meeting, Charley confesses that he and Frank gave their money to the Widow Weston. He hopes that Captain Sedley will give him back the money, but when the Captain understands Charley's motives, he puts away his wallet. He seems to recognize that Frank's motivations are different than Charley's, and goes on to counsel: "It was a noble sacrifice, Charles. . . . If *from a worthy motive* we sacrifice our inclinations for the good of others, we are always sure of finding our reward—indeed, the act is its own reward" (41, emphasis original). When Charley tells his story to his parents, Charley's father and mother recognize immediately that their son is no longer happy about the good he has done. His mother points out and his father agrees that Charley's gift was given hypocritically. The narrator, intriguingly, tells the reader something different. When Charley gave the money, the narrator insists, it was given in the right spirit; however, Charley's anticipation of the Fourth celebration and his quickness in giving up the money demonstrate that he had not yet considered the consequences or the reality of the sacrifice he chose happily to make. Charley wavers between the philanthropic donation and his continuing desire to go to the Boston celebration, and in seeking out Captain Sedley, he, like the father figures to whom the Know-Nothings look for citizenship guidance, searches for a suitable compromise.

The text constantly grapples with Charley's citizenship, and finally uses the regulatory nature of the club to develop a citizenship for him that is situated somewhere between Frank's unerring goodness and Tim Bunker's badness. Until the end of the text delivers a verdict on Charley's type, he is described as occupying a rather shifting and complex set of citizen positions. The text emphasizes that although some boys like Frank might seem to be entirely good, others, like Charley, refuse to be typified as a "kind" of boy and consequently operate as both good and bad characters, stable and unstable citizens. In Charley's case, the fragmented, opposing, and tangential desires that compete with each other are spurred on by his lower-middle-class status. It is more difficult for him to give up his spending money than it is for Frank—he has less and it is not as readily available to him. His location in a suburb city of Boston and his liminal association with boys who operate according to rubrics different from his own and also different from each other's make it difficult for him to be as generous as Frank or as hard-working as Tony. Optic's obsession with Charley's "type" of character invites readers to participate in this ordering of the chaos, and Charley's ability to land on the side of right by the time he is an adult constructs law-abiding American citizenship as something that is partially obtained by relationships with other stable citizens. In Charley's case, Frank and the club help him to find a workable citizenship.

Charley, at least in the early pages of the book, does not make any independent decisions. He gives his money to the widow in part because he recognizes that Frank's idea is good and generous, but the idea is not his own. He also joins in the fight with Tony, but only after he notices that Tony has an approach that is working. Before he joins in, he decides between Frank's nonviolent approach and his own inclination to fight back. His one idea, that of both giving money to the widow and going to Boston by being reimbursed for his generosity, is one that, rather than following an American model of work and payment, follows the European peasant/noble model of reward and recognition. Charley in many ways expects reward, while Frank does not desire any such reward for his good deed. Charley's lack of original ideas hints that he may not succeed in an American capitalistic system where quick independent thinking and creativity are the middle-class keys to stability. Even Charley's plan to raft to the widow's house is one based on the Bunkers' behaviors. Charley does not seem to fit into the American model built around the Bunkers, Tony, and Frank.

The Boat Club and its sequel tell the story of Charley's journey toward American boyhood and subsequent manhood. The first book, which begins by declaring Frank a good boy and by leaving readers to decide what kind of boy Charley is, compromises on Charley's type with a final textual assessment: "Charles, in spite of his hypocritical character, was a well meaning boy. His desire to appear well, and to be first and foremost, sometimes led him astray, and the discipline of the club finally worked a 'great improvement in him'" (250). Charley's ambivalent commitment to the good of the larger group and his tendency to choose self-gratification over self-sacrifice interfere with the way he is perceived by other members of the club. As an American boy who expresses his Americanness by participating in a small, exclusive democracy, he needs to find ways to compromise on his pleasure and power-seeking tendencies and to locate "good" or "sound" motivations so that he can maintain citizenship within the club and the town.

The club, like the *Young American's Magazine of Self-Improvement*'s recommended reading lists designed to improve working-class factory boys, works to "improve" Charley.[29] His worth as an individual improves in part because he decides to abide by the forms and codes of the small boat club. These forms lay bare the kinds of hypocrisies that Charley brings into most of his everyday practices. Tim Bunker, who is eliminated from belonging in the club without any discussion of whether or not he is a good boy at heart, must go to a "house of correction" to benefit from a similar kind of transformative alternative domestic space. The boat club's codes provide Charley with parameters that enhance his ability to successfully participate in the club and in other parts of society. In the sequel, *All Aboard*, Optic reveals that the club has taken all of the bad out of Charley. He becomes a preacher when he grows up. Whether or not the "house of correction" will work in similar ways for Tim Bunker is not specified within the text, although the sequel reveals that Tim is untransformed.

As the boat club organizes, the rules and directives from Captain Sedley allow the boys to find compromises for their differences. With these rules, order is maintained without directly insulting anyone or making a violation of the rules grounds for a personal disagreement. One example of this can be seen when the boat club has a parliamentary meeting where the members of the club draw up their constitution. The format of the meetings is modeled after adult town models:

> Captain Sedley had instructed Frank in some of the forms of conducting a public meeting, and the matter had been made the topic of conversation among the others, so that they had a tolerable idea of parliamentary usage. They were all enthusiastic and eager to learn, and some of them had attended a special town meeting a few days before, for the purpose, as they expressed it, of "seeing how the thing was done." And when Captain Sedley came in to breakfast on the morning of that eventful day, he found Frank intently perusing the pages of Cushing's Manual (134).

At the meeting, everyone agrees to abide by the rules. Most of the written laws are designed to enforce obedience and peace: "No member shall provoke a quarrel with another person, but shall do all he can to prevent fighting and unkindly feelings one towards another. No member shall use tobacco, or ardent spirits as a beverage in any form. All members shall obey the coxswain while in the boat" (142). Another rule is that any disruption must be reported to Captain Sedley: "all violations of spirit of our organization, set forth in Article II., whether in word or in deed, shall be reported to our director, and the delinquent shall be subject to such penalty as he shall determine" (142). Like the Know-Nothing Party's endeavors to increase government stability through rules that established belonging and prevented outsiders from gaining legislative power, Captain Sedley's rules help to maintain the peace of the club. One of the aims of the Know-Nothing Party was to extend the naturalization period because they feared that new immigrants would corrupt the elections with the leisure-time activities sometimes associated with election days—districts with heavy German populations, for example, were accused of using alcohol to corrupt election day. In carefully controlling the boys' leisure in an environment that is connected to government, Captain Sedley teaches them the correct Rippleton response to government processes.

The members test the stability of the rules and the power of their parliamentary club meeting by heading out for their first club excursion in their new sailing uniforms. Charley, who before the meeting tries to oust Tony from the club because he is under suspicion of having stolen a wallet, asks Frank, the coxswain, whether or not they can stop off at Rippleton and parade through the streets. Frank refuses, because he thinks something might happen to the boat while they are gone. Charley sulks, and refuses to row, and Frank heads back to the boathouse.

Charley repents when he comes closer to the boathouse, but Frank still feels obliged to inform his father of the disruption. Captain Sedley wants to pull Charley off the boat, but Frank pleads his cause, and Charley apologizes for his argumentative behavior. Charley's knowledge of the written constitution prevents him from being angry with Frank for telling his father, and also leads him to a quicker repentance because he knows that the disagreement will lead to possible suspension of the outing. The laws maintain peace in this instance by encouraging leadership-based compromises that minimize verbal disagreements and prevent them from escalating into physical violence.

Elections provide another area for boy citizenships to be constructed and tested. Captain Sedley points out when the club convenes to elect a new coxswain that it is important to elect individually without electioneering. This emphasis on conscience-based voting also relates to the platform of the Know-Nothing Party. The Know-Nothings were convinced that speechmaking politicians and immigrants were rigging elections in the United States. Because of increased anxieties in the South and national anxieties about secure boundaries in the 1850s, local and national elections were surrounded by rhetorics of conspiracy and dishonesty.

Within the club, Captain Sedley sets rules for the election because he wants the boys to have practice in the responsibilities that they will inherit as members of a republic. In the first book of the series, especially during the time of the election, the boys move toward a more chaotic state when many of them want to be elected coxswain, but not all of them want to admit to the desire. Frank suggests, by way of following Captain Sedley's guidelines, that the election not be talked about. Captain Sedley sets the following rules for the election:

> In the first place, I do not wish to have any unpleasant feelings excited by these elections; and in the second place, I wish you to learn the duty of a republican

> citizen—to cast an independent vote. Among boys, as among men, there is often one or more who wield an influence over others—an influence that is not always directed by truth and justice. One by his mental power or social position, controls others. They follow his example without always imagining whether it is good or bad—I want you to think for yourselves; to make up your minds, without any assistance from others in regard to the fitness of the person for whom you vote (245–46).

Although Captain Sedley approves debating as a form of leisure activity, he does not seem to believe that debating about elections will guarantee that the best candidate will win. Indeed, he seems to think that the less talk there is about such an issue, the better the position of the voters to make an unbiased decision. The members of the club are supposed to select the next leader of the club based on their own consciences. Frank and most of the others follow this rule, but Charley resists it. Charley wants desperately to be coxswain, and he talks to one of the fellow members about the election, all the while denying the truth of his actual desire. When the fellow member confronts Charley, he again denies his desire to win the election. Throughout the text, Charley is constructed as a figure whose power does not necessarily stem from the quiet, conscience-based democracy that Frank and Captain Sedley try to enforce in their election.

When the votes are finally counted, there is one vote for Fred and one vote for Charley. The rest are for Tony. It turns out that Tony voted for Fred, and although the club members do not discuss the election beforehand, they seem to feel no qualms about discussing it afterward. It is determined that in all probability Charley voted for himself. Fred tells Charley ahead of time that he thinks voting for oneself is not right, because it amounts to arguing that one is the best member of the club. Charley says it merely indicates that the person voting for himself is desirous of the position.[30]

The Boat Club's delineation of elections procedures suggests then that there should be something selfless about democratic citizenship. Selfishness or the desires of the self need to be either ignored or erased in order for the stable club to have enough confidence in a candidate for him to win. Tony, who is poor, improves his chances of winning the election by seeming to take no interest in winning the election himself. Other members such as Charley deny their desires. The club member who wins Tony's vote and also works to ferret out the fact that Charley has voted for himself takes such an interest in the election process that it is difficult to believe he has no interest in winning. In fact, when he discusses the possibility of winning with Charley, he admits honestly that he would enjoy winning. Charley is unwilling to admit his interest while all the while having an inordinate amount of interest in winning, so much so that he votes for himself, an act which seems to be, in its lack of self-confidence, the ultimate act of self-devaluation.

In the text, both Tony and Frank appear to be totally unaware of the power of the elected position; they are elected not for politics but for merit. The text suggests, in its treatment of club elections, that democracy works best, then, when the citizens decide on the winner without debate. The text conveys that the exclusive nature of the club, made up of controlled and obedient members, guarantees that no inadequate member could be elected, and it also indicates, with the election rules, that even the most exclusive clubs might need some methods of preventing their weakest members from rising to leadership. In the careful negotiation of elections in *The Boat Club* and the subsequent admittance of an ostensibly reformed Tim Bunker to the club in *All Aboard*, this text signals an awareness of the near impossibility of maintaining an entirely "nativist" government. The delineation of election rules offers boys practical ways to manage their citizenships in the face of the inevitable intrusion of "outsiders" into their clubs and local governments.

The concept of the club dramatizes anxieties Americans have in the late 1840s and early 1850s about just anybody joining the "club" that is America. Optic's text explores how wealth can change the status even of someone who "belongs" legitimately. When George Weston, Tony's long lost brother, returns from the gold rush, he builds Tony's status by trying to match Tony's possessions to Frank's. George feels ashamed that his mother lived in poverty all the years he was absent, and he does not understand her relative contentedness. When he learns about Frank and Charley's gift of money on the eve of the Fourth of July, he insists that their generosity will not go unrewarded. In the end, although Captain Sedley does not reimburse the boys for their generosity as Charley hopes, they do receive their money.

The club's membership rules are tested when Tony falls under suspicion of having committed a theft for which he is not responsible. Charley, who is initially tempted to drop Tony from the club because of appearances, is glad that he has not when the town rallies behind Tony at the time of the trial. What Charley begins to learn from this is not that it is best to believe the best of all people, but that it is a wise idea to follow the opinions of those with the most power. In other words, even though Captain Sedley's election rules call for silent, conscience-based voting, the outcomes of the text suggest that the wealthiest members of the small-town organizations are usually "right" and in turn, those who are friends of the wealthy, will, like Tony, be protected and perhaps rewarded. Captain Sedley's whole motivation for providing the boat is so it can be used as a safe substitute for the Bunkers' raft. The exclusive nature of the club also keeps Tim Bunker from participation in the club. Tony, though, whose behavior is approved by Captain Sedley, is always welcome, even when he is under suspicion of having stolen a wallet. In contemplating Tony's position in the club and Tim's exclusion from it, Charley has trouble gauging the worth of certain social behaviors, and he often wants to go for short-term immediate gratification that will protect his citizenship position at the expense of others. What he begins to learn when Tony is elevated to a position of power is that this kind of self-centered shortsightedness does not always pay. Even as *The Boat Club* participates in national moves to tighten admittance to citizenship, it demonstrates, in the lessons that Charley learns about possibilities for sudden changes in status, that exclusionary regulations need to be applied respectfully and with caution. As it depicts how potential status changes might call for renegotiations of power relationships, this text points to the usefulness and necessity of compromises on citizenship issues.

In this text, both the sudden changes in fortune and the nature of the rewards that are given to good boys suggest possible origins of Optic's reputation as a writer of cheap sensation stories. Tony's rise from poverty provides some insight into how Optic's endings might be read as partly sensational. On the surface and in the first few chapters, character seems to be what is valued in defining good citizenship, but ultimately, money is the reward for the demonstration of character. The importance of reward to Optic's construction of small-town boyhood is heightened by the reward's placement at the end of the text. Alcott's complaint that Optic sensationalizes his texts by offering the moral that the person who is smart gets rich rather than the person who is good gets happiness seems to be partly true in the case of Tony. The death of Tony's father makes him poor, and the death leaves Tony's mother to provide for the two children who remain at home. When Tony is discovered at the scene of the wallet theft, his social status declines even further although it is somewhat salvaged by Captain Sedley's loyalty and detectival perseverance. Tony is raised instantly to almost equal status with Captain Sedley when George Weston returns from the California gold fields. With the help of his brother George's fortune, Tony moves from being patronized by Captain Sedley to being the one to do the patronizing. He owns a club boat and forms a rival club so that the two boat crews can have races. In the end, Tony, who demonstrates his smartness by behaving in a retiring and deferential manner toward the Sedley family, ends up having a boat himself.

The only time when Tony is not smart is in the wallet incident, and his responses here indicate his citizen position in relationship to Frank. Tony insists the wallet should be left alone rather than carried to the owner. The decision and argument, in Tony's case, seem to be based on the fact that he is a member of a lower economic class and his motives for taking hold of the wallet might be questioned. But his unwillingness in this case to follow the directives of his economic superiors lands him in court, although his stellar behavior on all other occasions ensures him the help of his friends. He also has some amount of far-sightedness when it comes to election strategies in the boat club and about his own desires to own a boat versus the advisability of discussing the measure with the all-knowing and wise Captain Sedley before making the decision with his brother. Charley, on the other hand, loses out on the election, by thinking too highly of himself, which does not work in this community that values humble boys like Frank and Tony.

Even as it makes Tony's change in fortune "sensationally" large, *The Boat Club* tempers Tony's rags-to-riches story with Tim Bunker's decline from any access to citizenship. When Sedley suspects Tim of stealing the wallet, he gives Tim every opportunity to confess his crimes, but Tim sticks to his story about Tony and refuses to be grateful to Tony for saving him from drowning. When this happens, Captain Sedley quickly diminishes Tim's reputation even further by making sure that his involvement in the wallet theft is known and by insisting that Tim be sent to a house of correction. This ending reinforces Captain Sedley's fatherly assessment of Tim Bunker as a boy who is too "bad" to be allowed to enter the club that is designed to give his boy a forum to practice good citizenship.

Other sensational tendencies on which Alcott's objections might be based have to do with systems of reward that complicate the "goodness" of boy citizenships. Captain Sedley allows Frank's generosity (as well as Charley's less altruistic generosity) to go unrewarded for the Fourth of July celebration, but then he buys Frank something much more expensive as a delayed reward. At the same time, Charley is punished for his lack of genuine generosity by not being allowed to take on a definite leadership role in the club. So, although the text promotes unrewarded generosity, it simultaneously rewards every "good" boy with material goods. As part of this system of material rewards, it is important to note that it is only the good and wealthy American boys who get promoted to leadership positions in the clubs that imitate local and national democratic systems.

Alcott's arguments that Optic's texts recount rewards sensationally suggest her discomfort with the combination of good-boy government and material goods. Perhaps her criticisms come because his regularly produced series texts create American boyhoods that show leadership positions only being available to good-because-wealthy/American-because-wealthy boys. The text seems to suggest that one cannot be good, American, and perpetually poor. Since Alcott comes from a persistently poor but intellectually middle-class family, she also might have wanted to resist the idea that goodness, boyness, and Americanness needed to be so tied up with wealth and goods. Her texts also create characters who receive rewards from wealthier characters, but she does not often provide such wealth and generosity as a means of solving all of her character's citizenship problems.

In *All Aboard*, the text that is next in the series, the elaborate reward systems with which Alcott finds fault continue even while the emphasis on belonging and keeping bad citizens out shifts. In this text, Tim Bunker, who has served his time in the house of juvenile correction, is asked to be a member as a way of preventing him from returning to his bad ways. When Tony Weston's boat club wins money for its daring rescue of a sinking carriage, the boys move to buy another boat so that there can be a fleet of ships all under the command of Frank Sedley. Rather than keeping the club numbers small, the emphasis in this text is on how well membership within the club works to ward off "dangerous" behaviors. This both reflects the Manifest Destiny tendencies of Optic's politics, which are indicated in his celebration of Tony's brother's return from the West with a wealth to rival Captain Sedley's old money. The club's strucure also suggests that "others" following the laws of the United States were better than "others" working against those laws.

The boat club depends for its success on a kind of collective exclusivity. There is a parallel between the kind of collective exclusivity promoted by the club and the kind promoted by the Know-Nothings who are elected to the United States government during this time period. The government is concerned with maintaining its borders against the influx of too many immigrants and with establishing rules for anyone in a position to claim citizen rights. States—especially Southern states that had become restless in the post-Jackson era—began to resist following the forms and codes of the "Union." As indicated in my previous discussion of the *Young American's Magazine of Self-Improvement*, the importance of Union is emphasized as a way to convince those who might not follow rigid forms and codes easily (i.e., members of the newly immigrated classes, members of the working classes) that there is a kind of collective good that simultaneously benefits the individual whenever the forms or codes are followed. This happens in the boat club when the boys, in order to reap the individual benefits of belonging to the boat club, must follow the rules of inclusion/exclusion and punishment/reward established by Captain Sedley and Frank. Optic's text mimics the forms and codes of locally democratic spaces (the town meeting, the public school, the trial by jury) by working to build an exclusive, privately funded but "democratically" operated club, one that strives to make sure that "bad" boys do not get in. These rules, with their rewards and punishments, reflect fears of and the awareness of the inevitable necessity of opening up democracy to "all" rather than to privileged white men.

Like the "club" that Oliver Optic's *Boat Club* series posits as the solution to small-town tensions between good boys and bad boys, law-abiding citizens and thieves, the "club" of children's literature as a discipline has also experienced anxieties about establishing rules for membership and good standing. In order to define their own literary citizenship and to convince more established literary disciplines that they too were serious scholars, members of the children's literature division of the Modern Language Association set up a Canon Committee in the 1980s. The committee's main purpose was to designate which children's texts were "important" enough to study. This committee replicated, in its valorization of texts that explored paradoxes and individual encounters with societal "evils," the project of the New Critics.[31] As the discipline decided and continues to decide which authors and texts should be studied—which ones "belong"—texts like Optic's *Boat Club*, which advocates compromise by club committee, continue to occupy unstable canonical positions. Optic's series books present boys who are good, bad, and in-between, and the texts complicate Optic's reputation as a dime novel writer. They remain relatively unexamined because of the power of this received reputation and because of the kinds of boyhoods they construct. The stories Optic's texts tell about prosperous middle-class boys and their exclusive clubs are not necessarily the ones that histories of children's literature want to remember, possibly because the descriptions of obedient and privileged white club members hit too close to home for comfort.

The boyhood texts that have been elevated to canonical status by histories of children literature tend either to have more explicit ties to already validated "adult" texts or to explore individual boyhood citizenships instead of group citizenships. One such canonical text is Thomas Bailey Aldrich's *Story of a Bad Boy*, which has ties to *Tom Sawyer* and *Huckleberry Finn*. In chapter four, we will see that in such postwar reconstructions of prewar boyhoods as *Story of a Bad Boy*, individual boys can shift the way they have been "typed." This text and other late 1860s texts demonstrate that later-nineteenth-century boyhood clubs are remembered as being constructed separately from parental guidance. In contrast to *The Boat Club*, the boys admitted to membership in the clubs described in the texts of the 1860s enter on the merits of their mischief rather than on their obedience to town rules and regulations. These reconstructions of mischievous small-town boyhoods fit more readily into the later-nineteenth-century construction of the boy as an "individual" endowed with youthful powers that can challenge and change the rules of the adult world.

NOTES

1. Jane Tompkins discusses the widespread popularity of these two novels and notes that *Uncle Tom's Cabin* was the "first American novel ever to sell over a million copies" (124).
2. British literature fares far better during this decade with texts such as John Ruskin's *King of the Golden River* (1852) and Charles Kingsley's *Westward Ho!* (1855) coming onto the literary scene.
3. I am thinking here of *Story of a Bad Boy*.

4. Gene Gleason in "Whatever Happened to Oliver Optic?" reviews this quarrel and notes that another magazine editor from the nineteenth century, Emily Huntington Miller, also attacked Optic by saying that his books were a "bad influence" (649).

5. As the articles by Darling and Gleason demonstrate, articles have been written about Optic, but most of these grapple with the Alcott–Optic quarrel. Delores Jones has written a bibliographic book titled *An "Oliver Optic" Checklist*. More recently, Sarah A. Wadsworth has published an article in *The Lion and the Unicorn* titled "Louisa May Alcott, William T. Adams, and the Rise of Gender-Specific Series Books," but few other studies have been made.

6. I am thinking both of the participants in the project of constructing American literary history around American boyhood and participants in the discipline of children's literature.

7. *Ragged Dick* was serialized in 1867 in *Student and Schoolmate*, a magazine edited by Optic, and published in book form in 1868.

8. The Know-Nothing Party's policy was that in order to be native one's family had to have lived in the United States for two generations.

9. These rules included, according to MacLeod, honesty, hard work, and respectability, as well as thrift, punctuality, and regularity of habit (121).

10. The received opinion about these reputations is that both series are "cheap," not "real," literature in the sense that John Ruskin's *King of the Golden River* would be.

11. From Peter Hunt's *An Introduction to Children's Literature*.

12. I am working here with Antonio Gramsci's concept of hegemony, which he suggests can be carried out culturally, intellectually, and ideologically to reinforce what seems to be common sense, "fact," or cultural myth. See Gramsci's *Selections from the Prison Notebooks*.

13. See this chapter's opening quotation about Optic and libraries.

14. Howard Zinn discusses this in *A People's History of the United States*: "The Texas boundary was set at the Rio Grande; New Mexico and California were ceded. The United States paid Mexico $15 million, which led the *Whig Intelligencer* to conclude that 'we take nothing by conquest. . . . Thank God'" (166).

15. The Know-Nothing Party had complete control of Massachusetts by 1854. See discussion of Know-Nothings in *The Age of Jackson*, 469–87. See also Tyler Anbinder's *Nativism and Slavery: The Northern Know-Nothings and the Politics of the 1850s*.

16. The term *Conscience Whigs* is used by Schlesinger to describe Northern antislavery members of that party. See 470–71.

17. See Stephenson's *A History of American Immigration* 112–13 and John R. Commons' *Races and Immigrants in America* 117.

18. For discussions and examples see Nina Baym's *Woman's Fiction*, the proliferation of *Godey's Lady's Book* images of beautiful mothers tending docile children on the covers of recent studies of American literature and Americanness, Gillian Brown's *Domestic Individualism*.

19. See Ryan's discussion of mothers as agents of "social production" in *The Empire of Mother* (18).

Linda Kerber also posits that mothers were central organizers and educators of young citizens in her essays "The Republican Mother: Women and the Enlightenment" and "'History Can Do It No Justice': Women and the Reinterpretation of the American Revolution."

20. Mary P. Ryan offers a fascinating study of the importance of associations and clubs to the maintenance of small-town identity in *The Cradle of the Middle Class*. See especially 145 and following. Rippleton, which in Optic's text responds to the influence of Boston and also the West, uses the club to maintain and foster the "face-to-face" bonds of their younger generation.

21. This was the case with Henry Wilson, who was elected to the senate in Massachusetts in 1855 because of his Know-Nothing status. See Stephenson's discussion of the short life of the party (113–15).

22. The party sought to control cities in addition to responding to the ways the sale of land in western territories to immigrants might drive down the prices of land in their eastern states.

23. Chapter two discusses the Young American movement and its connection to boyhood.

24. See Shelley Streeby's *American Sensations: Class, Empire, and the Production of Popular Culture* for a discussion of how sensational literature and story papers negotiate northeastern citizenship anxieties and reflect empire building projects in Mexico and the Americas and reveal the ways in which popular culture forms reflect the complexities and contradictions of citizenship. See also Michael Denning's *Mechanic Accents: Dime Novels and Working-Class Culture in America*.

25. See "Self-Reliance": "I tell thee, thou foolish philanthropist, that I grudge the dollar, the dime, the cent I give to such men as do not belong to me and to whom I do not belong" (180).

26. David Savran's writes of masculinity and masochism in *Taking It Like a Man*: "modern white masculinities are deeply contradictory, eroticizing submission and victimization while trying to retain a certain aggressively virile edge, offering subjects positions that have been marked historically as being both masculine and feminine, white and black" (9). Frank seems to take genuine pleasure in giving up his Fourth of July celebration, but only so long as it is closeted and unrewarded by his father.

27. See Smith-Rosenberg's discussion of attitudes toward change and social order and their connection to father and son conflict (91). See also Michel Foucault's discussion of nineteenth-century obsessions with naming, classifying, and typing in *The Order of Things*. If discursive practices construct the world, Optic's series participates in the construction of types of boys, types that become more connected to canonical success and Americanness in subsequent decades: good boys like Fauntleroy are noncanonical and only tenuously American; bad boys like Huck are canonical and American.

28. This earlier Ben compares to the sailor Ben who appears in *Story of a Bad Boy*.

29. In chapter two, I offer a reading of the *Young American's Magazine* in order to suggest that tightly controlled reading lists for working-class boys were designed both to improve their citizenship status and to improve the quality of the Union of the states.

30. If the club constructs and explores an embodied set of boyhoods, Charley's voting for himself might be read as a form of written autoeroticism and the club's outcry and ridicule a rejection of this form of self-making. I am thinking here both

of Calvin Thomas's discussion of writing, the body, and masculinity in *Male Matters* and of Foucault's "technologies of the self" in his *History of Sexuality, Volume 1: An Introduction.*

31. See Suzanne Rahn's discussion of the Canon Committee in *Rediscoveries in Children's Literature* (xv). See also U. C. Knoepflmacher's cartoon of children's literature's admission to MLA division status in *PMLA* 115.7 (Dec. 2000): 1729.

4

Necessary Badness: Reconstructing Postbellum Boyhood Citizenships in *Our Young Folks* and *The Story of a Bad Boy*

> This is the Story of a Bad Boy. Well, not such a very bad, but a pretty bad boy; and I ought to know, for I am, or rather I was, that boy myself (3).

Thomas Bailey Aldrich's *Story of a Bad Boy* was serialized in 1869 in *Our Young Folks*, one of the few children's periodicals to begin production during the Civil War. This periodical ran from 1865 to 1873 and finally merged with *St. Nicholas Magazine*.[1] Aldrich's position as a "man of letters" who influenced the reception of other pieces of American literature by sitting as editor of the *Atlantic Monthly* sets him apart as more "canonically" privileged than roughly contemporary authors such as Oliver Optic and Horatio Alger. The opening of Aldrich's text explicitly sets it apart from other boys' books written in the past:

> Lest the title should mislead the reader, I hasten to assure him here that I have no dark confessions to make. I call my story the story of a bad boy, partly to distinguish myself from those faultless young gentlemen who generally figure in narratives of this kind, and partly because I really was *not* a cherub. I may truthfully say that I was an amiable, impulsive lad, blessed with fine digestive powers, and no hypocrite (3).

In addition to proclaiming itself different from the earlier stories of "faultless young gentlemen," *Story of a Bad Boy*'s direct connections to Mark Twain's *Tom Sawyer* and *The Adventures of Huckleberry Finn* have given it a place in American literary histories, as is demonstrated by Albert E. Stone's argument that "there is an especially close link between Tom Sawyer and his literary cousins: Aldrich's Tom Bailey, Howe's Ned Westlock, Warner's John, Howells's 'my boy,' Shillaber's Ike Partington, and the others" (63).[2] Originally published by Ticknor and Fields, *Our Young Folks* was edited by John Townsend Trowbridge, Lucy Larcom, and Mary Abigail Dodge.[3] While Optic's boyhood texts published in the 1850s demonstrate how stability-promoting compromises are worked out at the local small-town level, texts published in the post–Civil War 1860s focus on the need for the larger regions of the North and South to learn to compromise. Aldrich's text serves as a guide that helps boys left fatherless by the war to find out what such compromise means, and it suggests that compromise is critical to establishing boyhood that is national and not just regional.

Aldrich's serialization demonstrates, when read in conjunction with other *Our Young Folks* material, that after the Civil War, texts about prewar boyhoods were serialized and distributed in periodical form, thereby defining peacetime boyhood and delineating proper responses to it. Indeed, the periodical material surrounding Aldrich's canonical precursor to *Tom Sawyer* indicates that older male writers, and the editors who chose to publish their stories, felt the need to actively capture lives of prewar boys to "reconstruct," through reading material, postwar boyhoods. These texts chart for readers the territories of boyhood citizenship by narrating possible permutations of boys' leisure activities, friendships, and work, all of which could be imitated and carried out in postwar economies. Written in the aftermath of the Civil War by an author with ties to the North and the South, *Story of a Bad Boy* illustrates how narrative interpretation can textually diminish the repercussions of sectional violence and make possible peaceful and productive participation in reconstructed national citizenships. The mischievous bad boyhood that Aldrich's text describes mixes Northern and Southern conventions of boyhood to ultimately locate compromises between the two regional cultures; these regional compromises prepare boys to become citizens in a reconstructed nation. The surrounding *Our Young Folks* material joins in *Story of a Bad Boy*'s reconstructive project as, in texts about prewar boyhoods, it repeatedly shows boys and men encountering people who are "other" than American as a means of presenting and negotiating prosperous and stable American citizenships in the postwar period.

The project of "reconstructing boyhood" that seems to be central to *Our Young Folks* in the direct aftermath of the war in some ways contradicts the earlier, pre-Reconstruction, abolitionist stance of the magazine. In a national context, the position of *Our Young Folks* during the early Reconstruction period parallels the position of Andrew Johnson, the president in charge of implementing the Reconstruction policies established by Abraham Lincoln prior to his assassination. After the war, Johnson, from the South but a supporter of the Union, provided pardons to supporters of the Confederate government with a speed and thoroughness that disturbed Union supporters who wanted retribution for what they defined as treason. In his State of the Union Address in 1867, Johnson drew the Southern states back into the United States by looking to the textual authority of the Constitution and claiming that the war and the Confederacy never dissolved the Union. When Johnson claimed that "the Union is not only undissolved, but indissoluble," he made the point that the textual construction of the "Union" in the Constitution prevented it from ever having been dissolved, even as the physical evidence presented by the aftermath of the war suggested that the dissolution of the Union was very real (rpt. in Stalcup 46).[4] In a linguistic move similar to Johnson's claim that the textuality of the Constitution reifies the Union's stability, the title chosen for *Our Young Folks*, with "Our" as its opening word, suggests that the editors, backed by the consensus-seeking Congregationalist publishing house Ticknor and Fields, have formed a "union" with the magazine's young subscribers, who come from a variety of regions and backgrounds.

The union between the readers and the editors of *Our Young Folks* is strengthened when readers are offered a "Letter Box" forum for their opinions and stories. Letters from Southern readers, which are carefully selected by the editors to print, emphasize readers' desires to be seen as members of the Union and not as dangerous rebels while simultaneously acknowledging the rebellious impulses still in existence in other children. One reader writes about herself and her "rebel" brothers: "I am a Southern girl, but you must not think any the worse of me for that, for I am not a rebel. I have five sisters and four brothers (two of them younger than I am), and they all are bitter against the North. I used to be before I came up here, but I have heard both sides now, and am as strong a Republican as anybody" (*Our Young Folks* 4.7 448). *Our Young Folks* strives, then, to reach out to readers from its Southern states and to smooth out remaining conflicts, in part by looking to the past to understand regional principles in a national context. The texts that include stories of boys and men grappling with the violence of the past illustrate how narrative interpretation can smooth out differences and encourage identification with national rather than just regional communities.

Material in *Our Young Folks* indicates that boyhoods are recollected and thereby reconstructed through discursive treatment of how North–South regional principles intersected and diverged in the pre-, mid-, and postwar years. In its investigations of regional characteristics, this periodical gives local constructions of boyhood national presence; its portable form gives these constructions influence among a variety of classes of readers. These discussions of regional differences explore acceptable and unacceptable aspects of boy culture. In one such exploration of boy culture, Aldrich's text opens with a suggestion that Tom Bailey's boyhood was defined by his being (even in childhood) "A Northern man with Southern principles." In an early address to the readers, Tom uses his biregional background to explain his reluctance to be sent North to school:

> You see I was what is called "a Northern man with Southern principles." I had no recollection of New England; my earliest memories were connected with the South, with Aunt Chloe, my old negro nurse, and with the great ill-kept garden in the centre of which stood our house—a white-washed brick house it was, with wide verandas—shut out from the street by lines of orange, fig, and magnolia trees. I knew I was born at the North, but hoped nobody would find it out. I looked upon the misfortune as something so shrouded by time and distance that may be [sic] nobody remembered it. I never told my schoolmates I was a Yankee, because they talked about the Yankees in such a scornful way as to make me feel that it was quite a disgrace not to be born in Louisiana, or at least in one of the Border States (8).

What does it mean to be a Northern man with Southern principles? The placement of this explanation early on in the serialized text resituates the pre-Reconstruction abolitionist politics of *Our Young Folks* by addressing regional identities and tensions without mentioning slavery and by placing a boy in a situation that requires him to confront the biregional nature of his background and heritage.

The principles for boyhood that *Our Young Folks* promotes by printing this "Northern story with Southern principles" in the immediate aftermath of the war include recognizing the links between regions and employing the links in the service of the Reconstruction project. Aldrich's text uses the word *principles* to describe culturally informed approaches to everyday situations. The term *principles* might also be read as signaling the kind of hegemonic values and actions that are usually so "naturalized" that participants cannot describe or locate the pressures to conform to a "whole way of life."[5] In its self-aware naming of region, this early discussion of Tom's principles contains some counterhegemonic pressure that recognizes the complex nature of boyhood not as a world apart but as that which is always joined with citizenship and the loyalties that shape it at the same time that the lighthearted dismissive tone of the surrounding narrative participates in the Reconstruction era's hegemonic moves to maintain United States' citizenship for white male citizens. Tom's self-description sheds light on what being "Northern with Southern principles" means for the rest of the bad boy's story and for the surrounding "character" of the periodical for which it was first produced.

In the passage cited above, the "Northern man with Southern principles" remark is immediately followed with an elaboration on the power of recollections to shape regional loyalties. For Tom, recollections form and shape principles tied to regions and more specifically to domestic persons and scenes: nurse, ill-kept garden, and white-washed brick house. Memory serves to shape principles not just in *Story of a Bad Boy* but also in *Our Young Folks* as a whole. In the years immediately following the end of the war, *Our Young Folks* allots space to fiction and nonfiction about childhoods from before the war as a means of capturing the interests and subscriptions of readers from a wide variety of regions. Texts built around remembered childhoods include Elijah Kellogg's *Good Old Times; or, Grandfather's Struggles for a Homestead*, which was serialized in 1867. Others that focus on past adventures and recollections of wildness (safely tamed in the narrator's present) include *Round-the-World Joe* (George Eager) and *Cast Away in the Cold: An Old Man's Story of a Young Man's Adventures* (Isaac I. Hayes).[6] John Townsend Trowbridge's *Half Hours with Father Brighthopes* and *The Adventures of Jack Hazard* focus on what younger generations can learn by looking back to grandfathers and grandfatherly figures. These are stories told by men about past boyhoods—they are made up of didacticisms, reminiscences, and survival techniques. They actively reconstruct boyhood for the younger, postwar generations who, as they read *Our Young Folks*, contemplate boyhood and manhood without the guidance of fathers/brothers who were lost in the Civil War.

Listening to grandfathers during the Reconstruction era and knowing what grandfathers knew became important for both literate and illiterate boys as the nation and the individual states debated how citizenship would be restructured and redefined to incorporate the "freedmen" into suffrage systems. While maintaining widely differing opinions about suffrage for emancipated slaves, Northerners and Southerners both agreed that any new suffrage laws needed to provide "grandfather clauses" so that white citizens who could not read or write would not lose their voting privileges.[7] Carl Schurz, who was sent by Andrew Johnson in 1865 to gather information about the Southern response to Reconstruction, writes about a Louisiana man's views on suffrage for emancipated slaves: "He declared himself ready to vote for an amendment to the constitution of his State bestowing the right of suffrage upon all male citizens without distinction of color who could furnish evidence of their ability to read and write, without, however, disenfranchising those who are now voters and are not able to fulfill that condition" (rpt. in Stalcup 55). C. Vann Woodward notes that laws such as the "'understanding clause' for illiterate whites and the 'grandfather clause' enfranchising all who had voted in 1857 as well as their sons and grandsons" were used to prevent disenfranchisement laws from affecting white voters.

Just as grandfather clauses become important during the postwar years, so do grandfather stories. "The Turning of the Leaf," written in June 1865 by *Our Young Folks* editor John Townsend Trowbridge, takes a position that seeks to smooth over past conflicts.[8] The older character, Uncle Rodman, argues that although many in the North were in favor of abolition, they were not in favor of war: "the most the Northern people expected to do, when they made Abraham Lincoln President, was to keep slavery out of the new States that were coming into the Union" (399). Uncle Rodman explains: "Unjust and unwise as it was to keep human beings in bondage, they did not feel that the law gave them any right to take slaves away from their masters by force" (399). Slaveholders spreading slavery into the new states is what Uncle Rodman cites as being one of the main causes of the war. He ends his history with an exhortation: "You especially, who are young, belong to the new era of justice and human brotherhood; and O let the fact inspire you now and henceforth with high aspirations, noble motives; and all generous thoughts and hopes!" (401). In *Our Young Folks*, the grandfathers' recollected pasts that provide boy readers with working knowledge of their histories, then, both sidestep and participate in current politics by exploring boyhoods or young manhoods that occurred forty years prior to the war.

Many of the serialized tales use elaborate narrative frames to provide reasons for their recollections.[9] The older, sedate narrator of *Cast Away in the Cold* lives in a home for aged mariners and, to a group of interested children who come on weekly visits, he tells story after story of his survival in the Alaska territories. The somewhat younger storyteller of *Around-the-World Joe* (sometimes described as a boy) seems to enjoy shocking the children with stories of foods, clothes, and practices he has observed on his travels. Like the narrator of *Story of a Bad Boy*, who establishes authority over and connection to boyhood with his claim "I am, or rather I was, that boy myself," the adult "Joe," in part because of his travels, still exhibits boy characteristics: "being one of those boys that give all their mind to a thing, and even pare apples with enthusiasm, he had thrown off his jacket and rolled his shirt-sleeves up to the shoulder" (41). In one episode, Joe spends a considerable amount of time explaining the friendliness of a cannibalistic group and arguing that it is important for the children to be aware of the power of their own customs:

> it's all Tradition and the Custom of the Country, and education has nothing to do with it. If it was the fashion in this country to dine on one's neighbors, you'd be catching all the little children that strayed into the yard, and fattening them in coops; and the greediest cannibals in this land would be subscribers to the "Home Journal" (329).

Joe's equation of subscription to the "Home Journal" with fashions of cannibals draws attention to dangerous and frightening historical traditions in the United States. His reference to capturing and fattening children obliquely hints at slavery as one such tradition and points to the work periodicals do to spread messages about both traditions and customs in ways that influence the responses of the subscribers.

Both *Round-the-World Joe* and *Cast Away in the Cold* focus on the survival of the American characters. In these serialized texts, the exploratory missions and their sometimes violent use of the lands and peoples they encounter are never questioned, and the "otherness" of the encountered cultures reinforces the "Americanness" of the narrating characters.[10] The reactions of the children within the text who listen to the stories told by the older narrators suggest what the magazine readers' own responses to the stories of the enactment of antebellum "Manifest Destiny" should be. These "survival" responses seem designed to help young citizens, who are experiencing the economic and legislative upheaval of Reconstruction, stay alert to their citizenship status and the privileges that status confers. In *Story of a Bad Boy* and other *Our Young Folks* texts, some of these strategies include standing up for citizenship rights with violence if necessary, reaching out to those less fortunate while marking individual territory and property, and proving membership or loyalty through ritualized or challenge-based feats. Most of the "stories-from-the-past" texts in *Our Young Folks* use the presentation of survival strategies to participate in the (re)construction of national citizenship.

The fashion-based power of periodicals that *Round-the-World Joe* highlights is a power that influences efforts to reconstruct national citizenship in the postwar years. Writing about the antebellum years in *A Fictive People*, Zboray argues that the sharing of periodicals and other kinds of texts (an act that sometimes took the place of letter writing) intervened in the construction of national and regional identities: "The suppression of individuality in conformance with fictional social types became a mainstay of national cultural life as Americans increasingly read fiction and became themselves not just a little fictionalized" (121). Zboray goes on to suggest that readers participated in this fictionalization of identity in ways that often diverged from the publishers and editors' conceptions of how their offerings would be received:

> Through their individualized, locally grounded re-interpretations, readers constructed texts very differently from how authors and publishers intended them to. In this way readers used the new leisure time economic development afforded them not only to self-construct but also to orient themselves outward, to engage a larger republic of letters, in which they acquired a citizenship equal to that of publishers and authors (193).

Our Young Folks, in its endorsement of *The Story of a Bad Boy*, offers fictionalized explorations of one boy's reunion with the North and his subsequent entry into the realm of American manhood. The subscribers to *Our*

Young Folks, invited by the title of the magazine to consider themselves members of a larger community, have the opportunity to interpret Tom's North–South–North citizenship shifts and to apply the interpretation to their own regionally influenced boyhoods. The serialized production of the text encourages the kind of participatory self-construction Zboray claims was available before the war.[11]

In *Story of a Bad Boy*, the sidestepping of the present via memories of the past reconstructs boyhood as valuable, necessary to recapture, and above the fray of regional politics and economies even as it reinforces the significance of regional politics through its emphasis on the importance of region to "proper" boyhood. The narrator's explanation of how his principles are tied specifically to memories of his nurse points, without mentioning slavery, to how the nurse/slave's understanding and dissemination of warning tales about "mean" whites from the North who were not gentlemen shape young Tom's views. Aunt Chloe tells Tom that the North is a terrible place: "'Dar ain't no gentl'men in the Norf noway,' and on one occasion terrified me beyond measure by declaring, 'If any of dem mean whites tries to git me away from marster, I's jes' gwine to knock 'em on de head wid a gourd!'" (8). The sources for Aunt Chloe's attitudes are tales similar to those used to prevent slaves from running away to the North. The connotations of the word *mean* in the narrator's repetition of the nurse's assessment of the North include the cheapness, cheating, theft, and cruelty that were part of the reputation of the antebellum Yankee overseer and the Northern principles of the postbellum carpetbaggers and scalawags.[12] The Reconstruction Acts of 1867 prevented members of the Confederacy from voting and holding office, and these Laws encouraged mean,Northern exploitation of the Southern states. The text's inclusion of Aunt Chloe's comments about Northerners suggests how, prior to the war, perhaps because of the economic shifts in banking and investment procedures that led up to the Panic of 1837 as well as increasing abolitionist agitation, rhetoric that encouraged suspicion of those entering the South from outside its borders had been passed along to slaves. Ideas about the meanness of Northerners carry through the book; in a late episode, for example, the text describes an adult "mean white" from the North, a man named Conway, who is Tom's arch enemy in Rivermouth, in terms that reflect the narrator's ongoing biregional conflict:

> Young Conway went into the grocery business with his ancient chum, Rodgers—[Rodgers & Conway]! I read the sign only last summer when I was down in Rivermouth, and had half a mind to pop into the shop and shake hands with him, and ask him if he wanted to fight. I contented myself, however, with flattening my nose against his dingy shop window, and beheld Conway, in red whiskers and blue overalls, weighing out sugar for a customer—giving him short weight, I would bet anything! (277)

Here, the narrator Tom responds as an adult to Conway's "meanness" with condescension. He does not shake hands with his old boyhood enemy, but instead puts his cheapness and red whiskers on display in a way that invites readers to respond with the same kind of smiling derision. The description of Conway, I would argue, is informed by Southern principles that call into question the "short weight" citizenship (characterized by the military rule established in 1867 and Radical Reconstructionists' calls for the revocation of citizenship privileges of former Confederate officers) provided by Reconstructionist intervention in Southern states' governments and economies.[13]

In a discussion of North–South regional biases, one of Aldrich's early biographers explores the subtle, regionally inflected class- and race-based attitudes that informed Aldrich's texts. Using biographical information about Aldrich, in *American Men of Letters: Thomas Bailey Aldrich* (1928), Ferris Greenslet writes about Aldrich's early life in New Orleans:

> For three years this was our poet's home, and it is perhaps not too fantastic a speculation to suppose that from those early days in the old Creole city, with its strange, tropical beauty, its exotic sounds and scents, he drew imaginative clues to a richer and more romantic life than was commonly to be observed among the dwellers upon the North Shore, with their preoccupations, commercial and transcendental. In the spring and fall the boy would be taken on trading trips up and down the Mississippi, and to the end of his life he could vividly recall the weird-flaring torches of the negroes who came down to light their landings (10).

Greenslet moves from this interpretation of the environment's shaping of the imagination to argue that the connection between New Orleans and the slave culture Aldrich experienced there influenced Aldrich's work and the mannerisms he carried with him throughout his life: "And, perhaps, in his childish relations with a subject race,—the reader will recall the affectionate kicking of little black Sam in 'The Story of a Bad Boy,'—we may find one secondary source of a certain amiable and engaging assurance that always marked his manner" (11). Pertinently, the "amiable and engaging assurance" has influenced Greenslet so much that he refers to the kicking of Sam as "affectionate," an evaluation that Aldrich's serialized text, as I will discuss below, seems to invite readers to make. The text of *The Story of a Bad Boy* grapples with the mixture of Tom Bailey's Northern manhood and Southern principles as it moves its character from boyhood to manhood, and as it does so, positions readers to respond to Southern encounters in similarly "principled" ways. *Our Young Folks* moves from its overtly abolitionist stance to a more complicated position that anticipates and responds to both Northern and Southern "principles" by mining the past for responses to the present. This mixture of regional influences, combined with the production format of the text, bring together hegemonic and counterhegemonic crosscurrents that complicate this text's and *Our Young Folks'* commentaries on American boyhood and its intersections with race, legislation, and rebellion.[14]

As noted above, one of this almost-all-white text's commentaries on regionally influenced race relations appears when Tom's immediate response to the news that his father intends to send him North to be educated is to kick Sam, one of Tom's slaves. Tom's action simultaneously combines the kind of "mean white" behavior Aunt Chloe seems to fear and Tom's "Southern principles." The illustration in the periodical version of the text seems to critique the violence by showing Sam facedown on the ground and Tom standing over him, looking unpleasant, but the text itself excuses the cruel, dehumanizing nature of Tom's response in a way that underscores the Southern principles of both *The Story of a Bad Boy* and *Our Young Folks*: their efforts to circulate reconciliatory, anti-activist responses to slavery and prejudice (see figure 4.1).[15]

The Southern-principled cruelty of the kick reflects Tom's unhealthy state

Figure 4.1. "Sam and Tom." Thomas Bailey Aldrich. *Our Young Folks* 5 (Jan. 1869): 3. Image courtesy of the de Grummond Children's Literature Collection, The University of Southern Mississippi, www.lib.usm.edu/~degrum

as a child dependent on slaves, and this highlights one of the reasons why his father wants to send him North. The text frames Tom's violent response with a history of Tom's Northern antecedents:

> I was only eighteen months old at the time of the removal [from Rivermouth], and it did not make much difference to me where I was, because I was so small; but several years later, when my father proposed to take me North to be educated, I had my own peculiar views on the subject. I instantly kicked over the little negro boy who happened to be standing by me at the moment, and, stamping my foot violently on the floor of the piazza, declared that I would not be taken away to live among a lot of Yankees! (7)

The narrator excuses Tom from the act of violence by explaining that Tom's understanding of the North was that it was uncivilized and dangerous, characterized by frontier violence, scalping Indians, and primitive log cabins:

> With this delightful picture of Northern civilization in my eye, the reader will easily understand my terror at the bare thought of being transported to Rivermouth to school, and possibly will forgive me for kicking over little black Sam, and otherwise misconducting myself, when my father announced his determination to me. As for kicking little Sam—I *always* did that, more or less gently, when anything went wrong with me. (9)

The heart of Tom's excuse, and the older narrator's remembrance and interpretation of it for young readers, emphasizes that the kick is not important in part because kicking Sam was something that Tom "always" did. The message to the previously abolitionist Northern readers and to the Southern subscribers is that the kick is just one of the "not [so . . .] very bad" specimens of mischief that they will encounter when reading the text. The "Southern principle" that comes through here for Northern white middle-class readers who face an influx of freed slaves into their communities is that violent treatment of persons of color is somehow natural—excusable because it has always been done.

The fact that Sam is only mentioned two other times in the text reinforces the white-centeredness that shapes the healthily mischievous bad boyhood the rest of the text describes, a white-centeredness I would argue is infused with a peculiar mixture of Northern and Southern principles.[16] The kick, while bad in the sense that it is cruel, is not purposeful; it is nonsensical, a display of anger, but not one designed to change the source of anger. When Tom says good-bye to his home in Louisiana, the narrator mentions that Sam does not appear to be sorry to see Tom go. The other comment about slavery comes near the end of the text when the narration mentions Sam's status as a slave more overtly; the opening episodes never mention that Chloe and Sam are, in fact, slaves. Sam is moved from Tom's father's home to a sugarcane plantation in Baton Rouge by his master, and since Sam does not like this change, he runs away to Canada. The text's description of Sam's fate comes in the closing episodes when Tom's mother returns to Rivermouth:

> Then there were old times to talk over, full of reminiscences of Aunt Chloe and little black Sam. Little black Sam, by the bye, had been taken by his master from my father's service ten months previously, and put on a sugar-plantation near Baton Rouge. Not relishing the change, Sam had run away, and by some mysterious agency got into Canada, from which place he had sent back several indecorous messages to his late owner. Aunt Chloe was still in New Orleans, employed as a nurse in one of the cholera hospital wards, and the Desmoulines, near neighbors of ours, had purchased the pretty brick house among the orange-trees. How all these simple details interested me will be readily understood by any boy who has been long absent from home (269–70).

The narration dismisses Sam's life-changing decision to run away and Aunt Chloe's dangerous work in the cholera wards as "simple details," a description that provides a reconstructive "Southern-principled" interpretation for the readers of *Our Young Folks.*

Other than lightly dismissing the kick, by which Tom treats Sam as a thing—not a human being—and thereby demonstrating his Southern principles, Aldrich's text does not linger on the issue of slavery or on how Sam's quest for manhood in Canada is as representative of boyhood at the time as Tom's quest for manhood in Rivermouth. While the illustration that accompanies the narrative of the kicking in *Our Young Folks* does attempt to drive home the horror of the "Southern principles" to which the text alludes, the periodical avoids the need to editorialize about the treatment, since the text sets up the "Story" as a series of fictionalized memoirs rather than present-day actions.

"The Story" begins in New Orleans, but the text suggests that Tom does not become a "boy" until he moves north. In Rivermouth, Tom is inculcated with regional interpretations of national histories until his boyhood is "Americanized" enough so that he can become a man. The surrounding periodical matter of *Our Young Folks* repeatedly illustrates how "Northern men with Southern principles" can work through encounters with people "other" than themselves to become "American" men with American principles. Along with *Cast Away in the Cold* and *Round-the-World Joe*, *Our Young Folks* provides reading recommendations for boys that highlight boys' encounters with "other landscapes" and recommendations that provide narratives of how boys from other cultures achieved manhood through an embrace of boyhood schooling: "For Boys who like stories of hardship and adventure, there is 'Lion Ben,' of which it is sufficient praise to say that it is by the author of 'Good Old Times.' Like that, it is the history of a boy's rough experience on the wild shores of Maine, and is the first of a series announced by Lee and Shepard as the 'Elm Island Stories'" (*Our Young Folks* 5.1 [May 1869]: 63).[17] *Story of a Bad Boy* joins these texts in encouraging encounters with the other. It is evident from Tom's father's insistence that Tom be educated in the North that he feels something is missing from Tom's education. The text makes the missing elements clear and the narrator (the older Tom) explains the missing elements in terms that focus on the character of masculinity and the aspects of daily life that shape it:

> Daily contact with boys who had not been brought up as gently as I worked an immediate and, in some respects, a beneficial change in my character. I had the nonsense taken out of me, as the saying is—some of the nonsense, at least. I became more manly and self-reliant. I discovered that the world was not created exclusively on my account. In New Orleans I labored under the delusion that it was. Having neither brother nor sister to give up to at home, and being, moreover, the largest pupil at school there, my will had seldom been opposed. At Rivermouth matters were different, and I was not long in adapting myself to the altered circumstances. Of course I got many severe rubs, often unconsciously given; but I had the sense to see that I was all the better for them (58–59).

Some of the "nonsense" that the text claims is taken out of Tom by his schooling at Temple Grammar School is the regional nonsense of slavery. As Tom narrates it, the sources of the nonsense have to do with Tom's hierarchical relationships to other household members and to other students. The not-so-bad, healthily mischievous badness that Tom learns and performs delineates his place in Rivermouth, his loyalty to his peers, and his knowledge of boy and adult institutions.

In addition to emphasizing the need to move Tom North in order to improve the quality of his education and to take the "nonsense" out of him, the text also suggests through images of permanent markings that boys are in danger of being permanently marked by their environment—in ways that would limit the possibilities available to them. When Tom meets Sailor Ben on his voyage to Rivermouth, the text emphasizes the permanent and simultaneously portable nature of Sailor Ben's tattoos. The narrator Tom describes Ben as a "perfect walking picture book" and he comments on the portability in the following way: "I imagine he was fond of drawings, and took this means of gratifying his artistic taste. It was certainly very ingenious and convenient. A portfolio might be displaced, or dropped overboard; but Sailor Ben had his pictures wherever he went" (21). This focus on the portability and convenience of some texts over others in a serialized text is significant, partly because periodicals were sold many times on the basis of their portability. The link between portable texts that can go anywhere and the story itself, as well as the surrounding stories "told" by old men to young boys, demonstrates a desire to make the boyhoods that these texts were recounting conveniently portable—able to move across the increasingly expanding American territories.

The frame stories of the older narrators speaking to a younger audience also mimic the portable narrative of the oral history. The told story is another portable text, although not necessarily an illustrated one in the way that Sailor Ben's body is. The text explains that in part, Ben's body, like the many serialized texts included in the 1867–1869 years of *Our Young Folks*, serves to commemorate past friendships and adventures, as well as past obligations.[18] The text describes Tom's reaction to the commemorative nature of the tattoos in the following way:

> The two hands on his breast, he informed me, were a tribute to the memory of a dead messmate from whom he had parted years ago—and surely a more touching tribute was never engraved on a tombstone. This caused me to think of my parting with old Aunt Chloe, and I told him I should take it as a great favor indeed if he would paint a pink hand and a black hand on my chest. He said the colors were pricked into the skin with needles, and that the operation was somewhat painful. I assured him, in an off-hand manner, that I didn't mind pain, and begged him to set to work at once (21).

The tattoo that Tom chooses, and almost has permanently inscribed on his body, consists of an image of two hands—for Tom, an image that supposedly will commemorate his love and devotion to Aunt Chloe. While it very well may have represented his love for her, the tattoo that Tom's father prevents him from receiving would also have commemorated his entanglement in the "peculiar institution." The fact that Tom is so accustomed to slavery as to want to mark his body with a token of his remembrance of it is perhaps an example of the kind of nonsense that Tom's father wants a Northern education to take out of him.

Upon entering the boy-making region of New England, Tom struggles to shed the "markings" of the South. Although he was not tattooed on the ship, his enemies at the Temple Grammar School foreground Tom's regional displacement by insisting that he is mulatto—marked visibly with the race of the people he has been accustomed to keeping as slaves. While Tom, before his entry into Rivermouth, was comfortable enough with his close relationship to his father's slaves to want to be marked with a reminder of the familial nature of one slave–master relationship, he does not want to be accused of having actual blood ties to slaves. Mixed blood becomes the cause of a fight with Bill Conway that ultimately seals Tom's membership in the boy community of Rivermouth. The fight with Conway over North–South differences, which occurs before the war but is recollected in the years immediately following, speaks to the ways that the violence and destruction of the Civil War settled the Union—everyone belonged—without settling the differences. The text uses a weather analogy to explain the difficulties Tom has in overcoming his regional differences from his Rivermouth classmates:

> So the days glided on, with fewer clouds and more sunshine than fall to the lot of most boys. Conway was certainly a cloud. Within school-bounds he seldom ventured to be aggressive; but whenever we met about town he never failed to brush up against me, or pull my cap over my eyes, or drive me distracted by inquiring after my family in New Orleans, always alluding to them as highly respectable colored persons (65).[19]

The cause of the problem between Conway and Tom—race—becomes part of the common cause of Reconstruction, with a central project including writing legislation that grappled with the citizenship rights of freed slaves. When affairs with Tom's enemy Conway come to a head after Conway thrashes Tom's friend Binny Wallace, Tom is goaded into continuing to fight by Conway's constant references to Tom's regional affiliations. These regional remarks are always connected to questions about Tom's race:

> "The thing must go on," said Adams, with dignity. "Rodgers, as I understand it, is your second, Conway? Bailey, come here. What's the row about?"
>
> "He was thrashing Binny Wallace."
>
> "No, I wasn't," interrupted Conway; "but I was going to, because he knows who put Meeks's mortar over our door. And I know well enough who did it; it was that sneaking little mulatter!"—pointing at me (113).

Conway fights with Tom because he is from New Orleans, which for Conway means that Tom is somehow contaminated by the race Tom's family has participated in exploiting. Tom fights with Conway, because while his narration claims that he loves his slaves, he cannot allow Conway to question his whiteness. Tom's strangely bifurcated position on race, which emerges as a result of Conway's comments, is one that is in line with the position of *Our Young Folks.* Comments on Reconstruction in the issues after the end of the war shift the abolitionist stance of the early issues slightly to protest the fact that any supporters of the Union ever meant to actually take slavery away from the slave states: the fight, they claim, was caused by Southern obstinacy—by Southern states' desires to expand slavery territory. The war has settled this difference, the editorial comments seem to say, and now subscribers and editors alike can get about the business of belonging and contributing to a unified nation. Written in the aftermath of the Civil War by an author with ties to the North and the South, the Conway episode in *The Story of a Bad Boy* illustrates how diminishment of violence through narrative interpretation can clear the way for belonging to a larger community.

Like the smaller scale war between Conway and Tom, another "war" in *The Story of a Bad Boy* echoes the final battles of the Civil War and stages for readers the same kind of losing battle that Confederate soldiers felt the need to fight. In "The Snow-Fort on Slatter's Hill," a battle begins between two groups of boys, significantly named "North Enders" and "South Enders," and finishes with the boys united against the adult members of the town watch in a battle the boys know they are destined to lose. Opening descriptions of the battle contain North versus South language that emphasizes regional differences in barely disguised commentary about the Civil War: "The memory of man, even that of the Oldest Inhabitant, runneth not back to the time when there did not exist a feud between the North End and the South End boys of Rivermouth" (139). The use of the term *feud* rather than *war* minimizes the severity of the Civil War and equates the national North–South differences with a regional feud between boys. In many ways, the fight over Slatter's Hill parallels national arguments about the territorial nature of the Civil War and the laws that applied to the Confederate states. William Whiting, one of Lincoln's experts on the laws of international war, writes that the Civil War was not a war about overthrowing the government but rather a war about territory:

> Hence civil war, in which the belligerents have become territorial enemies, instantly annuls all rights or claims of public enemies against the United States, under the Constitution or laws, that Constitution be called a compact, a treaty, or a covenant, and whether the parties to it were States, in their sovereign capacity, or the people of the United States as individuals (rpt. in Stalcup 40).

According to Whiting's understanding of the laws of war, fighting over territory shifts the war from being "Civil"—in this case, a dispute over government—to being a foreign/international war over territory. This shift erases citizenship rights and negates the constitutional contracts between the nation and the state. For a brief time, the feud over Slatter's Hill territory allows the boys of Rivermouth to create their own private "nation" and to subsequently divide it based on ownership and control of the fort. During this time, the feud weakens the boys' citizenship state in connection to the town, and eventually this diminishment of Rivermouth citizenship leads the North-Enders and the South-Enders to join their forces as they pursue a larger war with the men of the town.

Aldrich's text notes that the feud that this episode recounts escalates because of a territory dispute: "Great was the wrath of the South-Enders when they discovered that the North-Enders had thrown up a fort on the crown of Slatter's Hill" (139). Like the western territories that were part of the underlying tensions of the Civil War, Slatter's Hill is unassigned, belonging neither to the South or North: "Slatter's Hill, or No-man's-land, as it was generally called, was a rise of ground covering, perhaps, an acre and a quarter, situated on an imaginary line, marking the boundary between the two districts" (140). Although the text claims ignorance of the reasons for the feud, other names besides "South" and "North" suggest that some of the differences are class based. The North-Enders call the South-Enders "Puddle-dockers" and "River-rats," names that hint that the livelihoods of the South-Enders are connected to the physical labor of the port industries while the North-Enders are related to the owners of the ships, banks, and shops (141). The claiming of the unassigned territory by the already powerful North-Enders becomes ground for the ongoing feud to escalate into war.

The North–South war over the territory of the snow fort continues until the outside interference of the town watch. This interference unites the two sides in a few final battles that pitch the boys of Rivermouth against the men:

> The watch were determined fellows, and charged the boys valiantly, driving them all into the fort, where we made common cause, fighting side by side like the best of friends. In vain the four guardians of the peace rushed up the hill, flourishing their clubs and calling upon us to surrender. They could not get within ten yards of the fort, our fire was so destructive (149).

In this episode, the boys fight until they find a way to end the fighting, at which point they struggle to locate their new peacetime connection to members of the town, as well as their new peacetime relationships with each other. The move to resolve North versus South differences with images of united boyhood citizenships in this episode represents on a small scale the work the recollections-of-boyhood texts in *Our Young Folks* do to participate in the Reconstruction effort.

In writing *The Story of a Bad Boy*, Aldrich indirectly describes for his young readers the complexities of the Civil War as well as the intricate and inextricable links between North and South in both the pre- and postwar years. The best kinds of "bad" boys, that is, the ones with the most citizenship potential, are somehow miscegenated, marked with the differences, and connected in union against outside naysayers, infiltrators, and controllers. Aldrich's text uses his own mixed regional identity to involve boy readers and their adult counterparts as necessary participants in the unavoidably miscegenating project of Reconstruction—admitting to belonging, citizenship, and membership those that violence and oppression sought to prevent from entry.

Aldrich's text negotiates the complexities of belonging despite regional, economic, or conviction-based differences, and thereby attempts to reconstruct boyhood in the postwar years, by exploring the meanings of "contracts" at local, national, and international levels. According to explanations and commentary published in *Our Young Folks* about the causes of the Civil War, the slaveholding states in the South did not understand the seriousness of national contracts about slavery and expansion into the western territories and new states. Aldrich's text shows men and boys encountering contracts and meeting their requirements; the repetitious presence of these discussions indicates that *Our Young Folks* participated in the Reconstruction effort in part by disseminating the importance of the contract to both American manhood and boyhood through serialized publication of "contract" episodes.

Tom first hears about the life-changing nature of contracts through his friendship with Sailor Ben. In terms of United States and Rivermouth citizenship, Sailor Ben is this text's marginal figure; his tattooed body marks him as a sailor without clear ties to the land, but his marriage to Kitty Collins and his friendship with Tom offer him immediate entry into the society of one of the town's older members—Tom's grandfather, Captain Nutter. In using the word *marginal* to describe Sailor Ben, I am following Victor Turner's suggestion that marginal figures, because they embody contradictions, can point to a culture's central concerns.[20] Marginal figures are "simultaneously members (by ascription, optation, self-definition or achievement) of two or more groups whose social definitions and cultural norms are distinct from, and often opposed to, one another" (Turner 233). Ben's joining of the ranks of married American men and his ongoing loyalty to the duties of sailing form two opposed sets of obligations. The text makes use of Ben's conflicting contractual agreements to comment on the South's similar position in connection to opposed contracts—its contract to the Union and its loyalty to the slave-based plantation economies. In the rhetoric of Reconstruction, concerns with oppositional contracts and the dangerousness of reconciling them emerge in the debates over postwar distribution of plantation lands to slaves. Individual ownership of property, one of the near sacred qualities of United States' citizenship, comes into conflict with another citizenship right—compensation for labor.[21] In a speech to the House of Representatives in 1867, Thaddeus Stevens, a leader of the "Radical Republicans" (the party that most desired to enact revenge on the Southern states) argued that plantation lands should be distributed to former slaves because they had earned their ownership: "I do not speak of their fidelity and services in this bloody war. I put it more on the mere score of lawful earnings. They and their ancestors have toiled, not for years, but for ages, without one farthing of recompense. They have earned for their masters this very land and much more" (rpt. in Stalcup 154). The importance of making restitution for unjust contracts that Stevens notes can also be seen in *The Story of a Bad Boy*. Ben's successful reunion with Kitty after years of breaching his contract provides a one-man model of how the previously oppositional contracts between the North and the South might be renegotiated and reconciled through postwar narratives. In *The Romance of Reunion*, Nina Silber suggests that about ten years after the war middle- and upper-class Northerners actively participated in producing "metaphors and cultural images of reconciliation" (2). Part of the project Silber describes makes gender central to its narratives of reunion—mainly by feminizing the Southern man and by increasing the masculinity of the Northern: "The union of hearts became a wedding of the North and the South, a marriage which, when described by northerners, almost always paired the feminine South with the masculine North" (65). I would suggest that the reunion "romances" or narratives began to be seen in children's periodicals almost immediately after the war, and that the reunion stories both emphasize heterosexual images of marital faithfulness, as they do in the case of Ben's reunion with Kitty, and contemplate the reconciliatory power of homosocial friendships. I would also point out that rather than only being a "Northern" project, Aldrich's text weaves its reunion "romance" from a biregionalist position. Sailor Ben lays claim to his citizenship, and thereby his manhood, by weaving narratives about his struggles and by sticking obstinately to contracts he makes.

Ben's strategy for repairing breaches in his conflicting contracts is to narrate his intentions regarding his contracts. Ben uses his marriage contract with Kitty to explain why he cannot take a sailing job, even though he needs the money: "I've signed papers as keeps me ashore, an' the parson has witnessed the deed" (191). When Kitty looks at him questioningly after his return ("What right had he to look for a welcome from one he had treated so cruelly?"), Ben tells about this assertion to convince Kitty of his attempt to be faithful to his contract (186). Narrative repairs the harm caused by the long separation in Kitty and Ben's marriage, and similarly, this text's demonstrations of the restorative power of narration, like similar demonstrations in other *Our Young Folks*' texts, participate in resolidifying the Union of the states and healing the fissures caused by the Civil War.

In addition to providing narrative possibilities for renegotiating broken or weak contracts, *The Story of a Bad Boy* also explores the reasons why even an immoral or bad contract must sometimes be followed. Ben's discussion of forced contractual labor and his unwilling participation in it gestures to the inhumanity of the forced labor of the slave economies as well as to the Southern states' contractual embroilment in that economy. Ben participates in a forced contract when he encounters a man who uses drugs and alcohol to convince sailors to sign onto ships: "I was signalled by one of them sleek, smooth-spoken rascals with a white hat an' a weed on it, as is always goin' about the piers a-seekin' who they may devower" (190). Even though Ben recognizes the impressment officer for what he is—a version of a slave trader—he cannot escape him. Ben's narration attributes his and other sailors' responses to these contractors to a lack of manhood: "We sailors know 'em for rascals from stem to starn, but somehow every fresh one fleeces us jest as his mate did afore him. We don't larn nothin' by exper'ence; we're jest no better than a lot of babbys with no brains" (190). Ben describes his response as babylike (not even childlike); the persuasive and slippery language of the contractor renders Ben powerless, with the powerlessness resulting in forced labor.

Ben's story emphasizes that one way to claim manhood after being turned into a powerless "babby" is to uphold the contract. Claiming the signature as his own is one way for Ben to move back to manhood: "But I done my duty like a man, seein' there was n't no way of gittin' out of it. I told my shipmates of the trick as had been played on me, an' they tried to cheer me up a bit" (192). For Ben, fulfilling this contract (acknowledging ownership of his signature) prevents him from admitting to being enslaved and permits him to perform his work "like a man." Like Tom, the readers of *Our Young Folk* see demonstrated here that labor can be classified as forced or unforced, and by association, enslaved or free. Further, they learn that understanding the force of contract, and claiming participation in it, can provide participants in even the most degrading and menial labor some semblance of power and control, both of which are constructed by Ben's narrative as being attributes of manhood. Since slaves could not enter into contracts because they lacked the civic identity to do so, this text, written in the early years of Reconstruction, responds to slavery in the manhood it inscribes by educating the readers about the necessity of the contract in claiming manhood.[22] In the postbellum era, former slaves are reminded of this, so their "manhood" can be affirmed.

The text further explains Ben's dedication to the idea of "contract" in the episode that recounts Tom's running away to Boston. Ben buys a train ticket to Boston in order to follow Tom. When Tom inquires why Ben did not stop him in Rivermouth, Ben explains that he viewed buying the ticket as a contractual agreement: "having purchased a ticket for Boston, he considered himself bound to the owners (the stockholders of the road) to fulfil his part of the contract. To use his own words, he had 'shipped for the viage'" (260). According to Ben's philosophy, upholding contracts helps to keep the machinery of the American economy in good working order. Although this is a humorous scenario, Tom takes the multiple lessons about contracts to heart, fulfilling contracts when he plans the refurbishment and firing of Rivermouth's collection of 1812 cannons. In this episode, Tom uses money to buy contractual power in the planning and implementation of the cannon firing:

> It was unanimously agreed that a plan should be carried out in the handsomest manner, and a subscription to that end was taken on the spot. Several of the Centipedes had n't a cent, excepting the one strung around their necks; others, however, were richer. I chanced to have a dollar, and it went into the cap quicker than lightning. When the club, in view of my munificence, voted to name the guns Bailey's Battery, I was prouder than I have ever been since over anything (208).

When money is tied to the plan, the firing of the cannons moves from being a simple plan to being an act of mischief in which the boys own stock. Tom's significant monetary share allows his name to be associated with the project; and, just as Ben's signature obligates him to fulfill his duties as sailor, the association of Tom's name with the cannon project strengthens the power of the contract and the obligation to carry it out.

The serialized format of *The Story of a Bad Boy*'s production also demonstrates the power of the contract and the power of buying and selling in the years after the Civil War. Aldrich's biographer Greenslet explains that, having been contracted to write the serial, Aldrich does, and the magazine adds thousands to its subscription list because of the fact that they know *The Story of a Bad Boy* will be finished in its pages:

> In the early months of 1869 "The Story of a Bad Boy" was issued serially in "Our Young Folks," a juvenile magazine ably edited by Mr. J. T. Trowbridge and published by Fields, Osgood and Co. as the firm had then become. So great was its success in the periodical that several thousand subscribers were promptly added to the circulation, and after its publication in book form in the autumn of 1869 (dated 1870), it speedily ran through some eleven editions, a notable record for a book of its kind in those days (92).

In promising to tell the story of a bad boy that is different from previous texts about boys, their friendships, and pursuits, Aldrich and the editors of *Our Young Folks* establish a powerful contract that not only boosts circulation of the periodical but offers Aldrich, whose poetry has never achieved canonical status, the chance to obtain a lasting reputation in annals of American literature.[23]

Interestingly, *Story of a Bad Boy* hints at the power that subscribing to a periodical can confer in a description of Captain Nutter's use of his subscription to the *Rivermouth Barnacle*:

> Captain Nutter was at home reading the Rivermouth Barnacle. He was a reader to do an editor's heart good; he never skipped over an advertisement, even if he had read it fifty times before. Then the paper went the rounds of the neighborhood, among the poor people, like the single portable eye which the three blind crones passed to one another in the legend of King Acrisius (183).

Captain Nutter's sharing of his paper connects him through a kind of custom-based contract to his neighbors and gives him control of the flow of information. Another indication of the power of the periodical comes in the terminology Jack Harris uses to describe the lighting of the 1812 cannons. When he realizes that there is the possibility of lighting more than one, he exclaims: "We'll give 'em a broadside, to be sure, if we die for it!" (207). While the term *broadside* is used for unexpected attacks, it is also a word linked to cheaply produced and widely distributed periodical material. The broadside, often illustrated and used for political purposes, had the power to shock, to enthrall, and to persuade. Aldrich's text "broadsides" its readers episodically with narrative prescriptions for conducting a bad and simultaneously reconstructive boyhood.

In addition to reconstructing boyhood through meditations on the influences of large-scale regions on small-town boyhoods and the exploration of the man-making power of contracts, Aldrich's text continues and extends Oliver Optic's obsession with clubs as keys to developing "good" American boyhoods by suggesting that clubs can both contain (subdue) and permit the sorts of rebellions that end up solidifying and stabilizing larger civic bodies and economies.[24] After living in Rivermouth for a while and participating in the festivities of the Fourth of July, Tom becomes a member of the Rivermouth Centipedes, "a secret society composed of twelve of the Temple Grammar School boys" (100). Tom's entry into the Centipede club signals the boys' acceptance of him: "This was an honor to which I had long aspired, but being a new boy, I was not admitted to the fraternity until my character had fully developed itself" (100). His membership in the club makes him a member of the Rivermouth community rather than an outsider from New Orleans.

Several of the club's activities center around play/mischief-motivated interpretations of patriotic or American actions that challenge the authority of the adult members of the Rivermouth community:

> [T]here was a tacit understanding among us that the Centipedes were to stand by one another on all occasions, though I don't remember that they did; but further than this we had no purpose, unless it was to accomplish as a body the same amount of mischief which we were sure to do as individuals. To mystify the staid and slow-going Rivermouthians was our frequent pleasure. Several of our pranks won us such a reputation among the townfolk that we were credited with having a large finger in whatever went amiss in the place.

Tom is admitted to the Centipedes club in part because of his willing participation in burning the town's old stagecoach at the traditional Fourth of July Rivermouth bonfire.[25] That the town's response to the boys' mischief is that "boys will be boys" becomes particularly clear in the scene where Tom slips out of his grandfather's house to participate in the town square bonfire tradition. He encounters a member of the town watch, who observes his actions and apprehends him:

> "What on airth air you a-doin'?" asked the man, grasping the collar of my jacket.
>
> "I live here, sir, if you please," I replied, "and am going to the bonfire. I didn't want to wake up the old folks, that's all."

> "Boys is boys," he muttered. He did not attempt to stop me as I slipped through the gate (76).

Here, the town watch sanctions an activity that is outside of the law in part because it is an activity that reinforces known and understood conceptions of boyhood in the Rivermouth community.

Part of being a boy in Rivermouth is being willing to join in with the other boys in the community—to participate willingly in whatever mischief they concoct. When Tom is asked to join in, he partially establishes his eligibility for the Centipedes by not questioning the suggested activity. After the bonfire (mischief approved by the town), the boys decide to set an old stagecoach on fire. Rivermouth boys are supposed to be "ripe for anything," and since this activity involves destruction of a Rivermouth citizen's property, participation in the burning gives Tom a chance to prove his willingness to belong (78). The kind of mischief at work in the stagecoach burning is destructive, but it does not necessarily damage human beings. Book reviews published in *Our Young Folks* encourage boys to buy books that celebrate the "harmless" mischief that this periodical seems to see as necessary in constructing boys who will become useful citizens. One such 1867 review urges boys to buy a book of poetry written by Alice Cary: "The second has a real *snap* to it, and will go straight to the hearts of all the youngsters. But remember, it only asks that boys should be *boys*,—not hectors, or turbulent troublesome fellows. A great distinction there young gentlemen!" (752). Cary's poem, titled "Plea for the Boys," emphasizes the importance of play to boyhood citizenship:

> Young men must work, and old men rest,—
> They have earned their quiet joys;
> And everywhere, from east to west,
> The boys must still be boys. (752)

When Aldrich's boys play, they do so in "troublesome" ways that challenge the town's nostalgia for the past. The description of the stagecoach is intriguing because it draws attention to the town's economic stability, the power of individual investments, and the relationship between tradition and change, all issues that intersect with the function of recollections of a past boyhood in *The Story of a Bad Boy*:

> We glided out from the crowd and silently wended our way through a neighboring alley, at the head of which stood a tumble-down old barn, owned by one Ezra Wingate. In former days this was the stable of the mail-coach that ran between Rivermouth and Boston. When the railroad superseded that primitive mode of travel, the lumbering vehicle was rolled into the barn, and there it stayed. The stage-driver, after prophesying the immediate downfall of the

> nation, died of grief and apoplexy, and the old coach followed in his wake as fast as it could by quietly dropping to pieces. The barn had the reputation of being haunted (78).

The stagecoach, left behind by the railroad, haunts the barn until the town's young citizens come to burn away the remainder/reminder of the past.[26] The boys who are not "ripe for anything" are asked to forfeit their rights to discuss the incident—to silently step aside without protesting or tattling. If they speak, the implication is that they will no longer be considered members of the boyhood community. "'The old trundle-cart isn't worth twenty-five cents,' said Jack Harris, 'and Ezra Wingate ought to thank us for getting the rubbish out of the way. But if any fellow here doesn't want to have a hand in it, let him cut and run, and keep a quiet tongue in his head ever after'" (78–79). Together, the boys of Rivermouth take a grassroots action that ratifies the age of the train while simultaneously deciding which boys have what it takes to "have a hand in it."

After Tom proves himself during the Fourth of July burning of the stagecoach, he is inducted into the Centipedes and thereafter participates wholeheartedly in all of the club's official and unofficial activities. One such activity is the previously discussed battle over the Slatter's Hill snow fort. The Centipede club members are also all North-Enders, and they use the organizational and mischief-planning skills gained through membership in the club to carry out maneuvers during the fight. Jack Harris, one of the leaders of the Centipedes, is also the general of the North-Enders. His leadership skills galvanize the Slatter's Hill snowball fight when it turns from a North–South dispute to a rebellion against the leaders of the town:

> The selectmen of the town awoke to the fact of what was going on, and detailed a posse of police to prevent further disturbance. The boys at the foot of the hill, South-Enders as it happened, finding themselves assailed in the rear and on the flank, turned around and attempted to beat off the watchmen. In this they were sustained by numerous volunteers from the fort, who looked upon the interference as tyrannical (148).

For a while, the Centipede club members' superior organizational skills daunt the members of the town watch. But, eventually, the boys—both the members of the club and the united North-Enders and South-Enders—realize that they are fighting a losing battle. They come to terms with this realization with a final display of their rebellious spirit:

> Perceiving that it was impossible with their small number to dislodge us, the watch sent for reinforcements. Their call was responded to, not only by the whole constabulary force (eight men), but by the numerous body of citizens, who had become alarmed at the prospect of a riot. This formidable array

> brought us to our senses: we began to think that may be [sic] discretion was the better part of valor. General Harris and General Ames, with their respective staffs, held a council of war in the hospital and a backward movement was decided on. So, after one grand farewell volley, we fled, sliding, jumping, rolling, tumbling down the quarry at the rear of the fort, and escaped without losing a man (149).

In its description of the capitulation at the battle of Slatter Hill, the text depicts boyhood as a battle that will always lose to manhood. The fort on Slatter's Hill becomes one of the Foucauldian heterotopias, or "everyday places that are charged with ideal purpose as private citizens are publicly bound to people they scarcely know," which Kathleen Diffley argues shape national identity (191).[27] The war descriptions in the Slatter's Hill episode comment on connections between region and nation as they express both the border state between childhood and manhood in which the North-Enders and South-Enders reside and the delicate balance between war–peace spatial and territorial relations. The text shapes the Slatter's Hill fort into a spatial repository of boyhood and asks readers to imaginatively invest themselves in the extraordinary impact of the fort on Tom's understanding of boyhood. Diffley explains how war recollections can make spaces sacred: "seemingly ordinary places, even the most private were infused with political urgency when stories of war were told" (191). I would argue that the "war story" of the fort on Slatter's Hill uses spatial recollection to indicate the tenuous nature of the Rivermouth boys' relationships to each other and to the adult members of the town. The depiction of this tenuousness comments on the fragility of national and regional citizenship "contracts." The scene of the final volley illustrates that losing a rebellion, or moving back into a law-abiding relationship with the men of the town, does not have to be a scene of shame or discouragement. For participants in the battle, the shape of the entire rebellion, not just the final retreat, provides recollective fuel for the boyhood Reconstruction project in which this text participates.

The cannon resurrection offers a final example of how rebellion can define and impart purpose to boyhood citizenship. The mischief narrative of the Centipede Club's refurbishment of the old cannons supplies images that illustrate how texts can re-repair material and lives that are buried in the past:

> These guns ('old sogers' the boys called them), had their story, like everything else in Rivermouth. When that everlasting last war—the war of 1812, I mean—came to an end, all the brigs, schooners, and barks fitted out at this port as privateers were as eager to get rid of their useless twelve-pounders and swivels as they had previously been to obtain them. Many of the pieces had cost large sums, and now they were little better than so much crude iron—not so good, in fact, for they were clumsy things to break up and melt over. The government

> did not want them; private citizens did not want them; they were a drug in the market (202).

One Rivermouth man, the text explains, believes that the war will begin again soon, and he buys the cannons to make a future profit. When he dies, the cannons are left behind in Rivermouth. In calling the cannons "old sogers," the text links the weapons to male bodies and in particular to the bodies of soldiers—like the guns, these bodies are worthless and impotent after the war. The text emphasizes the silenced story-telling potential of the guns with language that personifies the cannons as silenced male bodies: "They were famous fellows in our eyes. What a racket they had made in the heyday of their unchastened youth! What stories they might tell now, if their puffy metallic lips could only speak! Once they were lively talkers enough; but there the grim seadogs lay, silent and forlorn in spite of all their former growlings" (205). The boys of Rivermouth decide to resurrect the "old sogers" that had helped the young "Sons of Liberty" defend themselves against the British fathers in the early years of the nation. If the snow fort on Slatter's Hill demonstrates that boys lose to men, the resurrection of the boyish nation's weapons of victory revisits this conclusion and suggests that remembering the past can alleviate present-day losses.[28] Tom's idea to "set one of the old sogers on his legs and serve him out a ration of gunpowder" brings the Centipede Club together in an act that consists of a surprise attack by the boys against the adult men of the town (206).[29] In giving voice to the past, the boys recognize their own connectedness to the rebellious history of the port town and the nation while simultaneously displaying their potential power. When Tom Bailey and the other Centipedes draw lots to choose which one of them will light the fuse, the words printed on the slips claim manhood, not boyhood, as the status of the one chosen to complete the prank. Tom is chosen; his slip of paper reads, "Thou art the man" (211).

The Story of a Bad Boy remarks, after Tom survives the dangerous task of lighting the fuse, that "There is a special Providence that watches over idiots, drunken men, and boys" (212). Here, the text participates, in its tone of affectionate indulgence, in establishing, along with other texts that recollect boyhoods of the past, a kind of textual "providence" for American boys who will become American men. *Our Young Folks* and *The Story of a Bad Boy* give space to scenes that recount the ingenuity and rebelliousness of younger generations while acknowledging through their narrative frames that rebellious boys become stable and productive citizens. In its comparison of the "unmanly" badness of slavery to the healthily mischievous badness of mixed region boys and in its discussions of the man-making power of contracts, *Story of a Bad Boy* contemplates the reconstructive changes that are necessary to make the white boyhood citizenships it describes available to African American readers, who, like Sam, use reading and writing to mark their freedom. Readers facing the aftermath of the large-scale rebellion of the war, an aftermath that left many fatherless, find textual re-embodiments of American men and manhood that provide written guidelines for harnessing their own "badness" into successful local and national citizenship.

As this text recollects one New England boyhood, it provides for young readers powerful images of how the rebellion and violence of regional splits can culminate in renewed or new contracts that establish stable citizenships that allow for participation in renewed/renewable economies. The moves made by the contributing authors of *Our Young Folks* to recollect where they had come from as boys participate in the work of Reconstruction in part because of the circulation of this magazine and the number of reprints of its best-known canonical text. The magazine as a whole and the text specifically meditate on violence and survival as ways of reassuring themselves and young readers that the regional reunions demanded by Reconstruction could be made textually possible.

Periodicals for boys published in the 1870s indicate that the Reconstruction of boyhood through written recollection had been successful. Although there had been a few gender-specific titles of magazines before the Civil War, magazines for boys proliferated between the 1870s and 1880s. Some of the titles given by R. Gordon Kelly in *Children's Periodicals of the United States* include: *Boys' Ledger* (1872), *Boys' Own* (1873), *Frank Leslie's Boys of America* (1875), *Boys of New York* (1875), *Boys of the World: A Story Paper for the Rising Generation* (1875), *New York Boys* (1877), and *Young Men of America* (1877). There are even more titles than these, and I would suggest that the reconstructions of boyhood that occur in *Our Young Folks* work to create a separate reading world that is designated for boys.[30] Writing stories for boys, it seems, is a lucrative and powerful business. Writing about the authors who contributed "boy" stories to the magazine industry (W. D. Howells and Stephen Crane among others), Albert Stone explains: "A favorite vehicle [for the boy book] was the new children's magazine, which in the fifteen years after the War sprang into prominence and popularity and proved so formative an influence on a whole generation of Americans like 'Teddie' Roosevelt" (ix).[31] By the 1880s, magazines for boys were commonly available, and they provided forums for both men and women authors to tell a variety of stories about boys.[32] Between 1885 and 1886, two American boyhoods emerge from these scenes of magazine production: *The Adventures of Huckleberry Finn* and *Little Lord Fauntleroy*. Extending the kind of rule-breaking mischief participated in by Tom Bailey and the Centipedes, Huck interrogates the laws governing slavery and establishes his brand of citizenship by deliberately breaking them. While *Huckleberry Finn* contemplates the rejection of citizenship altogether, *Little Lord Fauntleroy* explores not the power of badness, but the power of goodness that makes its influence felt through bodily display and persistent conversation. These two "Gilded

Age" boyhoods extend their influence to shape constructions of Americanness and boyhood throughout the twentieth century.

NOTES

1. See Joan Brest Friedberg's discussion of the magazine's history in R. Gordon Kelly's *Children's Periodicals of the United States* (329–41).

2. Stone also notes that "Comparing Tom with his fellow anti-prigs uncovers some striking parallels as well as differences equally significant" (63).

3. Subsequent publishers include Fields and Osgood from 1868 to 1870 and James Osgood from 1870 to 1873. See Henry Walcott Boynton's discussion of the religious affiliations of the Boston-based publishing houses in *Annals of American Bookselling 1638–1850.*

4. See Brenda Stalcup's *Reconstruction: Opposing Viewpoints.*

5. I draw here on Raymond Williams's discussion of the multiple definitions of culture in *Keywords: A Vocabulary of Culture and Society.*

6. Both of these begin serialization in 1867.

7. Tony Badger's "The Rise and Fall of Biracial Politics in the South" and C. Vann Woodward's "Post-Reconstruction Periods Compared, 1890s and 1990s" discuss how Southern states used literacy (basic literacy and also legislative literacy) to enfranchise and disenfranchise certain segments of the voting population.

8. See *Children's Periodicals of the United States* for discussion of other treatments of the Civil War in *Our Young Folks*. James Marten has published two significant studies of the children's literature of the Civil War. See *The Children's Civil War* and *Lessons of War: The Civil War in Children's Magazines.*

9. The narrative voice in *Story of a Bad Boy* seems to shift between an older Tom and a younger Tom (but one slightly older than the boy Tom). Both are autobiographical characterizations/caricatures of Thomas Bailey Aldrich.

10. In "Global and Local Cultures," Mike Featherstone explains how cultural comparisons can serve as self-defining narratives as well as narratives that explore dependencies between cultures: "the 'we-images' and 'they-images', which are generated within local struggles to form an identity and exclude outsiders, cannot be detached from the density of the web of interdependencies between people" (176).

11. Zboray explains that readers of magazines often shared subscriptions with family members or others in their local communities, thereby proliferating the number of readers of any given subscription (120). For other discussions of reading practices and constructions of national and local identities see Cathy N. Davidson's *Revolution and the Word*, David D. Hall's *Cultures of Print*, and Susan Coultrap-McQuin's *Doing Literary Business.*

12. See the discussion of Reconstruction Acts in Stalcup (109).

13. The Wade-Davis Bill, which summarized the Radical Reconstruction Plan, asks for the following enactment: "No person who has held or exercised any office, civil or military (except offices merely ministerial and military offices below the grade of colonel), State or Confederate, under the usurping power, shall vote for or be a member of the legislature or governor" (rpt. in Stalcup 36).

14. Gramsci's theories of hegemony provide useful ways to read Tom's narration of his coerced move to the North and his subsequent embrace of Rivermouth life and culture. See *Selections from the Prison Notebooks.*

15. The woodcut depicts Tom standing over Sam. Sam, dressed in ragged shirt-sleeves and bare feet, appears to be trying to get back up after being kicked over. Tom, in a jacket and long pants, still looks angry. The background shows Lake Ponchartrain, which emphasizes, I would suggest, the environment's influence on Tom's actions.

16. In my use of the term *white-centeredness,* I am thinking of Dana Nelson's discussion of how whiteness and maleness were used to create bonds of citizenship in the United States. See also Toni Morrison's *Playing in the Dark* and David Roediger's discussions of whiteness as it impacts class and citizenship in *Towards the Abolition of Whiteness* and *The Wages of Whiteness.*

17. Another recommendation reads: "'Tom Brown's School-Days at Rugby' is a standard for boys" (63).

18. Susan Bordo argues in her book about cultural constructions of the male body that "when we look at bodies (including our own in the mirror), we don't just see biological nature at work, but values and ideals, differences and similarities that *culture* has 'written,' so to speak, on those bodies" (26). Sailor Ben marks his body with a history of its forced docility and with marks of his own loyalty to other comrades. Tom's father interferes with Tom's desire to record the history of his Southern principles on his Northern body.

19. Historians of the Civil War have used similar weather analogies to describe the years leading up to the Civil War. See *The Approaching Fury: Voices of the Storm, 1820–1861.*

20. See Victor Turner's discussion of marginality and liminality in *Dramas, Fields and Metaphors: Symbolic Action in Human Society.*

21. See my discussion of Jacob Abbott's "Rollo" books and their 1840s serializations in the *Youth's Companion* for further descriptions of prewar obsessions with property laws and citizenship.

22. Here, again, the text indicates its mixed principles, because by claiming that manhood does not exist without contracts, it insists that slaves cannot be men at the same time that it declares and thereby educates readers about the man-making power of the contract.

23. In "Reading for Profit *and* Pleasure: *Little Women* and *The Story of a Bad Boy,*" Ellen Butler Donovan argues persuasively that Aldrich's narrative perspective invites readers to participate in his textual world: "Alcott and Aldrich offered to child readers the opportunity to experience another child's reality, to see the world or events from a child's point of view. The narrative strategies used by the authors also provided the readers an opportunity to think and judge independently" (151).

24. See my discussion of the "boat club" in chapter three.

25. As they do in Jacob Abbott's books and in Oliver Optic's books, patriotic celebrations disrupt the everyday flow of events in Aldrich's Rivermouth, particularly among the boys.

26. In some ways, the burning both resists and celebrates (or at least acknowledges) the past, which is what Aldrich's poetry also tended to do. For an elaboration

of how moving to New York as a young man allowed Thomas Bailey Aldrich to both escape from and connect with his New England fathers (Whittier and Longfellow among others) see Ferris Greenslet's *American Men of Letters: Thomas Bailey Aldrich*.

27. See "Home from the Theatre of War: The *Southern Magazine* and Recollections of the Civil War," an essay about postwar descriptions of Baltimore in magazine serializations.

28. See David Pugh's *Sons of Liberty* for a discussion of how Revolutionary heroes continued to shape views of masculinity (filtered through the lens of Americanness) throughout the nineteenth century.

29. The club uses their knowledge of the power of the contract to enlist Ben's help in the plot to surprise the town with the explosion: "The Admiral had a sailor's love for a joke, and entered at once into our scheme. He volunteered to prepare the fuses himself, and I left the labor in his hands, having bound him by several extraordinary oaths—such as 'Hope-I-may-die' and 'May-I-sink-first'—not to betray us, come what would" (210).

30. Kirsten Drotner notes about British reading boys during this same time period: "the sons of skilled workers, while rarely having regular employment outside school hours generally received pocket money for saving up. Some of their school savings were undoubtedly spent on commercial weeklies whose contents not only seemed more exciting and accessible than books but whose very possession often formed a covert protest" (148). The number of American boy magazine titles during this time period suggests that in the United States there were parallel expansions in the numbers of boys buying or borrowing reading material that seemed to belong to them alone.

31. Roosevelt subscribed to *Our Young Folks*.

32. See Beverly Lyon Clark's treatment of Julia A. Matthews's *Jack Granger's Cousin* (1877) in *Regendering the School Story* (197–221).

5

"Shall I Be Your Boy?": Conversational Citizenships in the *St. Nicholas* Serialization of *Little Lord Fauntleroy*

In 1885, Frances Hodgson Burnett serialized *Little Lord Fauntleroy* in *St. Nicholas Magazine*. This text, one of her best-known rags-to-riches tales, was published twenty-two years after the Emancipation Proclamation, in the middle of the United States' "Gilded Age," an age characterized by the conspicuous consumption of nineteenth-century industrialists.[1] Describing the age, Robert W. Cherny writes:

> The burnished locomotives spewing smoke and steam, the scintillating life of the expanding cities, the cornucopia of bright industrial entrepreneurs—all came to typify "progress" for many Americans, providing the gleaming surface of the Gilded Age. Just below that golden surface, however, lay twelve-hour workdays in factories, the widespread use of child labor, and large-scale business dealings so ethically dubious as to earn some entrepreneurs the designation "robber baron" (4).

In 1885, *St. Nicholas* was owned by the Century Company, and was one of the first children's magazines to solicit material from established authors such as Charles Dickens and Louisa May Alcott in order to produce an illustrated magazine that was suitable for children without being overtly didactic. The Century Company's endeavors made *St. Nicholas* a beautifully packaged and highly successful magazine.[2]

The spirit of *Little Lord Fauntleroy* certainly matches the generous nature of the saint of the magazine's title. The name *St. Nicholas* associates itself with the custom of gift giving at Christmas, and this tale of an American boy suddenly "gifted" with aristocratic lineage and immense wealth explores the possibilities of the beautifully packaged and androgynously engendered potential of what I will call a "conversational" citizenship. *Little Lord Fauntleroy* tells the story of Cedric Errol, the son of an English aristocrat and an American woman, from the "servant-companion" class. At the beginning of the text, Cedric lives in relative poverty in New York City, until Mr. Havisham, a lawyer from England, arrives to tell him that he is the next in line to become an earl. The Earl, Cedric's grandfather, who is described in the first episode as "a nobleman, with a very bad temper and a very violent dislike to America and Americans," sends for him because he wants to train him to run the estate (4). The episodes tell the story of how Cedric, who has been carefully trained by his close relationship with his mother, upsets the Earl's preconceived and negative definitions of America, by using his new economic powers to make benevolent changes in the lives of the workers he knows, first in New York and then on the estate. The text filters Cedric's benevolent expressions of citizenship, which I will discuss below, through his appearance and his conversational capabilities. The packaging of Cedric's boyhood transforms the Earl from a cantankerous American-hater to a more responsible estate owner whose new principles are informed by Cedric's conversationally conveyed lessons in benevolent citizenship. This citizenship manifests itself through the functions of generosity, beauty, relationship, and ownership as they come together in the figure of Cedric Errol. I suggest that the comments this text makes about the possibilities of conversational citizenship link to the conversational aspects of the magazine as a "scene of reading" that allows for explorations of the citizenships of young readers.[3] The letters sent in by the reading children shed light on the mostly positive reception of Fauntleroy's boy-citizenship in the 1880s and provide insight into subsequent and ongoing rejections of Fauntleroy's androgynous conversational citizenship.

Significantly, the serialization of *Little Lord Fauntleroy* began in 1885, the same year that Mark Twain's *The Adventures of Huckleberry Finn* was published, in another Century Company publication, the *Century Magazine*.[4] Despite the fact that both boys experience sudden access to wealth and power, the two depictions contemplate diverging strains of Americanness and American masculinity during the Gilded Age.[5] One boy, Cedric Errol, heads east, while Huckleberry Finn, who has become the quintessential textual personification of the American boy, heads west. Huck has maintained his status as an importantly original American boy because of the way he grapples with the manhood and citizenship of the enslaved Jim, and by association, then, with the citizenships of others who have been denied access to its privileges. Burnett's construction of Fauntleroy's boyhood suggests that she resists the boyhood promoted in Huck's retreat from "sivilization" in favor of other expressions of citizenship. Burnett's Fauntleroy, remembered neither for his boyishness nor for his Americanness, embodies aspects of American citizenship available to children and especially to women in the 1880s. Burnett explores in the figure of Fauntleroy the possibilities of conversational citizenship, which are embodied in the ambiguously gendered "accessories" of beauty and generosity. The practical capacities of the accessories associated with conversational citizenships are employed by Burnett and by other women writing for children's magazines in the 1880s.

Burnett, who was born in England and moved to the United States as a child, first wrote to improve her quality of life in rural Tennessee, and then to support herself and her children. She separated from her husband soon after publishing her most successful adult book, *Through One Administration*, and after her success, moved between the United States and England.[6] In *Little Lord Fauntleroy*, Burnett takes the culturally constructed womanly ideal of her childhood, the benevolent true woman, and transforms the woman into a boy. Claudia Nelson argues in *Boys Will Be Girls* that when women writers use the "angel in the house," a version of the true woman, in discussions of manliness and womanliness in stories for children, they do so as a "critique of capitalist individualism" (4). I would suggest, however, that Burnett's "true boyhood" both participates in the angel's monopoly and critiques it by using the monopoly to escape from the confines of the "house." As Carroll Smith-Rosenberg points out in *Disorderly Conduct*, the "new" women of the turn of the century, who "challenged existing gender relations and the distribution of power," were looked on with suspicion, and were classified by the medical profession of the time as being less than women, androgynous, and "unnatural" (245). Burnett's freedom to pursue a "new woman" existence comes in part through her creation of a powerful "true boyhood" in the form of *Little Lord Fauntleroy*. In her biography of Burnett, Ann Thwaite writes that "Frances said, more than once, 'The one perfect thing in my life was the childhood of my boys'" (80). Burnett employs "this perfection" to create a text that becomes one of the best-selling books of 1886, and in her creation, gifts herself with the kind of material comforts that provide her with her reasons to write. Cedric's "perfect childhood" and the safeguard that material wealth provides for it indicate that one response to dramatically shifting economic climates in the United States is for women to embrace the possibilities for quick and enormous wealth by proliferating "true boyhoods." Burnett's creation of best-selling characters who live lives of gentle generosity gives her the means to obtain a culturally sanctioned independence from her husband. She benefits from the textual benevolence of her characters in ways that allow her to experience transatlantic citizenship on her own terms.

St. Nicholas uses the "gift" significance of its title, with its year-round reminder of holiday generosity, to encourage unselfish kindness in its young readers, but of almost more significance than the generous saint is the physical beauty, the "wrapped" package of the magazine. Earlier nineteenth-century children's magazines had saved production costs by crowding words onto pages and by leaving very little margin. *St. Nicholas* uses a fairly large font and leaves plenty of margin space, making its pages attractive and easy for younger readers to access. Where earlier magazines contained few illustrations to relieve the text, illustrations accompany almost all of *St. Nicholas*'s serialized novels, and portraits and cartoonlike picture stories are scattered throughout the magazine. Readers' drawings and pictograms are published in almost every issue.

In *St. Nicholas*, texts with more abundant illustrations attract readers, and these illustrated texts have a greater chance of influencing readers and a better possibility for sales success outside the magazine. Readers writing to the magazine mention the illustrated texts most often, and some letters suggest that readers pay close attention to the outside appearance of the magazine as well. A reader from Washington, D.C., who is the first to have a letter published about *Little Lord Fauntleroy*, comments on the importance of the details of the "package" to her reading experience:[7]

> I take you every month and always enjoy reading your interesting stories. Your November number came the other day, and I was surprised to see such a different cover on you, but I like it much better than the old one. Then too, it will be very nice to look for the sign of the Zodiac every month. I have read your first chapter of "Little Lord Fauntleroy," and I think it is very interesting indeed. It does not take me long to read you, and then when I finish I wish it was time for your next number to come. I must not write any more, for fear of making my letter too long for your valuable space. Your affectionate reader, Mary R. C. (235).

As Mary points out in her letter, the cover changes add to the suspense of waiting for the magazine, and readers enjoy the surprise of seeing a slightly varied cover each month. The element of suspense, waiting for "the next number," indicates one way the magazine extends the "gift" aspects of its title to include both outside and inside content. Because the 1880s are characterized by the repackaging of resources and the celebration of technical innovation, the children of this world are culturally prepared to look for what Cedric's friend, Dick the bootblack, calls the chance to "start out fair," that is, the chance to start with the right accessories in order to enhance the possibilities for discovery, advancement, and success.[8] In Dick's case, these accessories translate into good brushes, boot-blacking territory, and a sign (89). In the 1880s, the emphasis on the glory of surprise makes sense in a country that uncovered immense wealth by mining and then refining the plain materials of the earth that had previously been "wrapped" as wilderness or farmland. *St. Nicholas*, then, schools its budding industrialists and entrepreneurs in the arts of suspense and discovery, both arts that are useful in advertising and packaging an industrialized product for public consumption.

The serialized format of *Little Lord Fauntleroy* also emphasizes the beauty of the package. The images of Cedric printed in the serialization suggest that Cedric's beauty has a power that extends beyond its intrinsic aesthetic value. As frequent letters to *St. Nicholas* indicate, the texts that generate the most comment are the ones that are the most heavily illustrated.[9] Cedric's illustrated "package," like the beautiful package of *St. Nicholas*, provides him with powers to which an unattractive body might not have access. The 1885–1886 issue of *St. Nicholas* has the first episode of *Little Lord Fauntleroy* as its lead story, and it is accompanied by a full-page illustration. This Reginald Birch illustration is one of the images that has helped to proliferate the notion that Little Lord Fauntleroy is a feminized and excessively good boy.[10] It is the accessories that make the illustrated Cedric look very much like a delicate girl. In the illustrations, Cedric wears knee breeches, sashes, large collars, and small slippers, and his hair reaches down to his shoulders; his appearance blurs gender boundaries, inviting readings that contemplate the homoerotic implications of the tale. Arguing that the illustrations are "the exemplary locus of the text's homoerotic energy," Anna Wilson writes:

> In Birch's original work, a small, velvet-covered Fauntleroy with flowing locks is repeatedly depicted astride or beside some gigantically virile animal. The effeminate boy caresses his phallic friend, equivocally both laying claim to and appearing separate from the masculinity beside him. In picturing Cedric, Birch renders evident the dichotomy that structures Fauntleroy's representation, the absent masculine possibility that the boy's effeminacy calls forth (244).

The large animals or men with whom Cedric is depicted convey, I would argue, not so much the "effeminacy" that Wilson reads, but the extension of Cedric's androgynously "packaged" influence. In an illustration that explores Cedric's innovative combination of feminized accessories and his more masculinized, conquestlike approaches to the world around him, Birch depicts Cedric lying prone on a tiger skin, an image I read as masculine, while he charms a cat, gendered in the text's caption as "she," by stroking her fur (see figure 5.1). The situation of Cedric's body (lying on the masculine rug, stroking the feminine cat) positions him to participate simultaneously in the homo- and heteroerotic elements of the scene; this image situates Cedric's embodied boyhood as powerfully androgynous. The accessories of this androgyny and the both/and sexuality suggest that playing

Figure 5.1. "Cedric and the Cat." Illus. Reginald Birch. *Little Lord Fauntleroy*. *St. Nicholas*. 13 (Feb. 1886): 256.

with the performance boundaries of boyhood opens possibilities for Cedric that extend the powers of gender to make practical changes in the citizenships of those they encounter. While they foreground Burnett's descriptions of Cedric's beauty and the details of his wardrobe, Birch's plentiful illustrations package the text into memorable images of Cedric's graceful, fearless, and mesmerizing androgynous citizenship.

Drawing on the homo- and heteroerotic power of Fauntleroy's body, the text of *Little Lord Fauntleroy* always emphasizes Cedric's outward beauty before it demonstrates the other "transformative" aspects of his citizenship. The first episode spends most of its time giving the history of Cedric's father, but one of the first descriptions of Cedric points to his physical beauty: "When he was old enough to walk out with his nurse, dragging a small wagon and wearing a short white kilt skirt, and a big white hat set back on his curly yellow hair, he was so handsome and strong and rosy that he attracted every one's attention" (5). Significantly, the text balances the descriptions of Cedric's beauty with allusions either to his strength or to his manliness. Angus McLaren suggests in *The Trials of Masculinity* that the word *manly* "was in the Victorian age increasingly employed as the antonym of the feminine or effeminate" (33). According to McLaren, reading material helped to reinforce shifts in the understanding and definition of manliness: "The nineteenth-century reading public was led from the stress on Christian manliness that marked the fictional works of Charles Kingsley and Thomas Hughes to Henty and H. Rider Haggard's depiction of robust heroes driven by brutal energy and dominating wills" (33). In describing Cedric as strong and beautiful, the text positions him somewhere outside the two kinds of manliness that McLaren describes.

While the text praises Fauntleroy's manliness, it is careful to show his boyishness as though to avoid any suggestion that his associations with adults have worn away his innocence. In one scene that signals an anxiety about precocious masculinity, Mr. Havisham, the Earl's attorney, comments to Mrs. Errol that Cedric seems mature because of his serious interest in adult conversations and his adult, possibly "foppish" mannerisms. She is quick to point out that Cedric is "a very boyish little boy, sometimes," an observation that is followed in the text with a description of him winning a footrace with the neighborhood boys (86). Cedric's body language and position, especially when he converses with adults, imitate men's mannerisms: "He sat well back in the depths of his big seat, his curly head against the cushioned back, his legs crossed, and his hands thrust deep into his pockets, in a quite Mr. Hobbs-like way" (87). Cedric continues to use these adult mannerisms on the ship: "when he sat down and nursed his knee with his chubby hands, and conversed with much gravity, he was a source of great entertainment to his hearers" (252). Cedric's adult body language during his conversations is set against his boyish enjoyment of physical activities such as racing and riding, and the balance provides him with a citizenship power that allows him to change the lives of others.

Interestingly, while the text insists that Cedric is a boyish boy, in the first stage productions of *Little Lord Fauntleroy*, girls always played the role of Cedric. Reviews of the first stage version suggest the importance of Cedric's appearance to the acceptance of his character. Elsie Leslie, who, according to Thwaite, had also starred in Twain's *The Prince and the Pauper*, is said to have played the role with enough "strength" to please the *Boston Transcript*: "her full-faced rosy beauty helps to make her Fauntleroy the more real—a distinct advantage when it is considered the slightest touch of pallor and fragility would turn this impossible little lord into a pure idealization" (qtd. in Thwaite 116–17). Evidently, the right kind of "rosy beauty"—the beauty that characterizes "true boyhood"—cannot be located in the body of a boy.

While descriptions combine Cedric's beauty with his strength or his rosiness, there seems to be an unreal quality to his beauty that reminds readers of the constructed nature of this get-rich-quick text. One older reader, who calls herself "Yum-Yum," ponders the impossibility of Cedric's beauty:[11]

> I have taken you ever since I was a very "small girl," and now, I am sorry to say, I am a very large one of eighteen. I am told that I ought to abandon dear old ST. NICK: for some "grown-up magazine," and I feel that it is indeed sad to grow old if giving up ST. NICHOLAS is one of the penalties, which I shall take care that it shall not be. I have just fallen in love with "Little Lord Fauntleroy," and I wish the "small boy" of the present day would copy after him, but I fear that would be too "pretty a state of things" (635).

This eighteen-year-old does not explain why she feels that copies of Lord Fauntleroy would create "too pretty a state," but perhaps, even as she admits to having fallen in love with Fauntleroy, "Yum-Yum" recognizes that Fauntleroy does not look like or act like the "small boys" she knows, and that if there were other beautiful Fauntleroy copies, his power to make changes, if only within the space of an episode, would be dramatically decreased.

The beauty that garners Cedric attention carries enough power to help him to befriend his decidedly unfriendly grandfather. Cedric's physical appearance comes up for discussion almost immediately when Mr. Havisham makes a report to the Earl after locating Cedric in New York:

> "Healthy and well grown?" asked my lord.
>
> "Apparently very healthy, and quite well-grown" replied the lawyer.
>
> "Straight-limbed and well enough to look at?" demanded the Earl.
>
> A very slight smile touched Mr. Havisham's lips. There rose up before his mind's eye the picture he had left at Court Lodge,—the beautiful, graceful child's body lying upon the tiger-skin in careless comfort—the bright, tumbled hair spread on the rug—the bright, rosy boy's face.
>
> "Rather a handsome boy, I think, my lord, as boys go," he said (255).

Here, Mr. Havisham's understated description of Cedric's beauty prepares the way for the Earl to respond to Cedric in a positive manner.[12] The Earl asks about Cedric's appearance in part because he believes that this appearance will predict whether Cedric will display his father's good traits or his uncles' bad ones. Early on, the text conveys its interest in the idea of a genetically transferred aristocracy: "But it so happened that Nature had given the younger son gifts which she had not bestowed on his elder brothers. He had a beautiful face and a fine, strong, graceful figure; he had a bright smile and a sweet, gay voice; he was brave and generous" (4). The uncles, on the other hand, who are older than Cedric's father, use their wealth to pursue leisure activities that display their bad breeding and endanger their health: one dies in a riding accident and the other of a fever. This emphasis on "breeding" and heredity pervades the text and indicates the influence of Charles Darwin's ideas about natural selection and Herbert Spencer's ideas about social evolution on the dominant cultural milieu.[13] By the late 1880s and 1890s, the ideas of social Darwinism are being contemplated in children's literature in ways that tie national origin to a kind of innate royalty or purity. Twain explores ideas of natural selection and environment in *A Connecticut Yankee in King Arthur's Court* (1889), *The Prince and the Pauper* (1881), and *Pudd'-nhead Wilson* (1894). Burnett uses Fauntleroy's beauty and health as evidence of his superior breeding.

The presence of other articles about social evolution in the *Century Magazine*, the adult counterpart of *St. Nicholas*, suggests that breeding was a topic of interest to readers during the time of *Fauntleroy*'s serialization.[14] An 1885 article by John Burroughs on the topic of "British Fertility" warns readers about the dangers of the dropping birthrate in the United States and the ways that the United States might learn lessons from British fertility to counteract the infertility supposedly brought by industrialization:

> The New Englander who sees with evil forebodings the rapid falling off of the birth-rate in his own land, the family rills shrinking in these later generations, like his native streams in summer, and who consequently fears for the perpetuity of the race, may see something to comfort him in the British islands. Behold the fecundity of the parent stock! (42)

Burroughs's commentary points out one possible reason for the Earl's wariness of Cedric's "Americanness." Cedric's body, imported from the allegedly "shrinking" fertility of the United States, is supposed to save the Earl's family line, which does not seem to be quite as "fertile" as Burroughs argues the British parent stock is. The Earl's older sons, who die because of their self-interested, nonbenevolent pursuits of leisure activities, have not been successfully fertile. The Earl counts on Cedric's good "breeding" to forward his own interests in the estate, but he is anxious about the risk of Cedric's "American" stock.

When the Earl and Cedric finally meet, Cedric's appearance softens the Earl's behavior toward Cedric, whom he still views as a mistake of breeding since he is partly the product of a poor American woman. The text describes the Earl's feelings: "he still hated the gentle little widow and would not speak of her except with bitter and cruel words. He insisted that she was only a common American girl, who had entrapped his son into marrying her because she knew he was an earl's son" (84). He orders Cedric to be sent into the room to meet him alone, and the text emphasizes the mesmerizing attractiveness of Cedric's physical body:

> What the Earl saw was a graceful, childish figure in a black velvet suit, with a lace collar, and with lovelocks waving about the handsome, manly little face, whose eyes met his with a look of innocent good-fellowship. If the castle was like the palace in a fairy story, it must be owned that little Lord Fauntleroy was himself rather like a small copy of the fairy prince, though he was not at all

> aware of the fact, and perhaps was rather a sturdy young model of a fairy. But there was a sudden glow of triumph and exultation in the fiery old Earl's heart as he saw what a strong, beautiful boy this grandson was (334).

Cedric's body shifts the Earl's previous negative attitude toward him, and the beauty of his body makes it easier for the Earl to listen to Cedric and to make his stay in the castle pleasant. Cedric's beauty paves the way for him not only to make positive changes for himself, but also to improve the quality of life of the tenants and the Earl.

In many ways, the beauty that opens doors for Cedric and paves the way for him to be a powerful citizen parallels the kinds of beauty–power connections that the 1885 angel-in-the-house culture promoted for women as part of the social evolutionary process. Social evolutionists suggested that women with too extensive or lively an intellectual life would rob their bodies of the energies necessary to preserve the race. Instead of attempting to become intellectual citizens, women, these theorists argued, would better serve their nations by cultivating beauty and healthiness.[15] The beauty of women, which is part of the social evolutionary package, and their power to transmit this beauty to the physical possessions around them, supposedly made the home a safe haven and healthy space for men who had to encounter the world outside the home in their daily quest for material goods. Elaine Showalter points out that the ideal woman at this time is a woman who is "a Perfect Lady, an Angel in the House, contentedly submissive to men, but strong in her inner purity and religiosity, queen in her own realm of the Home" (14).[16] The beauty of the women and their influence on the space of the home gives them, in accounts promoting this kind of "true womanhood," a political power, since the attractiveness of the home provides space for women to converse with their husbands and to use their persuasive powers.[17]

Burnett's text grapples with the importance of beauty in women in its treatment of Mrs. Errol. When she is forced into an entirely new economic and social environment by her son's change in citizenship, Cedric's mother's beauty provides her with a kind of social evolutionary advancement.[18] When the Earl sees her, he is reassured of her value to him and to the health of the boy. Her physical connection to the boy helps the Earl to accept her once he decides to speak to her, and she uses her beauty's influence to soothe the Earl during their first encounter: "'I wish you would sit down,' she said in a soft, pretty, sympathetic way. 'You have been so much troubled that you are very tired, and you need all your strength'" (826). The repeated descriptions of the power of physical beauty suggest that this text explores beauty's influence in political situations, and in doing so, meditates not only on the power of children's beauty, but also on how women's beauty might add to or detract from their political power. Cedric's beauty makes his body a mesmerizing spectacle and his hold over the Earl mirrors the kind of hold that women are taught to believe beauty would bring to a marriage relationship. As an author confronted with the assessment of the success and failure of beauty in her own life, Burnett experiments, in what might be read as her answer to the boy book, with the possibilities and boundaries of constructing a kind of true boyhood based on what she knew about true womanhood. [19] Boys *can*, this text replies to Huck's flight, with the right amount of gender-bending feminization, join in the project of citizenship and use beauty and conversation to effect social change.

As the text moves from Cedric's first influential appearance-based impressions to the actual changes he makes in his grandfather's life, there continue to be parallels between the kinds of transformative power Cedric has and the kinds of power opportunities available to women at this same time period.[20] In America, and in Europe, after *Little Lord Fauntleroy* was produced for the stage in 1888, women began to dress their sons in Fauntleroy clothes, partly because of the changes his very appearance seems able to bring about.[21] Thwaite writes:

> All over America, reluctant small boys were forced by their mothers into black velvet suits with lace collars and other outfits based on Cedric's clothes. In Davenport, Iowa, an eight-year-old burned down his father's barn in protest at being dressed as Lord Fauntleroy. In Worcester, Massachusetts, a boy traded in his suit for some old patched clothes belonging to a gypsy. In New York it was reported that Stephen Crane gave money to two small boys and sent them to have their curls cut off; one mother went into hysterics, the other fainted (117).

The spectacle of Fauntleroy's appearance and the instant love and acceptance his body gives him become translated into the successful production of material goods that mothers give their sons, in hopes that there will be some transfer of Fauntleroy's power and also of the rewards of love. That the boys and some of the adults resist this Fauntleroy "look" suggests that outside of the text, Fauntleroy's wardrobe did not have the same transformative power to bring about change. Likewise, the anecdotes about the burned barns and the fainting mothers demonstrate that when women attempted to force their sons' bodies into the same sorts of fashion-based contortions that they themselves had been urged to follow, some of these bodies chose not to conform. Neither could the dressed boys duplicate the charming and powerful beauty of the partially text-based, partially illustrated character.[22]

Illustrations in *St. Nicholas* issues from the later 1880s suggest that the Huck look and the Fauntleroy look coexisted. The 1888 edition of *St. Nicholas*, for example, serializes Thomas Nelson Page's *Two Little Confederates*, which, like *Huckleberry Finn*, is illustrated by E. W. Kemble, who, as Earl F.

Briden points out, described himself as "a delineator of the South, the Negro being my specialty" (383). In "How a Little Boy Camped Out," also published in 1888, a little boy begs his mother to let him camp out. She has the hired man set up a tent in the backyard. In the illustration, the little boy, who has to come in because, he realizes, "[h]e was a very small boy, and somehow camping out was n't [sic] delightful in *every* way," is depicted in a black suit with a huge white lace collar (950). This text combines the dream of escape with the dress of Fauntleroy, and with the boy's retreat from the "territory" back to the house, conveys the power of the dress to tie a boy to house and mother and suggests that the adventure fantasy usually ends in such a return.

While Cedric's physical appearance may help those he meets to respond to him positively, it is his generosity with his conversation, his vocal benevolence, which makes him beloved, both in New York and in his grandfather's village. Cedric's conversational descriptions of his benevolent intentions demonstrate that he will be generous as an earl; this becomes especially evident when he has a choice about what to do with the money his grandfather tells Mr. Havisham to give him. When Mr. Havisham asks Cedric what he would do if he had a lot of money, he is startled by Cedric's comments:

> "there are so many things a person can do with money. You see, there's the apple-woman. If I were very rich I should buy her a little tent to put her stall in, and a little stove, and then I should give her a dollar for every morning it rained, so that she could afford to stay at home. And then-oh! I'd give her a shawl. And, you see, her bones wouldn't feel so badly. Her bones are not like our bones; they hurt her when she moves. It's very painful when your bones hurt you. If I were rich enough to do all those things for her I guess her bones would be all right" (88).

In some ways, the kind of benevolence that Cedric enacts is similar to that promoted by the millionaires of the Gilded Age. The connections to the wealth and power of the industrialists in the Gilded Age can be seen in the ways that Burnett's text complicates the true woman by making the angelic true woman an androgynously packaged boy and placing him in a castle. The castle that replaces the house in Burnett's version of "true boyhood" suggests that she is constructing a response to the castle building that occurred in America as millionaires like the Vanderbilts built mansions to showcase their power and wealth. Cedric's acts of true boyhood are generous and thoughtful, but they also reward only the kind of hard work that will enhance Cedric's own standing as a citizen. Cedric's first thoughts are always of what he can do for others in order to increase their productivity in the workplace.

When Cedric plans exactly which material possessions will help those less fortunate, the materials he gives usually reflect some evaluation of the "deserving" nature of the recipient. His attitudes about the deserving poor reflect cultural views of benevolence. In an 1884 *Century* essay titled "Three Dangers" that highlights the cultural importance of benevolence at this time, Washington Gladden explores the dangers of the wrong kind of benevolence: "Self-love and benevolence are the central forces of human life; both are essential to progress and happiness, but they are always in conflict; individual and social welfare is secured only when they are brought into harmony" (620). The "three dangers" of the title are "misdirected kindness," "sentimental philanthropy" or "indiscriminate almsgiving," and "pure egoism" (621). About the last, Gladden writes, "Pure egoism is the antithesis of society. Its impulse is to get everything and give nothing in exchange for it; while as Herbert Spencer says, 'the universal basis of cooperation (and therefore of social life) is the proportioning of benefits received to services rendered'" (621). In Burnett's text, Mrs. Errol schools Cedric in the kind of "proportioning of benefits" that Gladden calls for in his essay by teaching him to always evaluate the needs and the deserving nature of his beneficiaries. When Mary's sister Bridget needs help, it is easy for Cedric to help because Mary has provided so many "services" for him and his mother: "[s]he was willing to work early and late to help his mama make his small suits and keep them in order" (5). Cedric's mother also informs Mr. Havisham (and the readers of *St. Nicholas*) that "[t]hey are quite deserving" since "Michael is a hard-working man" (90). The deserving beneficiaries, this text suggests, will pay back in kindness, in service, and in protection of citizenship rights what they are given in material goods.

The generosity that *Little Lord Fauntleroy* celebrates is emphasized elsewhere in *St. Nicholas*. In the December 1885 issue, one satiric "jingle" titled "The Benevolent Boy" recounts the story of a boy who dreams of what he would do for others if he were to come into great wealth:

> A very benevolent boy, Oho!
> A very benevolent boy!
> He said, "Oh I wish I had silver and gold
> I'd fill a big house till no more it could hold
> With every nice candy and toy!"
> This exceedingly generous boy!
> "And my Christmas dollar? O pshaw! don't you see?
> I'll have to keep that to buy candy for me!"
> This very benevolent boy! (124)

Here, the boy is given a dollar, and he decides since it is only a dollar, he will spend it on himself. This jingle is also illustrated by Reginald Birch, and appears in the issue that publishes Fauntleroy's gift-planning episode, linking the two treatments of benevolence. The readers, who are probably more likely to have a dollar to spend than an inherited fortune, have the chance to think through the juxtaposition of the two kinds of benevolence, and to decide the nature of their own benevolence. Even though this piece critiques the kind of benevolence that applauds generosity but refuses to participate in it, the magazine itself allows children to adopt a benevolent attitude toward the needy. The attitude, safely contained between the red and gold covers of the beautifully designed magazine, costs nothing, and without Cedric's good fortune, readers can feel complacent knowing that they, at the very least, have good feelings toward the hardworking poor.

Cedric is benevolent before he learns he is a wealthy aristocrat, but he is not able to do very much with his benevolent tendencies. Once Cedric becomes Lord Fauntleroy, he has the economic power of the "robber barons" of New York industry, but pious, pure, and submissive, he seems to have the soul of the true woman of the 1850s. Andrew Carnegie writes about the reasons individuals need to retain rights over property and wealth in "Wealth," and admits that some surplus riches should be used for the good of the public, but that the distribution should be carefully controlled: "the surplus wealth of the few will become, in the best sense, the property of the many, because administered for the common good; and this wealth, passing through the hands of the few, can be made a much more potent force for the elevation of our race than if distributed in small sums to the people themselves" (qtd. in *The Industrial Revolution: Opposing Viewpoints* 89). Cedric's "manliness," his ability to handle the newfound wealth, is filtered through the generosity that has been a large part of his connection to his New York neighborhood.

Cedric's selfless response to his wealth is one of the ways that he demonstrates his ability to excel in a new citizenship position. In a discussion of what she calls "Benevolent Citizenship," Susan M. Ryan points out that Harriet Beecher Stowe, herself a proponent of true womanhood, advocated a benevolent citizenship as she thought through the changes abolition would bring to the country in the years before the war. Ryan explains:

> In the decades before the Civil War, Americans used the terms *benevolence* and *benevolent* with astonishing frequency, not only where one would expect, as in reports by charitable organizations and in sermons or religious tracts, but also in political pamphlets, newspaper articles, poetry, and fiction. Moreover, in much antebellum discourse, the nation was said to be legitimized through the benevolence of its politics (752).

The presence of this language of benevolence in *St. Nicholas* and in *Little Lord Fauntleroy* indicates that the needs for "benevolent citizenship" and the reasons to practice benevolence extended beyond the immediate aftermath of the Civil War and had entered the era of rapid industrialization and increased moves to urban areas. *Little Lord Fauntleroy* sends the message that wealth can and should be used to contribute to the welfare of others who are less fortunate but also deserving.[23] *Little Lord Fauntleroy* explores the possibilities of enacting benevolence by talking about it and making something so by saying it is so.

As the story of the Earl's redemption unfolds, the text offers many examples of Fauntleroy's oral and written benevolent reconstruction of reality. One example comes in a letter that he writes to the grocer, Mr. Hobbs, who has taught him about politics and who has claimed that earls are tyrants:

> My dear mr hobbs i want to tell you about my granfarther he is the best earl you ever new it is a mistake about earls being tirents he is not a tirent at all i wish you new him you would be good friends i am sure you would he has the gout in his foot and is a grate sufrer but he is so pashent I love him more every day because no one could help loving an earl like that who is kind to every one in this world (567).

Fauntleroy's verbal (re)inventions of his grandfather suggest possible responses to other kinds of inventions the industrialists of the 1880s brought to needy, eager-to-believe, but simultaneously doubtful consumers. In an age of promise and invention, the only possibilities for life-changing consumption that benefited the consumer lay in the hands of the abundantly wealthy patent-owners and industry kings.[24] Those with monopolistic control of the new technologies and inventions also had control over the extent to which these products and the wealth generated by them would benefit the much larger numbers of poverty-stricken citizens. Burnett's text asks whether wealth has any power when it is not backed by generosity and good intentions, and suggests that everyday citizens might intervene in the dispersal of the powers of the wealthy by making use of conversations that either enhance or disrupt their reputations. Especially in scenes showing Fauntleroy temporarily losing his claim to the earldom, this text meditates on the tenuousness of the power of title and the fragility of conversational invention and authentic generosity at the same time that it makes use of impossible fantasy to garner titles and the power of benevolence for its author.

Burnett's contemporaries confront the ambivalence of invention, technology, and industry in somewhat more direct ways. In *Lighting Out for the Territory*, Shelley Fisher Fishkin points to *The Gilded Age*, *A Connecticut Yankee in King Arthur's Court*, and *The Adventures of Huckleberry Finn* as texts that exemplify how Twain, Burnett's contemporary, responded to the changes brought by invention and industrialization: "Mark Twain knew firsthand that technology could kill. He knew it could backfire. He knew its realities often failed to keep pace with its promise" (179). One of the backfiring technologies that Burnett's text explores is the easy transfer of information as it combines with the speed of travel. Her treatment of these technologies suggests that a mastery of language, whether oral or written, is essential to the kinds of citizenship her text promotes.

Intriguingly, Burnett's text makes the point that the technology of the periodical is powerful in the episodes when a contender, who claims to be the son of one of Cedric's uncles, threatens Cedric's aristocratic title. The contender, whose mother manufactures the title based on partial information, is proved an imposter, not by the Earl and the lawyer, but by Dick and Mr. Hobbs, who back in New York, have been reading all the papers about the aristocracy that they can find: "They read the *Penny Story Gazette*, and many other interesting things, and gained a knowledge of the habits of the nobility and gentry" (735). When the two New York friends hear about the claimant, they promise to look into the problem. The solution comes in the form of a paper that Mr. Hobbs hands to Dick: "That particular morning . . . he had an illustrated paper, with pictures in it of conspicuous people and things" (827). Dick looks at the pictures and realizes that they hold life-changing information: "He pointed to the picture, under which was written: 'Mother of Claimant (Lady Fauntleroy)' It was the picture of a handsome woman, with large eyes and heavy braids of black hair wound around her head. 'Her!' said Dick. 'My, I know her better 'n I know you!'" (827). The newspaper's illustration has allowed Dick to recognize that the mother of the contender is actually the wife of Dick's brother. As a result of this discovery, Dick and Mr. Hobbs immediately put their speaking, reading, and writing skills to use to notify a lawyer of the fraud.

When Dick and Mr. Hobbs travel to England to see that Cedric's title is restored, the mother's response conveys that transportation has in this case backfired against her attempts to rise from poverty: "She had thought of these newcomers as being thousands of miles away. . . . She had never expected to see them again" (884). Dick's experience with the power of the New York working-class newspaper to change international fortunes points to this text's interest in demonstrating the power of language. This episode shows that rapidly circulated printed language conversationally can protect the property and titles of citizens. The possibilities and dangers inherent in technology's new approaches to old problems manifest themselves in *Little Lord Fauntleroy* through overt explorations of industrial innovation—the dissemination of image and text through printing technology—and also through examinations of how quickly money can change positions, living conditions, and relationships.

Burnett's text uses Fauntleroy's temporary loss of title to show how important it is to sweeten the path to success with strong familial relationships built on benevolent deeds. This text, which meditates on how conversational citizenship is connected to being "at home" with the beneficiaries, gestures, in its treatment of American politics, toward how political parties during the 1880s promoted themselves by using the language of strong familial relationships. Robert W. Cherny explains, "Americans then understood that 'politics' meant *party politics*, and that all meaningful political participation came through parties" (5). In one commentary on Cedric's citizenship, Mary, Cedric's nurse, explains that it is his investment in conversation that conveys his genuine interest in his own citizenship and that of others:

> "nobody cud help laughin' at the quare little ways of him—and his ould-fashioned sayin's! Did n't he come into my kitchen the noight the new prisident was nominated and shtand afore the fire, lookin' loike a pictur, 'wid his hands in his shmall pockets, an' his innocent bit of a face as sayrious as a jedge? An' sez he to me: 'Mary,' sez he, 'I'm very much int'rusted in the 'lection,' sez he. 'I'm a 'publican, an' so is Dearest. Are you a 'publican, Mary?' 'Sorra a bit,' sez I; 'I'm the bist o' dimmycrats!' An he looks up at me wid a look that ud go to your heart, sez he: 'Mary,' sez he, 'the country will go to ruin.' An' nivver a day since thin has he let go by widout argyin' wid me to change me politics" (5).

When he says "I'm a 'publican, an' so is Dearest," Cedric indicates his affection and loyalty for Mary by arguing with her to join the "family" of his political party of choice—his family's "'publican" party. Cedric's concern for the state of Mary's citizenship and its influence on the country conveys his belief in the fact that she has a "say" in the ruin of the country (even though without suffrage she does not). His willingness to use conversational persuasion to offer her the gift of what he believes is a better citizenship showcases how the multidirectional nature of conversation offers those previously without any ability to articulate their citizenship a means to do so. Cedric tries to get Mary to change her politics, but she remains true to her party, even though she is loyal enough to him to accompany his mother to England.

The importance of family to conversational citizenship can also be seen when Cedric moves across the Atlantic. When Mrs. Errol comes to understand Fauntleroy's newfound power in England, she plans to use conversation to wield her familial influence in order to increase the magnitude of his (and his grandfather's) benevolence:

> [A] bold thought came into her wise little-mother heart. Gradually she had begun to see, as had others, that it had been her boy's good fortune to please the Earl very much, and that he would scarcely be likely to be denied anything for which he expressed a desire.

> "The Earl would give him anything," she said to Mr. Mordaunt [the rector]. "He would indulge his every whim. Why should not that indulgence be used for the good of others? It is for me to see that this shall come to pass" (646).

This passage illustrates the power of the bond between mother and son in this text, and it also points to how the conversational influence of mothers, and other women without explicit citizenship privileges, can be used to gain access to those powers held by the son.

Like Cedric, who offers conversationally inspired gifts to the tenants of his estate, the authors who contribute to *St. Nicholas* are also figured as gift givers. The young readers, in this formulation, become grateful beneficiaries. Since the magazine publishes some of the letters it receives, children respond to the gifts of stories by writing to thank the authors or to thank the magazine. Sometimes, the readers focus mainly on themselves and the ways they benefit from the reading material in comparison to the other material goods that are available to them. Etta K. from Kansas City, Missouri, informs *St. Nicholas* about the importance of receiving the magazine as a Christmas gift:

> I was wishing for you before Christmas because all the girls at school say you are so interesting. I never had a hope of getting you. But what do you think! On Christmas, to my great surprise, among my presents was a [*St. Nicholas*]. I jumped around with glee. I sat down, left all my other presents, and commenced reading you. I am eleven years old. I think the covering of you very pretty. The picture in front is "Apollo, the god of the sun." I am very fond of mythology. Mama is going to have my [*St. Nicholas*] bound when this year is out, and I am going to take you next year. Hoping this letter will be printed (634).

The outside beauty of the cover is important to Etta, and like Fauntleroy, she is able to make her desires real, especially her wish to be published, by putting them into writing. As Etta's letter demonstrates, children writing in to *St. Nicholas* personify "St. Nick" and thank him profusely for his gifts or beg him for more. The saint, a generous man who in theory does not recognize class, in fact makes his bounty most available to those with enough money to buy gifts.

In addition to exploring their feelings about being the recipients of gift subscriptions, readers will also look for ways they can give back to the magazine. The readers, often in imitation of the adult contributors, will send in stories, games, and puzzles that they believe will please the other readers of the magazine. In the January 1886 issue, Effie H. sends in a picture as a gift to the other readers of the magazine:

> My papa has a friend who is an artist, and he came to see us the other evening and told us that he had been "studying up old costumes," and then he made a

> funny drawing for us children. He said it showed how "children used to dress three hundred years ago, when good Queen Bess was on the throne of England." We were all delighted with the drawing, and he gave it to us. The other day we asked him if we mightn't send it to St. Nicholas, for other children to see, and he said we might. So here it is. Isn't it funny? Mamma said the children's dresses were almost as stiff as the furniture. I think so too (235).

Both readers recognize by their awareness of the space devoted to their letters and by the extension of the picture for "other children to see" that the contributor-reader connection is not a linear one between the magazine and the child reader. The contributing writer, using the generous figure of "St. Nicholas," has the opportunity to connect to national and international networks of readers. Contributing authors can, like the child readers, spread their influence and messages across these complex networks.

As seen in these sample letters, the epistolary model of communication that reflects the impact of certain *St. Nicholas* texts also mirrors the citizenship possibilities available to women and to children in the United States. Without suffrage, women had to gain access to powerful men in order to have any real influence in state, national, or international lawmaking; even if these women were heard, action might never be taken to grant their wishes. The children who write to the magazine wish first for their letters to be published, but they also use the space of their letters to comment about the sections of the magazine they like best. Often, the letters will comment on their writer's home region, and these regional letters will point to the fact that there have not been any other letters published from those regions. In other words, children write in because the "Letter Box" section gives them a chance to be heard by the powerful editors and by fellow children in the United States and abroad. The interactive qualities of children's magazines in the 1880s promote conversational readerships and, as a by-product, conversational citizenships.

Burnett, who knew Washington, D.C., and who wrote a novel about the lives of the women whose husbands are involved in government, was familiar with the conversational model of citizenship, and in the figure of Fauntleroy, she shaped a gifted conversationalist, whose words almost always grant him his wishes.[25] As described above, the power of Fauntleroy's citizenship connects first to his physical body and secondly to the ideas about which he chooses to speak. Because of his beautiful body, Cedric can bring up subjects that, previously, his grandfather has not wanted to entertain.[26] When Cedric's grandfather first hears about Cedric's conversational abilities, he says, "American impudence . . . I've heard of it before. They call it precocity and freedom. Beastly, impudent bad manners; that's what it is!" (255). Cedric's ability to have his impudent ideas heard seems to be modeled on that of Burnett's son Vivian, who used conversation to his advantage to discuss political issues that would have been unpopular in adult mouths, particularly the mouths of women. Thwaite writes that "Vivian, aged five, pronounced himself a supporter of the movement in favor of female suffrage. 'I believe they ought to be allowed to vote if they like, because what should we do if there were no ladies?'" (83). Fauntleroy, like Vivian, broaches subjects that have not been mentioned to the Earl in years.

Fauntleroy's mother, who is very aware of her son's conversational powers, uses her influence over him to draw the Earl's attention to estate matters that she feels need to be addressed. In one instance, Cedric brings up the repair of some buildings on the estate because Mrs. Errol has brought his attention to the misery of the tenants:

> "There is a place," said Fauntleroy, looking up at him with wide-open, horror-stricken eyes—"Dearest has seen it; it is at the other end of the village. The houses are close together, and almost falling down; you can scarcely breathe; and the people are so poor, and everything is dreadful! Often they have fever, and the children die; and it makes them wicked to live like that, and be so poor and miserable! It is worse than Michael and Bridget! The rain comes in at the roof! Dearest went to see a woman who lived there. She would not let me come near her until she had changed all her things. The tears ran down her cheeks when she told me about it!" (570)

Fauntleroy extends his persuasion by conversationally making the Earl aware that he does not believe the Earl knows of the problem:

> "I told her you did n't [sic] know, and I would tell you," he said. He jumped down and came and leaned against the Earl's chair. "You can make it all right," he said, "just as you made it all right for Higgins. You always make it all right for everybody. I told her you would, and that Newick must have forgotten to tell you" (570).

Fauntleroy uses the power of his conversational citizenship not only to influence the Earl, but also in conversations he has with others about the Earl. The Earl is forced, in part through Fauntleroy's conversational, and thereby publicly vocalized, belief in his goodness, to live up to Fauntleroy's assumptions. Cedric's repeated conversations result in the Earl changing the way he governs his possessions. At the Earl's direction, Fauntleroy puts his conversationally conveyed ideas into writing, and, in this way, discovers the powers of his spoken and written citizenship. When Higgins arrives to thank Fauntleroy for helping him to stay on the farm, Fauntleroy insists that the good deed was not his doing: "'I only wrote the letter. It was my grandfather who did it. But you know how he is about always being good to everybody'" (505).

Like Fauntleroy, contributing readers put "conversational" pressure on *St. Nicholas* when they write to the magazine. In the April 1886 issue, one letter uses the fact that the writers have never submitted a letter before to encourage the editors to publish it: "We have never written to you before, and we hope to see this printed in the March number" (475). An April letter reminds the editors that the readers have particular favorites that are missed if they do not appear in a given issue. Remarking on the absence of the "Brownies"—tiny characters rendered by Palmer Cox and eagerly awaited by readers—one boy writes: "What has become of the Brownies for February? I miss them so much, especially the Dude, as he reminds me so much of a good many *(very) young men of this city*. You just ought to see them tripping down the avenue, with such big feet, and no legs worth speaking of" (475, emphasis original).[27] These letters remind the editors of the attitudes the children have toward the magazine, and they, like Lord Fauntleroy shaping the personality of the Earl, influence the content of the magazine. The editors answer Clyde's plea for more Brownies by writing: "The Brownies are crowded out this month, too, dear Clyde; but they will reappear in the midst of lively scenes, in our next number" (475). The answers the children receive from the editors, as well as the changes that they see in the magazine as a result, affirm for the readers that their interactive relationship with *St. Nicholas* is one in which they have a voice.

The power of Fauntleroy's androgynously beautiful body and his conversational use of it for improved citizenship are evident in the letters that readers write in about *Little Lord Fauntleroy*. Young girls, who exclaim over Fauntleroy and imagine how the actual embodiment of a boy like him would change their lives, write most of the letters praising the text. The number of letters from girls suggests that the plot of suddenly gaining access to empowering wealth through a familial relationship with those in another country is one that struck a chord with middle-class reading girls, who at this time are expected to go to school, but are also expected to marry and to possibly marry well. Many of the letters explore the power of "relationship" by establishing connections to Fauntleroy that provide them with ways to imagine the possibilities for change involved in such familial links.

The letters that contain comments about family relationships provide insight into how Fauntleroy's boyhood is understood by readers in the 1880s. Some readers writing in October 1886 wish that they could have Lord Fauntleroy over to play, and in their letters draw attention to *their* dress and physical bodies: "We are three little girls just the same age, for we are triplets. We look and dress just alike, and our big old brother calls us the 'three little maids from school.' We have a pony, a big dog, and a little cat, but we have no little boy to play with, and we wish that Little Lord Fauntleroy was a really, truly boy and could come and play with us" (954). Their wish that Fauntleroy was a "really, truly boy" suggests that the kind of "true boyhood" I am proposing Fauntleroy embodies is a kind of boyhood in which girls could imaginatively participate. It also indicates that they are aware, even as they wish for his presence, that his body, in its androgynous beauty, pushes against the embodiments of boyhood, especially that of their "big old brother," with which they are most familiar.

Many letters offer wishes that comment on the possibility of Fauntleroy's boyhood making changes in their lives. One reader, writing in May 1887, wishes not for a playmate but for a closer tie: "I am very glad to hear of Little Lord Fauntleroy. I wish he were my brother" (555). In the same May Letter Box, Harvey, from Montpellier, France, displaces desire for Cedric onto the body of his younger brother: "We do enjoy your book very much, and my brother wishes he was more like Lord Fauntleroy, he was so nice" (555). A family of readers attempts to establish a connection with the Earl's dog: "We have a big mastiff dog named Zippo. He weighs one hundred and forty pounds. He came from England when he was eighteen months old. He was raised by an earl. Perhaps it was Little Lord Fauntleroy's grandfather" (877). These letters establish conversational connections with the fictional Fauntleroy, and their publication in the magazine gives a power and a reality to the connections that would not exist if their wishes had not been "heard" by the editors.

The attempts made by these youthful readers to establish connections reflect other connection-making tendencies in the world of adult culture. In the decade after the new country marked its hundredth anniversary, the nation consciously reminisced about where it had been and what the past had looked like. Articles serialized in 1884–1885 in the *Century Magazine* examine colonial home life and social conditions.[28] Simultaneously, the 1880s saw an abundance of world's fairs, one in Philadelphia, one in Paris, and one in New Orleans. The world's fairs celebrate the machinery and industry of the present, the culture of the past, and the potential of the future, and, with huge displays, give visitors a chance to imaginatively walk through the past and to think through relationships with their revolutionary ancestors.[29] In this context, *Little Lord Fauntleroy* capitalizes on this United States' fascination with roots, especially the European roots that Fauntleroy's return to England reestablish. When readers write that they wish they were related to Fauntleroy, they reify the strength of the bond they feel to him through the public and published declaration of familial feelings. As we will see, Burnett also uses the strength of familial feelings to her own "new" woman advantage when she employs the best-selling character as a platform for her own political purposes, some of which involve making changes in international copyright laws.

Ultimately, the text of *Little Lord Fauntleroy* demonstrates the power of Fauntleroy's appearance and conversation to change the lives of those around him, and this power for change extends outside the text to include Burnett's uses for the character of Fauntleroy. One of the issues for which Burnett fights, as a woman writer with readerships on both sides of the Atlantic, is copyright protection, not just for her book, but also for other rights related to it.[30] When *Fauntleroy* is pirated and turned into a play by E. V. Seebohm, Burnett uses the popularity of her work to gain the ears of British lawmakers and public figures.[31] Before she begins to pursue the international copyright case, Prime Minister Gladstone asks to meet her because the book has impressed him. Burnett writes about the meeting: "I find Prime Ministers agree with me. He is a fascinating old man, and said the most lovely things. Fauntleroy has charmed him—he told me he believed the book would have great effect in bringing about added good feeling between the two nations and making them understand each other" (qtd. in Thwaite 107–8).

In explaining her need to pursue legal action, she claims her position as the "mother" of Fauntleroy and points especially to the importance of being true to Fauntleroy's appearance and character when the story is produced on stage. In a letter to Owen Lankster, Burnett complains about the theft of her text and the casting of Cedric: "A thief has quietly dramatized Fauntleroy and I am engaged in a fierce battle with him. A large young woman—possibly your size—is to play Cedric" (qtd. in Thwaite 108). In drawing attention to the largeness of the woman, who evidently does not have the right kind of "rosy" boy beauty that is necessary for dramatization, Burnett cites the nature of Fauntleroy's body, his "package," to convey the extent of her own loss of title. In the protest she raises about the contender to her own title, Burnett makes use of the power of Fauntleroy's conversational citizenship and its influence on readers and audiences to make positive changes in copyright laws. Burnett wins the case by demonstrating that large parts of her text are actually copied—not merely represented—in the production process of the usurped play.[32]

Burnett's case sets a precedent that grants extended copyright privileges to other writers, and her act of "benevolence" results in the Society of Authors recognizing her work on behalf of copyright law.[33] Burnett's production of the play is titled, significantly, *The Real Little Lord Fauntleroy* (Thwaite 112). When Burnett gains her rights and achieves the recognition of other authors by appealing to her authorial understanding of the character's beautiful boyhood body, as opposed to the usurping body of the "large woman," she extends the work that *Fauntleroy* does in the construction of American boyhoods for her own "new woman" benefit. *Little Lord Fauntleroy*, in

Mrs. Errol's conversational deployment of Fauntleroy's bodily power in the service of her own independent and generous citizenship, employs hegemonic discourse about mothers and their relationships with their sons; her discourse claims that the "best" woman is a devoted mother who raises a loving son. Simultaneously, with its emphasis on beauty and conversation, this text dislodges United States' interpretations of successful boyhood that valorize lonely independence, competition, and adventure. In *Toward an Intellectual History of Women*, Linda Kerber explains that women have sometimes been able to use the culture's dominant discourses to their own advantages:

> Unable to conceptualize a challenge to hegemonic language, woman seem to have played the role of a "historical bloc" in Gramsci's sense—a group not completely distracted by the prevailing cultural hegemony and permanently in the process of groping for a language to describe its own perception of reality. I would say in the long sweep of women's history there have been times . . . when women have been particularly aggressive and imaginative in seizing their culture's tools of expression (223).

As an author invested in writing and in profiting from it, Burnett draws on her own and her culture's fascinations with boyhood to purchase, using her "culture's tools of expression," both the rights of authentic authorship and recognition of the power those rights confer.

Just as Burnett uses her relationship with "Fauntleroy" to emphasize the need for clearer national and international copyrights, the text itself emphasizes that despite the fragile nature of some titles—the titles of the robber barons might be won or lost in a matter of days—some relationships extend beyond titles to create bonds that cannot be broken by usurpers and contenders. This becomes especially clear when Lord Fauntleroy learns that he is no longer Lord Fauntleroy. As he begins to contemplate the changes this transfer of title will bring, he has the following exchange with his grandfather:

> "That other boy," he said rather tremulously—"he will have to—to be your boy now—as I was—wont [sic] he?"
>
> "*No*!" answered the Earl—and he said it so fiercely and loudly that Cedric quite jumped.
>
> "No?" he exclaimed in wonderment. "Wont [sic] he? I thought—" He stood up from his stool quite suddenly. "Shall I be your boy, even if I'm not going to be an earl?" he said. "Shall I be your boy, just as I was before?" And his flushed little face was all alight with eagerness.
>
> How the old Earl did look at him from head to foot, to be sure. How his great shaggy brows did draw themselves together, and how queerly his deep eyes shone under them—how very queerly!

> "My boy!" he said—and, if you'll believe it, his very voice was queer, almost shaky and a little broken and hoarse, not at all what you would expect an earl's voice to be, though he spoke more decidedly and peremptorily even than before,—"Yes, you'll be my boy as long as I live; and by George, sometimes I feel as if you were the only boy I ever had" (823).

The Earl affirms and authenticates the citizenship relationship that Fauntleroy most longs for, a familial relationship between son and father, between America and England that is legitimated by a nonexpiring title.

In having the Earl embrace the familial relationship at long last, the text replicates the drawn out citizenship-seeking process experienced by immigrants who came to the United States to work during the 1880s. At the same time, the parallel story of the contender demonizes the body and soul of the mother, who had indeed married one of the earl's sons, without demonizing her boy. Indeed, the Earl offers Tom, the contender who turns out to be Dick the bootblack's nephew, the offer to light out for the territory with all his expenses paid. The story of Ben, the usurper's real father, and his son Tom emphasizes Tom's goodness:

> Mr. Havisham had an interview with [Ben] in which the lawyer told him that the Earl of Dorincourt wished to do something for the boy who might have turned out to be Lord Fauntleroy, and so he had decided that it would be a good plan to invest in a cattle ranch of his own, and put Ben in charge of it, on terms which would make it pay him very well, and which would lay a foundation for his son's future. And so when Ben went away, he went as the prospective master of a ranch which would be almost as good as his own, and might easily become his own in time, as indeed it did in the course of a few years; and Tom, the boy, grew up on it into a fine young man and was devotedly fond of his father; and they were so successful and happy that Ben used to say that Tom made up to him for all the troubles he had ever had (885).

The other boy is not the Earl's boy, but he, like Dick, is a respectable hardworking boy who, the text establishes, deserves some kind of affection and the opportunity to work and earn money.

In the final episodes, the character of the Earl, the tyrannical grandfather, seems to be replaced by the most loving and expansive kind of Uncle Sam, as he affirms relationships with those he had previously scorned and provides for sons who are not his own. The Dorincourt estate becomes, during Fauntleroy's birthday party, a miniature United States, with peasants, grocers, bootblacks, lawyers, and earls coming together to celebrate the freedoms and privileges wrought from the strength of "party" bonds. These freedoms, Burnett's text suggests, do not need to come, as they do in *Huck Finn*, with a flight away from towns and cities, six-thousand-dollar windfalls, and a dead "Pap"—they can be achieved in the midst of community and city, with money, loyalty, and a generous spirit committed to familial relationships.

One common factor between the seemingly divergent boy contemporaries, Huck and Fauntleroy, is the capital that both of them have at the end of the text. The boys move their separate ways, one west, one east, one into the academic classroom and one into the juvenile section at the library.[34] In an essay about what he terms *Huckleberry Finn*'s "hypercanonization," Jonathan Arac points to some of the institutional forces that have contributed to its canonical elevation, and he tries to dismantle some of the most prevailing myths about Twain's "unfettered individuality" and *Huckleberry Finn*'s absolute originality (22). Writing about the text's twentieth-century status, Arac notes that "[b]ooks published in 1992 are praised for resembling *Huckleberry Finn* but not, I believe, any other single work of the later nineteenth century" (15). Arac connects this peculiarity to American understandings of "nation" and "literature" and suggests that *Huckleberry Finn* has been canonized in part because of the "allegorical" nature of the Americanness that is presented in the text:

> It is possible to link *Huckleberry Finn* to fundamental national historical experiences, but the link can be made only allegorically, that is, only through an aggressively active process of reader's interpretation, about which readers, in fact, differ very widely. My name for this interpretive process is the nationalizing of literary narrative, and it seems to me the means by which hypercanonical idolatry takes place (18).

As Arac understands it, hypercanonization becomes possible only when there is enough interpretive room for readers to draw their own "allegorical" or imaginative links to the "national historical experiences" that are not addressed directly by the text. *Huck Finn* treats slavery and westward expansion, but according to Arac's argument, leaves room for readers to imagine their own responses to these historical experiences.

So why has *Huck Finn* become a hypercanonical boyhood while *Fauntleroy* has not? Arac offers a hint at one of the reasons when, in his attempts to question *Huckleberry Finn*'s canonicity, he emphasizes the text's connection to the other serialized texts produced in 1885:

> A moment of American literary history that has still not been adequately thought through is the period of early 1885 when the *Century Magazine* published excerpts from *Huckleberry Finn*, while also serializing Howells's *Rise of Silas Lapham* and James's *Bostonians*. Subsequent institutional forces have prevented us from seeing how limited an event nineteenth-century literary narrative was, and the same forces account for the peculiar twentieth-century status of *Huckleberry Finn* (18).

In Arac's view, the "forces" that have given *Huckleberry Finn* its status are connected to American efforts to experience nation from an imaginative distance: "Americans in the twentieth century have adopted as national exemplars precisely those works that were written at a distance from national narrative" (17). In other words, the reason, as Arac presents it, that *The Bostonians* and *Silas Lapham* are not hypercanonical and are not even very "national" is that they connect too explicitly to the politics of the time without offering space for the kind of imaginative interpretation of nation that contributes to *Huck*'s canonicity. Arac's arguments about political distance and imaginative space are convincing, but I would like to extend his analysis of the causes of hypercanonization to argue that perhaps some of the resistances to texts like *Silas Lapham*, *The Bostonians*, and also *Little Lord Fauntleroy*, which was a best-selling text at roughly the same time, have to do with their treatments of gendered citizenships.[35] All of these texts, even the seemingly "original" *Huck Finn*, explore success and its connections to boyhood and manhood.

The nonfiction of the 1880s also links success to powerful citizenships, but this success is not always tied to wealth. In *Character Is Capital: Success Manuals and Manhood in Gilded Age America*, Judy Hilkey argues that success manuals proliferated during the Gilded Age partly to build a new kind of man who identified with the success of the "captains of industry" and worked to reinforce the dominant goals of the rest of the country. These manuals "democratized success when they insisted that true manhood, like character, was a goal within the reach of the poor as well as the rich, the humble as well as the great" (142). The serialized texts of the 1880s function like success manuals when they explore scenes of success: Huck's decision to go to hell and Fauntleroy's willingness to just be a boy. Hilkey also suggests that success manuals help boys who had been raised by women to make the transition to men's work and men's worlds—"Success manuals—especially their emphasis on self-reliance and the stigma they attached to dependence on women—may have had special appeal and provided emotional guidance to boys and youths who had to deny the world of their mothers in order to join the world of their fathers" (163). Cedric, who has to separate from his mother in order to prove himself to his grandfather, enacts the kind of self-reliance that these success manuals promote. Although Cedric provides a model of successful boyhood citizenship, it is Huck's citizenship that is more frequently remembered as representative of Americanness.

The American boyhood constructed by *Huck Finn* has been celebrated as being completely revolutionary and, as Arac suggests, "countercultural" (19).[36] Significantly, Burnett's text has also become countercultural in some ways, but it has not achieved a similar kind of canonicity or recognition as a text that explores issues of national experience. *Little Lord Fauntleroy*'s countercultural currents can be found in its emphasis on wardrobe and on vocally affectionate homosocial, if not homoerotic, relationships that exist across class lines.[37] While *Fauntleroy* has escaped any kind of hypercanonicity, some of Burnett's other texts, *The Secret Garden*, for example, provide *Fauntleroy* with enough children's literature canon status to keep it in print. Arguably, the allegorical national narratives that Arac claims contribute to the canonical stature of *Huckleberry Finn* are also present in *Little Lord Fauntleroy*, but, in this text about the power of party and the privileges of citizenship status—that is, being someone's boy—no matter what, the accessories of boyhood interfere with its national and canonical reputations.[38]

The accessories of Fauntleroy's embodiment materially reinforce Fauntleroy's androgynously constructed boyhood. These accessories, with black velvet and lace as the displayed signs of wisely accrued and dispensed wealth, which make *Little Lord Fauntleroy* a celebrated best-seller of the Gilded Age, are rejected in the early 1900s and have continued to be rejected throughout the twentieth century.[39] The wardrobe cloaks the national narrative of sudden wealth as the key to citizenship while providing the countercultural androgynous boyhood image, which continues to prevent Fauntleroy from entering histories of the construction of American boyhoods. This text inverts national narratives about finding citizenship in the wilderness since the main character goes back to England. Along with this inversion, the text's impossible fantasy about gaining title and wealth also makes it difficult to provide direct allegories for historical experiences. Although it is not accepted as an allegorical and canonical narrative about American citizenship, *Little Lord Fauntleroy* does provide Burnett with enough countercultural economic power to change laws (even without the vote) and to provide herself with loyal allies and semi-citizenships on both sides of the Atlantic. For Burnett, with her "perfect boyhood," revised for publication, and her fairly successful brand of "new womanhood," these authentications of national and literary citizenship are enough.

NOTES

1. The "Gilded Age," often used to refer to the last thirty years of the nineteenth century, was a term coined by Twain in his book (coauthored by Charles Dudley Warner) of the same title: *The Gilded Age: A Tale of the Present* (1873).

2. For more about the production history and the owners of *St. Nicholas* see Fred Erisman's history in *Children's Periodicals of the United States* (377–88), Frank Luther Mott's sketch in *A History of American Magazines: 1865–1885* (500–5, and Peter Hunt's discussion in *Children's Literature: An Illustrated History* (230–31).

3. Richard Brodhead uses the word *scene* to describe a variety of the aspects of the reading experience in *Cultures of Letters: Scenes of Reading and Writing in Nineteenth-Century America*.

4. Other texts serialized in the 1885 *Century Magazine* include William Dean Howells's *The Rise of Silas Lapham* and Henry James's *The Bostonians*. Burnett, who had a reputation as an adult author at the time she published *Little Lord Fauntleroy*, chooses the *Century*'s children's magazine as the forum for her version of the boy story, perhaps because it is easier for her to begin a conversation about boy citizenships with an audience of children than with an audience of adult arbiters of literary taste. See Ann Thwaite's *Waiting for the Party* for discussions of Burnett's writing processes and their connections to friendships with literary figures such as Henry James.

5. With Pap dead, Huck has access to the six thousand dollars Judge Thatcher has been holding for him. A text where versions of both western and eastern boyhoods come together is Julie A. Mathews's *Jack Granger's Cousin* (1877), discussed at length in *Regendering the School Story*.

6. After Burnett's first story was published in *Godey's Lady's Book*, she spent part of the money on alpaca for clothes for herself and her sister: "Fannie's was straw-color with blue scallops and mine was blue with straw-color straps" (Thwaite 35). Burnett divorces her husband in 1898. See Thwaite's discussion of the responses to this divorce at the time (176–77).

7. *Fauntleroy* begins serialization in November; the first Letter Box reference to it comes in January. This letter is from Washington, D.C., which is not very far away from New York. This lag in response time indicates the speed of the communication systems, and also, perhaps, suggests that younger readers took a longer time to make up their minds about a serialized text. The letters from Europe and other areas almost always contain comments about events in texts from several issues back.

8. The oil and steel industries were booming during this time and inventions proliferated: George Eastman's Kodak camera (1888); Alexander Graham Bell's telephone (1876); Thomas A. Edison's electric generating station in New York (1882).

9. According to Frank Luther Mott, illustrations became important to adult magazines during the 1880s and 1890s as well, so much so that the images sometimes became more prominent than the text: "the American general magazine went on increasing its pictorial content in richness and variety. 'Nowadays it is often the text which is illustrative rather than the pictures,' said the Kimball survey at the end of the century" (Mott on Kimball, Arthur Reed, *Journal of Social Science* 37 [1899]: 37. Qtd. in *A History of American Magazines, 1885–1905* [130]).

10. In *Waiting for the Party*, Ann Thwaite writes: "At the end of his life, Birch himself said they had ruined his career; no one ever let him forget them. They were based on a photograph of Vivian [Burnett's son] taken in Lynn in 1884. It is one thing to wear black velvet in a photographic studio or on Tuesday afternoons, as Vivian did; it is quite another to wear it when riding a pony or watching a bricklayer. The image was wide open to both admiration and ridicule" (92).

11. William Schwenck Gilbert wrote *The Mikado* in 1885, and evidently "Yum-Yum," who writes from New York, has some knowledge of the play.

12. In "Little Lord Fauntleroy: The Darling of Mothers and the Abomination of a Generation," Anna Wilson insightfully reads Mr. Havisham's "consumption of Fauntleroy's body" as homoerotic (243).

13. Darwin's *On the Origin of Species by Means of Natural Selection* was first pub-

lished in 1859 and Spencer's nine-volume *System of Synthetic Philosophy* was published between the years 1862 and 1893.

14. For a discussion of the emphasis on breeding in another text about a boy see David Gryll's treatment of Marie Corelli's *Boy* (1900) in *Guardians and Angels.*

15. In "Modern Girls and Masterful Boys," *English Children and Their Magazines, 1751–1945*, Kirsten Drotner points out that Herbert Spencer was "the key figure in popularizing an evolutionary theory of motherhood. As early as 1867, he voiced his anxiety about the physiological damage that could result from women's academic endeavors" (138).

16. See *A Literature of Their Own.* Claudia Nelson reviews theories of the impact of Coventry Patmore's angel in the house in *Boys Will Be Girls.* See also Carol Dyhouse's *Girls Growing Up in Late Victorian and Edwardian England.*

17. In *American Woman's Home* (1869), Catherine E. Beecher and Harriet Beecher Stowe write about the influence of beauty in the home on children's development (84). See Gillian Brown's *Domestic Individualism* and Nancy Armstrong's *Desire and Domestic Fiction* for more on subjectivity and domesticity.

18. See Kirsten Drotner's discussion of social evolution and "evolutionary motherhood" in which she points out that adolescent girls coming to adulthood in the late nineteenth century confronted mixed messages about "evolutionary motherhood" and their own educations, just when educational opportunities were beginning to expand (139).

19. Thwaite points out that newspaper reviews of Burnett's books often gave space to descriptions of Burnett's appearance: "Personally she is plump—almost too plump for her short stature. She wears her hair braided behind and frizzled in front to cover what she calls a horrid great forehead, which really is too square and too projecting for beauty" (qtd. in Thwaite 87).

20. In *You're A Brick, Angela!*, Mary Cadogan and Patricia Craig note that Burnett was fascinated by "Cinderellas and transformations" (61).

21. Thwaite notes that Burnett met Oscar Wilde at a party and suggests that his clothes inspired the suit Fauntleroy wears (82). Wilson also discusses this possibility (243).

22. Mark Spilka argues, in an essay treating Ernest Hemingway, *Little Lord Fauntleroy*, and *Huckleberry Finn*, that Hemingway's mother constructed him as a "Fauntleroy" in her "memory books" about his childhood (301). Spilka suggests, however, that "Ernest was like other American boys. He would eventually prefer Huckleberry Finn, whose frontier antecedents were at least secure, to Fauntleroy, the 'Fairy Prince' whose undeserved reputation as a prig and a sissy he spent a lifetime dodging and denying" (302).

23. Mary Cadogan and Patricia Craig note that Burnett wrote about Leland Stanford in a *Girl's Realm* article: "the article mentions her attraction to a youthful benefactor of mankind who has been cut off suddenly from life at the age of fifteen. Leland Stanford, the son of an American multi-millionaire, had expressed a wish that less fortunate young people could share his own educational opportunities: after his death Leland's parents had built Stanford" (61). Like Fauntleroy, the young Stanford does not have the spending ability of his parents, but he uses his wishes to increase the benevolent spending of his parents.

24. See William Graham Sumner's 1894 discussion of the importance of the manhood of the "captains of industry" to industrialist creativity and management (rpt. in *The Industrial Revolution: Opposing Viewpoints* [104]). See also Walter Lippman's 1914 argument that antitrust laws block the creativity of the "captains of industry" (rpt. in *The Industrial Revolution: Opposing Viewpoints* [124]).

25. The reception of *Through One Administration* placed Burnett's name on lists of important "American" authors alongside names like James and Howells. One such list appeared in the *Century* in 1883. See Thwaite's discussion of this article and Burnett's connections to other writers (86).

26. Fauntleroy speaks with his grandfather about Higgins, one of the tenants on the Earl's estate.

27. Mott writes that "The Brownies" are a fad during the 1890s (151–52). In the 1885 issues, they are very popular with letter writers. Since Cox indicates the nationality of the Brownies through their accessories (hats for example), the Brownies signal American preoccupations with using "dress" as a way to belong and to signal roots and national origin.

28. Edward Eggleston, author of *A Hoosier School Boy*, writes a series about life in the colonies in the 1885 issue of *Century*—one of the articles, "Colonial Home Life," provides illustrations of everyday items like silverware, bonnets, and shoes to prove that life was "lived."

29. See "New Orleans Exposition" published in the *Century Magazine*, which explains some of the aims of the world fairs (3).

30. Thwaite notes that Burnett had written to *Century* arguing for international copyright protection in 1886 (113).

31. Thwaite discusses Seebohm's play and Burnett's response to it in detail.

32. The verdict of Burnett's case provides protection for other authors. The ruling reads in part: "I grant a perpetual injunction to restrain the defendant from multiplying copies of his play. The plaintiffs further insist on an order directing the delivery up of existing copies of the play. . . . the costs of the action must be paid by the defendant" (qtd. in Thwaite 111).

33. Burnett is given a diamond bracelet accompanied by an elaborate thank you: "The undermentioned Men and Women of Letters desire to express to Mrs. Frances Hodgson Burnett their appreciation of the great service they believe she has rendered to British Authors by so strongly attracting public attention to the unsatisfactory condition of Copyright Law in England" (qtd. in Thwaite 114).

34. Compare assessments of the importance of the two texts: Ernest Hemingway writes in 1935: "all modern American literature comes from one book by Mark Twain called *Huckleberry Finn*" (22). John Sutherland writes in the *Stanford Companion to Victorian Fiction* that *Fauntleroy* was "too saccharine for some tastes. As Mrs. Elizabeth Riddell tartly noted, the story was a 'cross between a tract and a play. It appeals to mothers.'" P. W. Musgrove writes that *Fauntleroy* was "compelling, but even then seen as sentimental" (212).

35. Thwaite lists the best-selling books from 1884 to1886: 1884—*Heidi, Treasure Island*; 1885—*A Child's Garden of Verses, Huckleberry Finn, Little Lord Fauntleroy, King Solomon's Mines, War and Peace*—and she points out that all but *War and Peace* would now be considered children's books (95).

36. Arac writes that *Huck Finn*'s "very canonical prestige is connected to the sense that it is countercultural" (19). Forwarding the text's countercultural reputation, the form of this boy book and the problems it continues to present to interpreters (the ending, its presentation of race) help to emphasize its "specialness" and add to its canonicity.

37. Cedric establishes these affectionate connections with Mr. Hobbs the grocer, Dick the bootblack, and Jerry the sailor.

38. Edith Wharton's texts about upwardly mobile women contemplate class struggles with clever attention to the details of dress. While perhaps not experiencing hypercanonicity, her texts (unlike *Little Lord Fauntleroy*) do continue to resonate with American audiences as texts that provide credible examples of how the dressed body of Gilded Age womanhood gains social mobility.

39. Perhaps part of the reason for the rejection outside of dress and manners is that the ruthless investors of the 1910s and 1920s could not survive with Fauntleroy's unselfish benevolence as an example. Boys growing up in Depression Era poverty would not have been able to readily identify with the ease of Fauntleroy's rise to wealth.

6

Beeton's Boy's Own Magazine and *Boys' Life*: Serialized Directions for Boyhood Citizenships in the Twentieth Century

> [T]he boys of this country are not namby-pamby youths, devoid of imagination, and who know nothing and care nothing about the great world awaiting them. They want to read and know something beyond the dull level of their own street and town.
>
> —*Boys' Life*, March 1, 1911.[1]

The boyhoods recorded in periodicals for and about boys undergo several shifts over the course of the nineteenth century. In Jacob Abbott's representations of boys in the *Youth's Companion*, we see plodding and persistent experimenters, while in George White's editorials in the *Young American's Magazine of Self-Improvement*, boys become silent, somewhat pliable, and eager-to-learn consumers of texts. The boys constructed by Oliver Optic's series of the 1850s stay true to their locally defined types. In *Our Young Folks*, Aldrich and other writers for boys revisit their boyhoods and move away from the tendency to "type" boys; instead, they depict them as creatures with power to reconstruct themselves and their nations. In *St. Nicholas*, Frances Hodgson Burnett extends the transformative nature of conversational citizenship across the Atlantic as a way of demonstrating the power of American boyhood, an issue that Mark Twain also explores in *The Adventures of Huckleberry Finn*. These changes provide a genealogy for the serialized boyhood citizenships depicted in the 1890s and early 1900s. While they do not reveal direct connections to the textual boyhoods of the twenty-first century, the shifts in magazines for boys that occur between 1890 and 1911 offer some background and context for the current obsessions with boys and boyhoods in the United States.

During the late 1880s and 1890s, several boys' magazines began publication, and during the early years of the twentieth century, more boys' magazines were published.[2] William C. Sprague, the editor of *The American Boy*, promotes his magazine as being written for just for boys, especially those who are "turning the corner into manhood":

> This paper is for boys—American boys, the brightest and best boys on the face of the earth. It is not a family paper, tho' men and women with boys' hearts will read it. It is not a child's paper, of which we all know there are enough already. . . . the boy needs good literature—he is growing restless under restraint, dreams dreams, get aspirations and begins to do things" (qtd. in Reck viii).

Other magazines published specifically for boys include *The Boys' Champion* (1881), *Boys' Star Library* (1887), *American Youth* (1889), *Boys' Brigade Bulletin* (1892), *Youth's Realm* (1896), *Association Boys* (1902), *The Boys' World* (1902), *Our Boys' Magazine* (1908), *Young Knight* (1908), *Young Socialist's Magazine* (1908), *The Boy* (1909), *Boys' Best Weekly* (1909), *The Boys' Magazine* (1910), *Boys' Life* (1911), *Pioneer for Boys* (1915), and *American Boy—Open Road* (1919).[3] The length of this list suggests that gender-specific publishing was lucrative enough to keep several different magazines in business for at least a few years. Clearly, boys' reading material played an important role in constructing early-twentieth-century boyhood citizenships.

The longest running of these magazines for boys is *Boys' Life*. Writing in 1982, Alice Denham points out that "[w]hen *Boys' Life* started in 1911, it competed especially with several other popular magazines aimed at the same young male market, including *St. Nicholas*, *The Youth's Companion*, and *American Boy—Open Road*. *Boys' Life* alone survives—and if it were not for the Boy Scouts, it probably would not survive either" (41).[4] *Boys' Life* continues to be published even now at a time when most magazines read by boys are not designated as being specifically for boys. A late 1980s promotional flier claims: "Five million boys have one thing to say about *Boys' Life*: 'Oh Boy!' " (n. pag.). This flier argues that one of the reasons boys should read the magazine is because they need to learn what boys are doing nationwide: "How will your son, nephew, grandson, or kid brother find out what boys his age are doing around the country? *Boys' Life* will fill him in" (n. pag.). *Boys' Life* succeeds in part because it constructs boys in the United States as interested in the lives of other boys living in the nation; the magazine provides boys with a reading community that fosters a national boyhood citizenship.

Despite the claims of *Boys' Life* for its centrality in the lives of today's boys, these boys, if they choose to read at all, will often read mainstream magazines centered on sports, such as *Sports Illustrated*, or magazines associated with specific hobbies, like biking or skateboarding. Others choose periodicals without national circulations that publish articles related to highly specific tastes in music (Sonic Youth's fanzine *Sonic Death*), or to art (*Forced Exposure*, dedicated to experimental music and to personal comics).[5] These underground "zines," distributed through subscriber-initiated mailing list contacts or through independent book and music stores, explicitly reject national and mainstream culture in favor of stratified, local, and sometimes secretive, unreadable citizenships.

How did we get here from the widely distributed boyhoods circulated by the *Youth's Companion*, *Our Young Folks*, the *Century Magazine*, and *St. Nicholas*? The illustration and description of boy characters in magazines of the late 1890s and early 1910s show these serializations' connectedness to the boy figures in earlier periodicals, especially the quintessentially American Huck and the androgynous expatriate Fauntleroy. At the same time, the serializations demonstrate ways in which "global" magazines published in more than one nation reflect small shifts in boyhood citizenship; these shifts are apparent in the illustrations and in the scenes chosen for the adventures that serialize the moves from boyhood to manhood. In the 1880s, *Beeton's Boys' Own Paper* repetitiously produces white adventures featuring adult and young adult men; these serializations, which contain descendants of both Huck and Fauntleroy, reveal the sometimes-buried American embrace of imperialism that is an inextricable part of textual American boyhood. *Boys' Life*, the magazine associated with the Boy Scouts of America, responds to the imperialism in the magazines of the 1880s and 1890s by presenting domestic adventures contained within the United States. *Boys' Life* promotes a carefully organized, uniformed homosocial reading world that, in the later twentieth century, provides a model for other kinds of uniformed and serialized citizenships organized around the sameness of interests and talents. The serializations based on sameness of interests generate alternate scenes of homosociality that resist and blur previously marked gender boundaries. The points of connection and disconnection to serializations found in late nineteenth- and early twentieth-century periodicals provide partial histories of the process that has contributed to the withdrawal of some twentieth-century serialized boyhoods from the national and transatlantic publishing market into more particularized scenes of serialization. These increasingly stratified serializations open up ways for boys to participate in constructing citizenships that resist the controlling and constraining narratives provided about them by adults in the twentieth and twenty-first centuries.

In the 1880s and 1890s, magazines published specifically for boys profit from circulation on both sides of the Atlantic and, in some cases, circulation in colonized nations. Ward, Lock and Company published one such "global" magazine, *Beeton's Boy's Own Magazine*, in London, New York, and Melbourne. Edited by penny dreadful king G. A. Henty, the texts depict boys participating in the projects of empire. *Beeton's* declares that it is "profusely illustrated," and to some extent it is—a full-page illustration accompanies almost every serialized episode. Because of the emphasis on illustration, the boyhoods chosen for publication seem to be ones that are easily illustrated. The episodic moments chosen for illustration are usually ones that involve encounters between groups of boys or between boys and men, and these illustrated scenes construct the successful journey to manhood as one that embraces imperialist adventure wholeheartedly.

Many of the illustrated imperialist adventures reveal connections to the serialized boyhoods of the earlier part of the nineteenth century. Serialized texts include survival stories, such as James Greenwood's *The Adventures of Reuben Davidger, Seventeen Years and Four Months a Captive among the Dayaks of Borneo*, and Cecil Marryat Norris's *Never Say Die*, a text that moves the kind of river raft adventure that is central to *Huckleberry Finn* to the space of the ocean. In *Never Say Die*, the clothes the boys wear as they move through their adventures become more "Hucklike" as the text progresses: sleeves rip and jackets and shoes are discarded (see figure 6.1).

In this text, the illustrations focus on changes in clothing to indicate the extent of the survival efforts. The changes in accessories reflect the boys' determination to move toward manhood by "never say[ing] die." The extent to which the boys invest their physical bodies and divest their clothing in order to survive suggests that the more physical citizenship of Huck rather than the conversational citizenship of Fauntleroy is the construction of boyhood that is reinterpreted in the 1890s, although the fact that the boys survive together rather than alone indicates that cooperative, if not conversational, citizenship works as part of the survival equation.

In addition to including survival stories that construct imperialist boyhoods through survival narratives, *Beeton's Boys' Own* also serializes texts about more formal, career-based participation in imperialist projects. These texts draw on the Fauntleroy model of performing the duties of citizenship to illustrate how boys become men through their loyalty to imperialist occupations. Arthur Lee Knight's *Dicky Beaumont; His Perils and Adventures* shows Dicky moving from a position of envious longing for a place in his father's world of the navy to actively participating in conquest. The first serialized chapter provides an illustration of a Fauntleroy-inspired Dicky dressed for his birthday visit to a ship wearing a large lace collar, knee breeches, and a sash (see figure 6.2).

Subsequent chapters focus on Dicky's physical transformation and his

"NEVER SAY DIE."
Hoisting the Signal.

[Page A 54.

Figure 6.1. *Never Say Die*. Cecil Marryat Norris. *Beeton's Boys Own Magazine* 4 (1890): A257. Image courtesy of the de Grummond Children's Literature Collection, the University of Southern Mississippi. www.lib.usm.edu/~degrum

"'HE'S THE OLD 'RAL'S NEW FLAG-LIEUTENANT; AREN'T YOU, LITTLE MAN?'"

Dicky Beaumont.]

Figure 6.2. *Dicky Beaumont*. Arthur Lee Knight. *Beeton's Boy's Own Magazine* 4 (1890): A 305. Image courtesy of the de Grummond Children's Literature Collection, the University of Southern Mississippi. www.lib.usm.edu/~degrum

ability to use his body to gain control during his "perils." One description reads:

> His head, which is small and symmetrical, is well placed on his shoulders; and though tall and strongly built, his figure isn't by any means clumsy or awkward-looking, being, on the contrary, lithe and well proportioned, as befitted a boy who was fond of out-door exercise and field sports, which pastimes, however, he never allowed to interfere with necessary studies, or with his passion for reading romances of the sea and the Waverly Novels (314).

Here, reading boys are given a prescription for surviving the change from young boyhood to young manhood: exercise, study, and reading for pleasure. These, evidently, are the habits that will help Dicky to survive adventures that include sailing to Hong Kong and being captured by "Malay" pirates. Both *Never Say Die* and *Dicky Beaumont* draw on previous serialization models to construct boys who survive challenges and participate in imperialist conquest; these serialized constructions depend not only on the ongoing transformation of the characters but also on the characters' abilities to interact with groups of men who either advance their survival or work against it.

Throughout *Beeton's*, texts focus almost exclusively on all-male worlds. This can be seen in texts about the past like *Cressy and Poictiers; The Story of the Black Prince's Page*, which celebrates the imperialist motivations of the crusades, and in texts about late-nineteenth-century territorial expansion like *White-Faced Dick*. This is another adventure quest; set in the American gold mines, it is similar to *Dicky Beaumont* in its depictions of a younger man's relationships with older men. The regular serializations of homosocial boyhoods and manhoods in a variety of settings (Hong Kong, England, and California) construct citizenships that are made possible through both homosociality and imperial adventure.

While the profusely illustrated fiction in *Beeton's* emphasizes the adventures of young men who are nearing adulthood, the editorials recognize that some boys and young men stay at home; these editorials narrate solutions for and attempt to contain citizenships that differ from those serialized in the homosocial adventure quests. One editorial contrasts clerkships with the jobs of artisans and mechanics and argues that unless the clerkship is awarded by evaluations of class and education and is therefore well-paid, it is more profitable for boys considering careers to be skeptical about the respectability associated with the clerkship and to instead, work with their hands.

> The rise from the rank of what is called unskilled labour to that of the artisan or mechanic—the man who has to work with his head as well as his hands—is indeed a very great one; and I consider that there are few positions in life in

> which a man can enjoy a larger amount of happiness than in that of a skilled mechanic or artisan, provided always that he is a good specimen of his class—intelligent, steady, self-respecting, and contented (203).

The references to mechanics and clerkships in this editorial indicate that some of the readers of *Beeton's* come from an artisan/mechanic class that is similar to the class addressed by the earlier *Young American's Magazine of Self-Improvement.* In his commentary, Henty does his best to discourage these readers from entering clerkships by celebrating the work of the skilled laborer. Other editorials also treat issues of industrial labor. In one editorial, Henty denounces strikes as being examples of "partizan [sic] obstinacy": "The question of what wages the masters can afford to pay is one upon which the men cannot be so well qualified as to form an opinion as can the employer; and at least a very patient consideration ought to be given to the arguments on the other side. This, however, is seldom the case; it is assumed at once that he ought to be able to afford it" (460). These editorials demonstrate that even while the adventure tales focus on how places far away from London and New York can shape boyhoods into manhoods, the majority of the reading boys face decisions about work and the everyday issues surrounding it—labor of the head versus labor of the hands, fair wages, and the control of capital.

The working-class readers addressed in the editorials of *Beeton's* are also the target audiences of other adventure-centered magazines that are marketed to American boys in the 1890s. Some of the magazines that are the contemporaries of *Beeton's* include the illustrated *Happy Days* (another version of *Boys of New York*), edited by Frank Tousey and published from 1894 to 1924. Constance Grenmore writes, "Like *Boys of New York*, this publication appealed primarily to boys of the lower and middle classes who hoped to rise in the world. Shipwrecks, fires, factory and railroad accidents, and encounters with thieves and kidnappers provided the protagonists in the popular serial stories opportunities to become heroes" (Kelly 188).[6] Grenmore points out that both *Boys of New York* and *Happy Days* contain humor columns made up of accounts of jokes played on "outsiders" (by race or ethnicity), and on members of the middle classes and authority figures (parents and teachers):

> [t]hey were farcical accounts of boyish pranks—saddling horses backwards, setting booby traps, frightening adult victims with devices like firecrackers—tales of tricks and swindles and domestic quarrels and mishaps. Pranksters sought out their victims among the adult population, frequently picking on black men or knocking the stuffing out of priggish members of the middle class (56).

A magazine with similar audiences and purposes is the *Boys of London and Boys of New York*, edited by James Jackson. The 1886 edition contains such titles as *The Swamp Doctor or The Man Witch* by D. W. Stevens; *White Boy Chief!, or The Terror of the North Platte* by E. H. Kellogg; *In the Secret Service; or Young Counterfeiters of the West* by Frank Forrest; and *Pandy Ellis, the Prairie Prince; or, The Shadow Scout of Red River* by Marline Manly. As these titles suggest, this magazine is preoccupied with regional, mostly westward, expansion and the roles and positions ("chief," "prince," "counterfeiter") available to young men there. These positions are usually gained by the main character's collaboration with other men or boys. The collaborative citizenships promoted in these working-class magazines echo the emphasis on union seen in the *Young American's Magazine of Self-Improvement*.

About ten years later (1897), in the London-based *Boys' Own*, there continues to be a similar interest in heightening the adventure value of a given text by associating the white heroes with the dark Other—in this magazine the "Other" takes the form of the Native American. Titles include G. Manville Fenn's *Nic Revel: or, A White Slave's Adventures in the Alligator Land* and Harold Avery's *Mobsley's Mohicans: A Tale of Two Terms*. In these magazines with transatlantic audiences, during the 1880s and 1890s, there seems to be an effort to address the everyday concerns of reading boys by fantasizing about the possibilities for gaining titles and land through combinations of luck, survival skills, and violence, all of which are tested by forming relationships with other men. As *Mobsley's Mohicans* shows, some of these serializations domesticate the other kinds of men-only adventures by bringing names associated with expansion and conquest to bear on the matters of everyday friendship and rivalry at a boys' school.[7] Beginning in 1911, the adventures that George S. Barton's *Boys' Life* magazine publishes compete with the homosocial adventure stories based on American imperialism that can be found in these other boys' magazines.

The changes in magazine content that can be traced by comparing *Boys of New York* and *Beeton's Boys' Own* with *Boys' Life* mirror some of the shifts of citizenship in the United States. During the 1880s and 1890s, more than fifteen million immigrants came to the United States, the biggest influx since the 1840s. The 1880s and 1890s were a time of expansion in the United States, with plains states added to the Union, and over seventy thousand miles of railway constructed. Creativity and entrepreneurship were fostered by this expansionism and by the arrival of new citizens. The 1898 Spanish-American War was fueled both by a drive to expand and by a belief that violent expansion is a quick way to establish or reestablish the definition of nation and to give the nation "manly" vigor and purpose.[8] The United States' motivations in expanding the Pacific island territories were not especially clear before the war, and they became even more complicated afterwards when citizenship privileges in the conquered territories had to be decided.

By the early 1900s, the creativity and acquisitive entrepreneurial spirit that had made itself manifest in business ventures within the United States' borders began to be tempered by large corporations needing order and having the power to purchase it. In order to eliminate competition, John Pierpont Morgan used his monetary power to buy up railway lines and reorganize or "Morganize" them. This drive toward order also can be seen in the name John D. Rockefeller gave to his oil company; "Standard Oil" became the recognized brand of oil, and the orderliness and regularity of its production helped to keep it powerful. The depressions that struck the United States between 1894 and 1897 coincided with the violence of the Haymarket riot in Chicago, the Homestead strike in Pennsylvania, and the silver mine strike in Idaho in the 1880s and early 1890s. All of these disruptions added motivation to these moves toward order. *Boys' Life*, a magazine associated with an organized group, the Boy Scouts, offered a similar kind of soothing regularity to the boys preparing to enter the industrialized but increasingly isolationist world of the United States. The universe might not care that an individual exists, the world of *Boys' Life* seems to say, but perhaps a uniformed group of reading "peace scouts" with contacts nationwide might have a chance to exist safely and comfortably.[9]

Like the *Youth's Companion* and *Our Young Folks*, *Boys' Life* began publication in New England. The first editor, George S. Barton, writes about the magazine's aims:

> To furnish the Boy Scouts with a paper which they may consider their own . . . and to supply them with good, clean, stirring stories of adventure . . . to place in the hands of all boys a paper of which they may be proud, and one which they will not be afraid to have their parents see them reading (21).[10]

In this prospectus for a magazine that had a long and successful life in the twentieth century, Barton chooses to foreground adventure, ownership, and cleanliness, which he ties to a lack of shame. These aspects of boys' lives will be presented in what Barton describes as "good, healthy stories of adventure that will do their part toward building character in boys" (21). The first stories of the magazine do employ adventure, but they focus on making the dull, repetitious work that is available to many boys seem potentially exciting and heroic.

The March 1, 1911, issue opens with "The Lost Express," a domestic adventure story that examines the problems faced by owners of railroad companies. The owner's nephew has been a disappointment in the office because his privileged life has not given him the necessary initiative to move his uncle's company forward. His uncle, who had been going to put him in charge of the company, tells him not to return. The nephew catches a train and while he is traveling overhears some treacherous, double-crossing affiliates of his uncle's company making plans to nullify his uncle's railroading rights. He saves the day by taking control of the train and stopping it so that he can telegraph his uncle about the problem. The adventure, which is completely tied up with business concerns and legal contracts, reveals to the previously bored and unmotivated nephew just how exciting the paperwork of a large business can be. His adventure renews his interest and investment in his uncle's company, and he returns to be promoted as his uncle had originally planned. This episode rewrites the clerkships that many of the readers of the magazine had to look forward to in their adult lives and presents work organized around paper shuffling as courageous, dangerous, and powerful.

The story, with its violence and adventure, has some of the qualities of the dime novel, but these qualities have been displaced onto the relatively nonphysical and sometimes dull world of corporate management and are thereby domesticated. In "*Boys' Life*: The Real Beginnings" John T. Dizer writes about the history of *Boys' Life* and its connections to the more sensational dime novel:

> The true founder, publisher, and editor of *Boys' Life*, was not Joseph Lane but George S. Barton of Somerville, Massachusetts, a Boston publisher and early Scout. Barton was also a collector and researcher in the dime novel field, a fact which Franklin K. Mathiews, Chief Scout Librarian of the Boys Scouts of America and arch enemy of dime novels, would have deplored (39).

In its use of controlled adventure, *Boys' Life* responds to the "sensation" of the illustrated magazines of the late 1890s and to their dangerous physical humor with content that the editors deem to be simultaneously "healthy" and "stirring," both terms that indicate cultural connections between reading material and the physical body of American boyhood during the early years of the twentieth century. While the "stirring" does suggest erotic arousal, the material of the magazine keeps the content healthy by focusing on "wholesome" activities and adventures for boys to participate in at home and away.

As the turn of the century, the connections between health, boyhood, and future citizenship continue to preoccupy magazine publishers and other adults. In 1903, Theodore Roosevelt publishes his own ideas about health and work in *The Strenuous Life*: "a healthy state can exist only when the men and women who make it up lead clean, vigorous, healthy lives; when the children are so trained that they shall endeavor, not to shirk difficulties, but to overcome them; not to seek ease, but to know how to wrest triumph from toil and risk" (3). This curiously bigendered discussion of healthiness seems to allow for the fact that both men and women might lead the kind of "strenuous life" that Roosevelt argues will improve the nation. In other sections, however, Roosevelt focuses on manhood and urges men of the nation to colonize Hawaii, Cuba, Puerto Rico, and the Philippines. His theories are based both on the healthiness of American men and the healthiness of the nation:

> The timid man, the lazy man, the man who distrusts his country, the over-civilized man, who has lost the great, fighting, masterful virtues, the ignorant man, and the man of dull mind whose soul is incapable of feeling the mighty lift that thrills "stern men with empires in their brains"—all these, of course, shrink from seeing us build a navy and an army adequate to our needs; shrink from seeing us do our share of the world's work (7).

The healthiness that Roosevelt locates in work is related to the health he claims can be found in taking on global projects of empire. A similar emphasis on health can be found in early issues of *Boys' Life*. The scouting badges and activities that are described in *Boys' Life* prescribe ways to avoid the ease that Roosevelt describes as being dangerous to boyhood; the plans for leading an outdoor life that can be found in the pages of the magazine map out guides to the vigorous lives necessary for Roosevelt's brand of healthy citizenship.

Beeton's and *Boys of London and New York*, magazines with production ties to the late nineteenth century, tend to have more of an imperialist bent, while *Boys' Life* responds to isolationist moves away from imperialism by endorsing a uniformed and regulated homosocial reading world for boys facing increased coeducation and co-gendered civic space and work activities. The Maxims for Scouts section of *Boys' Life* emphasizes isolationist moves by focusing on what it terms "peace scouting": "You need not wait for war in order to be useful as a scout. As a peace scout there is a lot for you to do any day, wherever you may be" (23). At the same time, however, the recent expansionist enterprises of the United States are recognized: "If every boy works hard at scouting and really learns all that it teaches him, he will, at the end of it, have some claim to call himself a real man, and will find, if ever he goes on service or to a colony, that he will have no difficulty in looking after himself and in being really useful to his country" (18). The scouting projects offered by the magazine both recognize and retreat from imperialism by suggesting that the domestic versions of conquest and survival be carried out in the boys' backyards.

Much of the magazine devotes itself to the construction of boyhood citizenships that will ensure the likelihood of similar adult citizenships. Some of the maxims offered to the scouts attempt to connect scouting to the place of men in the United States: "The history of the United States has been made up of American adventurers and explorers, the scouts of the nation, for hundreds of years past up to the present time" (23). In much of the magazine, which in its early issues seeks to define scouting in its relation to America, there is a focus on group identity: "We are very much like bricks in a wall—we each have our place, though it may seem a small one in so big a wall" (37). The sameness of the scouts, demonstrated in their shared maxims and their uniforms (for which the magazine provides order forms), helps the scouts to find their places. In "An Appreciation of the Boy Scout Movement," Rev. Albert H. Wheelock extends the "brick in the wall" idea to discuss the way the Boy Scout movement is helping boys to find a place in the world. Wheelock "believe[s] in the American Boy Scout movement . . . because it is for boys as boys, without distinction. Material condition, creed, race, are ignored in behalf of the natural democracy of boyhood. The only things barred is [sic] moral or physical contagion" (37). As the court decisions upholding the Boys Scouts' right to bar gays from their leadership positions demonstrate, the "contagion" to which Wheelock alludes has continued to be anxiously barred from this particular "democracy of boyhood."

The space of *Boys' Life*, according to Alice Denham's history, remains relatively unchanged during the twentieth century, presenting a nearly all-white middle-class world to its readers. Reviewing the magazine's history in 1982, Denham finds that sexuality is one subject that is never touched; other potentially dangerous aspects of boys' lives, drugs and violence, for example, are rarely mentioned. By stubbornly depicting a uniformed and orderly world, the editors of *Boys' Life* establish "safe" boundaries for what life is and is not, and in creating such a textual world, they provide models for other groups with different agendas to establish parallel and counter citizenships.[11]

The privatized and regulated boys' world that can be found in *Boys' Life* has been replicated and improvised upon during the twentieth century at the local level in ways that serialize alternate kinds of homosocial citizenships. These homosocial citizenships are based on sameness in passions or obsessions rather than sameness in sex and gender and thereby challenge gender boundaries that continue to be constructed by adult assessors of boyhood. The late-twentieth-century treatises on boys offered by Michael Gurian and William Pollack argue urgently for the need to protect boys by maintaining and valorizing sex and gender boundaries. In *Raising Cain*, Dan Kindlon and Michael Thompson agree with Gurian and Pollack's "let boys be boys" pleas and further suggest that girls and women need to recognize that boys "naturally" exploit women.[12] Jill Bellas and Faye Arnett join in the interpretations of American boyhood in *The Son also Rises*, which is devoted to reassuring mothers that their boys will outgrow adolescence. These diagnoses of the problems with American boyhood have been produced alongside serializations that continually reinvent American boyhoods.

Some of these serialized boyhoods contain relatively easy-to-spot links to the serialized boyhoods of the past. The embrace of New England as the best site for American boyhood to turn to manhood and the concerns about community identity and the preciousness of youth that are explored in Optic's series and in *Story of a Bad Boy* in *Our Young Folks* continue to be serialized and proliferated, sometimes in surprising places. In the summer of 2000, the Warner Brothers' television network, which markets most of its prime-time programs to young adults, aired a series titled *The Young Americans*. This series, produced by Coca-Cola to be a product placement venue, was an hour-long drama, and was set in New England at a boys' school. Some of the main story lines play with cross-dressing and same-sex education. A girl dressed as a boy attends the school to get even with her mother and to access an education unavailable to girls. This character develops a sexual attraction to one of the other boys who spends several episodes believing he is uncovering a gay identity. Other aspects of "young Americanness" that are covered include class conflict (a town boy receives a scholarship to attend) and incest (a wealthy politician's son falls in love with a town girl, whom he discovers is his father's child and therefore his sister). These versions of boyhood are introduced in the first episode, and their various dangers and possibilities are explored throughout the episodes.

The *Young Americans* lasted for only the summer season, but it found an audience during its run. Interestingly, a petition to save the show, circulated on the Internet, echoes the language of some of the earlier prospectuses for the magazines of the nineteenth century. The petition demonstrates the extent to which the "issues" the show covered resonate with some viewers:

> It is not often that a television show touches the lives of the youth of America, nor one that creates situations that we can relate to—"Young Americans" provides us with not only something to look forward to on Wednesday nights and a release from summer re-runs, but also a new look on the 'teen scene' that no other television show (including "Dawson's Creek," and "Buffy") has touched in such a manner. Due to the show's daring topics, youth everywhere can place a connection between themselves and the characters. It gives us a chance to think about and solve problems we are to [sic] timid and scared to talk to others about. Leaving "Young Americans" on the air (fall, winter, spring, or even next summer) will give your network the chance to branch out to those for whom [sic] you have not yet touched. Please consider our request to save the unique and inspirational "Young Americans."[13]

The title of the series and its obsessions with masculinity indicate that the concerns of the nineteenth-century magazines for exploring boyhood and its connections to national citizenship have not entirely disappeared from twenty-first-century serializations. At the same time, the issues addressed explicitly by the series (homosexuality within a homosocial educational environment and incest brought on by cultural constructions of American fatherhood) demonstrate how these serializations construct boyhoods that reflect the desires of television producers to harness the ratings power of controversy while maintaining the interest and approval of a wide spectrum of viewers. The *Young Americans* does this by using New England, the boy-breeding ground explored in serializations by Jacob Abbott, Oliver Optic, and Thomas Bailey Aldrich, as a safely familiar setting to market the Americanness of Coca-Cola and the ostensibly gay-friendly nature of Warner Brothers' teen soaps.

In its serializations of citizenships, the show claims to explore new possibilities for American boyhood by depicting twenty-first-century responses to the old taboo against explicitly addressing the homoerotic possibilities of a homosocial setting, which are often implied but rarely named in prime-time network programming.[14] These possibilities are then contained by changing the boy–boy relationship into a cross-dressing girl–boy relationship. Similarly, the *Young Americans* proclaims its "twenty-first century-ness" and its need to hold on to a wide variety of viewers by approaching the current cultural taboo against incest and then retreating from it (the brother and sister uncover their relationship and curb its advance). This serialized forum names and presents possibilities for blurring the gender boundaries of citizenships (a careful performance can make an American girlhood an American boyhood) and then contains these androgynous serialized citizenships with story lines that uncover the ongoing power of gender to prevent the addition of new possibilities.

As evidenced in the *Young Americans*, scenes of serialization can occur outside of the print and paper world of the magazine, and these other sites of boyhood construction can vary the sorts of citizenships that are presented, depending on the power and intentions of the producers and sponsors. The Internet and other forms of technological entertainment have tended to extend the forms of periodical production and to substantially change reading behaviors. A variety of periodical arenas replace the magazine's function as a proliferator of boyhoods. An example of a semi-mainstream and popular boyhood citizenship can be found in MTV's *Jackass*, which became popular in the late 1990s and has inspired similar explorations of citizenship. The stars of this show, Johnny Knoxville and Bam Margera, reproduce the American boy adventure quest and configure the American boy not as a hero who confronts personal and national moral dilemmas, but as a "jackass," who disrupts the status quo of the adult world with exaggerated pranks. Some scenes of jackassdom from this regularly produced construction site of American boyhoods include boys marinating and barbecuing themselves and boys in the nude riding bicycles down a town's main street.[15] This successful construction site is not produced for boys by adult men, but for boys by other boys.[16] The success of the *Jackass* series suggests that both at the mainstream and the countercultural levels, boys are resisting the grand narratives being offered about them (in the help-for-boys manuals) by writing and visualizing alternate scenes of prank-based citizenship.[17] The corporate sponsorship then contains and disseminates these boyhoods as part of the grand narrative that "boys will be boys."

Internet websites, which change regularly, provide another periodical source for boys to explore citizenship possibilities. Not yet members of the workforce, but with access to computers, some young boys investigate alternate citizenships and boyhoods regularly by repeatedly visiting sites such as "The Trench Coat Mafia Website" that acquaint them with the parameters of such citizenships.[18] Some corporations, such as the Electronic Frontier Foundation, attempt to harness the knowledge of the Internet that excessive leisure time helps these boys to acquire by sponsoring "cracker" (like hacker but with highly developed code-cracking skills) contests to test the security of their websites. Interestingly, after discovering that most of the winners were under the age of sixteen, the companies changed the prizes of the contest from cars to cash.[19] These contests gave corporations a chance to replicate Huck's lighting out for the territory in a scene of controlled exploration. The boys are offered the chance to break the rules and to be rewarded for their outlaw talent. Although most of the cracker prize winners are boys, the term *cracker* is not specifically gendered in the way *jackass* is. The nongendered specificity of the term *cracker* opens the possibility for girls and boys to blur gender boundaries by taking on the nongendered subjectivity of cracker. The Internet-based forum for these contests also indicates that by using a name associated with the opposite gender, either a boy or a girl could uncover the potential of a blurred gender citizenship within the repetitious and simultaneously mutating world of the encrypted frontier.

In addition to the proliferating technological scenes that construct these boy-related but gender-blurring citizenships, independently published magazines also provide print forums for serializations. Like *Jackass*, but without corporate funding, these underground zines, which some boys read and write, give boys a chance to construct boyhoods for other boys. Most of the zines, which have limited numbers of printed editions, also have websites, which offer them slightly larger readerships. This is true of *ya'kuz'a*, a zine composed of partly handwritten and partly typed text, which covers independent music and the travel diaries of a young man.[20] The format and the content push against boundaries that conventionally define the meaningful, the publishable, and the marketable, and incredibly, these aspects of the periodical locate readers who find that the difficult-to-read format reflects citizenship possibilities that they too would like to explore.

Other zines that, unlike *ya'kuz'a*, do not have websites find wider readerships and technological outlets through archiving projects such as the Independent Publishers Resource Center, which has a website devoted to cataloging titles and interviewing publishers.[21] The space of the zines allows for expressions of citizenships that are not specifically gender bound and that have found no other organized outlet. This can be seen when the *IPRC Newsletter* discusses citizenship possibilities with Nicole Georges, publisher of a zine titled *Invincible Summer*, and asks whether publishing is a political act. She answers:

> In an abstract sort of way, yes. It's so different from what the majority of the people think possible. . . . It has nothing to do with money or fame. I didn't need anyone editing my work or doing it for me. People who know nothing about zines are amazed. We have our own world, communities, and connections. It is almost self-reliant. That seems political (2).

The act of publishing without the sponsorship of a large publishing house becomes for the authors of these zines the kind of "self-reliant" and independent act that Ralph Waldo Emerson claims should characterize the American citizen. Most of these zines are produced not by participants in mainstream culture but by those who embrace existing on the fringes of the fringe. This often means that the number of issues printed remains under five hundred and that the audience who reads the printed text is fairly limited. The cataloguers of this sort of subset serialized citizenship (groups like the IRPC) use web space to expand the reader base and to circulate the messages contained in the independent serializations. These uses of technologies provide venues for minutely differentiated interests that replace the nationally recognized uniforms and reading materials of the Boy Scout with other privatized manuals and accessories designed to be read and interpreted by fellow followers of the same interests. The "sameness" of the interests combined with the serialized manuals and accessories provide alternate kinds of homosocial citizenships that permit the boundaries of Americanness and boyhood to bend to admit other passionate and/or obsessed members into the "clubs" built around the sameness of interests.

Just as the shorts and the badges and the scarves allow Boy Scouts to be recognized as members, other kinds of replicable and readable uniforms have been established by images or written details published about members of other official and unofficial organizations. This is demonstrated in the "trench coat" uniform of the members of the Trench Coat Mafia, a youth counterculture organization that some have connected to the planners of the Columbine shooting.[22] Other accessories that mark participation in the late-twentieth-century serialized boyhoods include the emblematic jean jacket patches worn by fans of hard-core music and the "ironic" dress of the Indy rockers, with the "uniform" including high school gym shirts and empty backpacks covered with patches that only other fellow Indy rockers can interpret. An example of more regulated uniform can be seen in the highly particularized code of dress worn by punk rockers; this dress often includes some form of leather jacket, Doc Martens footwear, and a hyper-British (un-American) Sex Pistols look that has remained relatively static since 1977. This unorganized and unofficial but also relatively unchanging uniform signals membership and allegiance to a "punk" as opposed to a "scout" form of citizenship.[23] Gang accessories are even more organized and official; the bandanas and diamonds that are worn by members, in the absence of access to government and national organizations, signal and display the citizenship privileges of material goods and status, which the gang has helped the members gain.[24] The fact that these "uniforms" are not so uniform dislodges the kinds of boyhoods performed by their wearers from any sort of official analysis or reading, and this unofficial nature allows the wearers of the uniforms to shift and reinterpret their citizenship subjectivities to prevent outsiders from "reading" them.[25] These physical accessories are often accompanied, within the loose and constantly changing organizations, by other written serialized instructions for showcasing and enjoying affiliation with a group.

Some physical accessories of citizenship are recognizable, and responses to September 11, 2001, indicate this. Stickers and pieces of paper with United States flags printed on them were distributed or placed on cars, and T-shirts and other clothing items were also printed with flags. When these signs were worn or displayed (through coercion or by the choices of the individual citizens), they were read as gestures of patriotism, gestures designed to signal wholehearted support of the political administration or to deflect xenophobic suspicions about terrorism that were directed at citizens outside of the white middle class. Probably because flags and patriotic paraphernalia are so easily obtained, the Patriot Acts turn to less accessible signs to investigate potentially disruptive citizenships—library records, magazine subscriptions, and book purchases. This legislative surveillance of reading material suggests the power of serialized citizenships to reinforce dominant constructions of citizenship or to exert counterhegemonic pressure on national and regional citizenships.

While some serialized American boyhood citizenships have become so particularized that they are difficult for those without insights into the codes of serialization to read, nonfiction studies about the nature of American boyhood continue to strive to contain the sorts of blurred-gender citizenships that can be found in episodic shows like *Young Americans*, in cracker contests, in the hyper-stratified and accessorized audiences of underground zines, and in youth-organized and researched news blogs, which have emerged as significant challengers to the inaccuracies of corporate-owned and adult-produced news sources. As some of the best-selling texts published between 1999 and the present have demonstrated, boyhood has increasingly served as a convenient venue for locating the cultural problems of violence, drug abuse, and crime. As psychologists and social historians write treatises interpreting and diagnosing American boyhoods based on family histories (women not spending enough time with their sons) and gendered expressions of emotion (boys not being encouraged to speak or write about love, fear, and sadness), it continues to be important to examine how these treatises compare to sites of construction that invite possibilities for other forms of citizenship. Serialized boyhoods are, as I have contended throughout this study, among the powerful sites that call for such investigation. In the nineteenth century, serialized texts create textual boyhoods that intersect with and shape the reality of available citizenship possibilities in the United States. In the twentieth and twenty-first centuries, constantly shifting and potentially powerful serialized constructions of boyhood continue to be produced with technologies multiplying the possible permutations of these packaged boyhoods. These serialized construction sites offer boys ways to participate in the packaging of their own citizenships. The highly specific interests that the periodical scenes treat blur the lines of gender specificity so that the serialized citizenships are organized around text-based subjectivity "clubs" rather than around bounded and impermeable gender taxonomies. The periodicals of the nineteenth century and the serialization scenes of the twentieth offer records of available citizenships and indicate the extent to which adults intervened regularly in the production of periodical citizenships. Even as the serialized forms continue to mark the boundaries of American boyhoods, the constant shifts in these serialized citizenships suggest that the regularity and the possibilities for change inherent in the serialization process have blurred gender boundaries and have invited underrepresented citizens to use serialization to negotiate and package citizenship privileges and possibilities.

NOTES

1. This is in Round the Campfire, the message from the editor section of the magazine (21).

2. Franklin M. Reck's introduction to the *American Boy Magazine* suggests that one of the draws for this gender-specific magazine is the nonfiction texts about "real" American boys (viii).

3. R. Gordon Kelly's *Children's Periodicals of the United States* contains several useful appendices that catalogue the periodicals (alphabetically, by region). Here, I am drawing on the titles for boys given in the "Chronological Listing of Magazines" (557–60). The subtitle of the first edition of *Boys' Champion*, published in October of 1881, is *An Instructive and Entertaining Journal for Young America*. Titles of texts indicate that one of the main concerns of this magazine was working-class life in the cities: "Giles Evergreen; or Fresh from the Country" and "Captain Hal; or, The Rival Fire Companies." This magazine is full of large engravings of violent or supernatural scenes (men attacking each other with knives; skeletons riding horses).

4. Alice Denham's brief history and assessment appears in Kelly's *Children's Periodicals of the United States* (41–50).

5. The founders of *Forced Exposure* have formed a company that reviews and sells music and art. See www.forcedexposure.com.

6. Grenmore reviews both *Boys of New York* (53–57) and *Happy Days: A Paper for Young Americans* (187–90) in Kelly's *Children's Periodicals of the United States.* About *Boys of New York*, Grenmore writes: "To the boys who spent their days working in factories or scrounging for a living blacking boots, *Boys of New York*, with its comic and sensational stories and dramatic illustrations, provided some much needed escape. It also presented a view of the world that could leave them both hopeful and lighthearted. It assured them that through honesty, hard work, and daring they could rise in the world" (56).

7. American school stories in the 1880s focus on spending money, sports, and boys' "vices" such as smoking. *Jack Hall or The School Days of an American Boy* shows a boy negotiating the behaviors necessary to please the more experienced and wealthier boys of the town and his mother. In "How Jack Spent the Forenoon of Washington's Birthday," Jack rationalizes smoking "rattan" cigarettes by telling himself he will be honest with his mother about his new habit (1–28).

8. Roosevelt had these views of warfare: "the nation that has trained itself to a career of unwarlike and isolated ease is bound, in the end, to go down before other nations which have not lost the manly and adventurous qualities" (*Strenuous Life* 6).

9. I am thinking, of course, of Stephen Crane's poem:

A man said to the universe
"Sir, I exist!"
"However," replied the universe,
"The fact has not created in me
A sense of obligation."

10. *Boys' Life* 1 (March 1, 1911), 21–22. Denham also notes these aims in her brief overview (41).

11. The world of young adult literature is one through which adults have explored a variety of subject positions and citizenships available to youths. Karen Coats's *Looking Glasses and Neverlands: Lacan, Desire, and Subjectivity in Children's Literature* uses Lacanian and post-Lacanian theories to investigate the intricacies of subjectivity in children's and young adult literature.

12. See 198–202 of the section titled "Romancing the Stone" in which Kindlon and Thompson argue that at some levels it is "normal" for a boy who expresses his masculinity with exploitative sex to "leave many girl casualties in his wake" (201). Adolescent girls should not expect any better, they suggest.

13. See petition: www.petitiononline.com/SaveYA/petition.html.

14. The fact that *Young Americans* explores possibilities for gay and incestuous young adult citizenships while advertising Coca-Cola, a company that has consistently used American celebrations and patriotic emotions to sell its product, has not gone unnoticed by reviewers. Antonio Zerbisias of the *Toronto Star* writes, "with all those gorgeous boys, girls in drag and their beautiful teachers, it's really made for the gay crowd. I wonder if Coke and the other sponsors realize they have a homoerotic hit on their hands" (n. pag.).

15. Tom Freston, the MTV Networks chair, explains that he sees the show as an extension of skateboarding culture, which has "its own rules and ethos" (qtd. in Sally Beatty's "MTV Ratings Soar"). The use of these alternate rules to gain economic success suggests that some boyhoods if serialized allow the boys themselves to turn a profit from alternate citizenships that would otherwise not be accepted or rewarded.

16. Of course adult sponsors backed the show, but the pranksters themselves conceived the initial idea and the first episodes. Bam Margera has also had considerable success producing and selling his own skate videos, which showcase his dangerous stunts.

17. During the nineteenth century, homemade magazines and newspapers might have served as a similar kind of space for working out alternate citizenships.

18. This elaborate site contains links to "how to" manuals for building bombs, and it catalogues news reports and student accounts of the Littleton, Colorado, shooting. See www.everwonder.com/david/Rebldomakr/.

19. For a history of "cracker" contests and the Electronic Frontier Foundation, an organization concerned with revealing the weaknesses of encryptions, see www.eff.org/descraker/.

20. See *yak'uz'a*'s website at www.yakuzamag.com. A description of a similar zine can be found at *halana*'s site: www.halana.com.

21. See the Independent Publishing Resource Center's site at www.iprc.org/. See also the "Zine Resource" site at www.zinebook.com/main.html and "A Reader's Guide to the Underground Press" at www.undergroundpress.org.

22. The nature of the "Trench Coat Mafia" has been difficult for adult assessors to pin down. In an article published the day after the shooting, the *Detroit News* attempts to describe and interpret the Mafia in the following way: "trench coats serve as a symbol for everything from Hitler and the Nazis to mass murder to suicidal fantasies. Some of the Columbine group wore Nazi crosses. . . . Under the coats, they dressed in black, from head to toe—military berets, T-shirts, jeans, combat boots. Red shoelaces and the occasional Confederate flag patch" (detnews.com/1999/nation/).

23. For images and discussion of these subsets of music see "Insound" at www.insound.com. See also "Indy Unleashed" at members.aol.com/vlorbik/tenpage/indy.html and "Ancient Punk Rock History" at www.nstop.com/paloma/history.html.

24. I want to point out that my readings of these uniforms are outsider readings, and that because of the shifting nature of terms assigned to groups and the accessories themselves, my records of the details of dress are not the final word on the subject. I want to demonstrate here that the citizenship possibilities made available in print, music, film, or on the Internet are replicable and somewhat readable, even as they shift. Some of the anecdotal information about independent rock and the music subsets has been gleaned from two of my brothers who publish a music review zine titled *A = 1/f2* (Amplitude equals one over the frequency squared), which is devoted to "the exploration of noise, free jazz, independent rock, and lo-fi" (*IPRC Newsletter* 3).

25. A young adult might come home from an afternoon of work at Kinkos and exchange the required blue vest associated with that corporation for an old Sunoco service station shirt, embroidered with a name that is not his own, which will be the

leisure time uniform he wears for his evening activities. In 2003, I taught a student who wore a Dunkin' Donuts uniform one day and a U.S. Postal Service shirt the next. These are accessories of youth citizenship and commentaries on citizenships available to adults, but they are so specific and stratified that their precise meanings are difficult to decode.

Works Cited

Abbott, Jacob. "The Adventures of a Traveller." *The Boys' and Girls' Magazine* 1 (1843): 78–80.

———. "The Bee Hive." From *Rollo's Experiments. Youth's Companion* 13.42 (Feb. 28, 1840): 165–66.

———. *Caleb in the Country*. London: T. Allman, 1839.

———. *Caleb in Town*. London: T. Allman, 1840.

———. "The Contrary Boy." From *Caleb in Town. Youth's Companion* 13.2 (July 26, 1839): 41–42.

———. *Jonas a Judge*. New York: T. Y. Crowell, [1840?].

———. *Jonas on a Farm in Summer*. New York: T. Y. Crowell, [1840?].

———. *Jonas on a Farm in Winter*. New York: T. Y. Crowell, [1840?].

———. *Jonas's Stories: Related to Rollo and Lucy*. New York: T. Y. Crowell, [1840?].

———. *Marco Paul's Travels and Adventures in the Pursuit of Knowledge*. Boston: T. H. Carter, 1845.

———. "Possessions." From *Jonas a Judge. Youth's Companion* 14.30 (1840): 117–18.

———. *Rollo at School*. Boston: Weeks, Jordan, and Company, 1839.

———. *Rollo's Experiments*. New York: Sheldon, 1867.

Adams, Grace, and Edward Hunter. *The Mad Forties*. New York: Harper, 1942.

Adams, Henry. *The Education of Henry Adams*. 1906. Reprint. Boston: Houghton Mifflin, 1961.

Adams, William Taylor. *All Aboard or Life on the Lake: A Sequel to the Boat Club*. Boston: Lee and Shepard, 1855.

———. *The Boat Club; or, The Bunkers of Rippleton. A Tale for Boys*. Boston: Brown, Bazin, and Company [1854], 1855.

———. *In Doors and Out*. Boston: Lee and Shepard, [1858?].

———. *Little by Little; or The Cruise of the Flyaway. A Story for Young Folks*. Cincinnati, Ohio: Rickey, Mallory, 1861.

———. *Now or Never; or The Adventures of Bobby Bright. A Story for Young Folks*. Boston: Lee and Shepard, 1856.

———. *Oliver Optic's Magazine* (Sept. 1875).
———. *Poor and Proud; or, The Fortunes of Katy Redburn. A Story for Young Folks.* Boston: Lee and Shepard, 1858.
———. *Try Again or the Trials and Triumphs of Harry West. A Story for Young Folks.* New York: Hurst, 1857.
Alcott, Louisa May. *Eight Cousins.* 1875. Reprint. Garden City, NY: Doubleday, 1958.
———. *Jack and Jill.* 1880.
———. *Little Women: or, Meg, Jo, Beth, and Amy.* 2 vols. 1868–1869.
Aldrich, Thomas Bailey. *The Story of a Bad Boy. Our Young Folks* 5 (1869).
———. *The Story of a Bad Boy.* 1907 ed. *The Works of Thomas Bailey Aldrich.* Vol. 7. New York: AMS, 1970.
Alryyes, Ala. *Original Subjects: The Child, the Novel, and the Nation.* Cambridge, MA: Harvard University Press, 2001.
Althusser, Louis. "Ideology and Ideological State Apparatuses." *Lenin and Philosophy.* 127–86.
———. *Lenin and Philosophy and Other Essays.* Trans. Ben Brewster. London: New Left, 1971.
———. *Philosophy and the Spontaneous Philosophy of the Scientists and Other Essays.* Trans. Ben Brewster, James H. Kavanaugh, Thomas E. Lewis, Grahame Lock, and Warren Montag. London: Verso, 1990.
———. "Theory, Theoretical Practice and Theoretical Formation: Ideology and Ideological Struggle." *Philosophy and the Spontaneous Philosophy of the Scientists and Other Essays.* 1–42.
Anbinder, Tyler. *Nativism and Slavery: The Northern Know-Nothings and the Politics of the 1850s.* New York: Oxford University Press, 1992.
"Ancient Punk Rock History." May 7, 2001. www.nonstop.com/paloma/history.html.
Arac, Jonathan. "Nationalism, Hypercanonization, and *Huckleberry Finn.*" *National Identities and Post-Americanist Narratives.* Ed. Donald E. Pease, 14–33. Durham, NC: Duke, 1994.
Ariès, Philipe. *Centuries of Childhood: A Social History of Family Life.* New York: Knopf, 1962.
Armstrong, Nancy. *Desire and Domestic Fiction.* New York: Oxford University Press, 1989.
Arnett, Faye, and Jill Bellas. *The Son also Rises: Stories of Parents Getting Boys to Adulthood.* Baltimore: America House, 2001.
Avery, Harold. "Mobsley's Mohicans: A Tale of Two Terms." *Boy's Own Annual* 20 (1897–1898): 54–55 and following.
"The Bad Scholar Who Made Himself a Good One." *Youth's Companion* 13.38 (Jan. 31, 1840): 150–51.
Badger, Tony. "The Rise and Fall of Biracial Politics in the South." *The Southern State of Mind.* Ed. Jan Nordby Gretlund, 23–35. Columbia: University of South Carolina Press, 1999.
Barnard, Charles. "The Children's Exhibition." *St. Nicholas* 13 (Oct. 1886): 916–24.
Barton, George S., ed. "Round the Campfire." *Boys' Life* 1.1 (March 11, 1911): 21.

Baym, Nina. *Woman's Fiction: A Guide to Novels by and about Women in America 1820–1870*. 2nd ed. Urbana: University of Illinois Press, 1993.

Beatty, Sally. "MTV Ratings Soar Off Gross Humor, Sex—and That's Just the Tame Stuff." *Wall Street Journal*, April 20, 2001. Fwd by Stern MD. Online posting, April 20, 2001. Google. May 6, 2001. www.janda.org/b20/News%20articles/MTVratings.htm.

Bederman, Gail. *Manliness and Civilization: A Cultural History of Gender and Race in the United States, 1880–1917*. Chicago: University of Chicago Press, 1995.

Beecher, Catherine, and Harriet Beecher Stowe. *American Woman's Home*. 1869. Reprint. New Brunswick, NJ: Rutgers University Press, 1996.

Beecher, Henry Ward. *Twelve Lectures to Young Men on Very Important Subjects*. New York: D. Appleton, 1893.

Berger, Maurice, et al. *Constructing Masculinity*. New York: Routledge, 1995.

Berlant, Lauren. *The Queen of America Goes to Washington City: Essays on Sex and Citizenship*. Durham, NC: Duke University Press, 1997.

Berry, Jani L. "Discipline and (Dis)order: Paternal Socialization in Jacob Abbott's Rollo Books." *Children's Literature Association Quarterly* 18.3 (1993): 100–5.

Biber, Katherine, Tom Sear, and Dave Trudinger, eds. *Playing the Man: New Approaches to Masculinity*. Annandale, NSW, Australia: Pluto, 1999.

Birch, Reginald. Illus. "Benevolent Boy." *St. Nicholas* 13 (Dec. 1885): 124.

Blewett, Mary H. "Manhood and the Market: The Politics of Gender and Class among the Textile Workers of Fall River, Massachusetts, 1870–1880." *Work Engendered: Toward a New History of American Labor*. Ed. Ava Baron, 92–113. Ithaca, NY: Cornell University Press, 1991.

Bordo, Susan. *The Male Body: A New Look at Men in Public and Private*. New York: Farrar, Straus & Giroux, 1999.

Bourdieu, Pierre. *Distinction: A Social Critique of the Judgement of Taste*. Trans. R. Nice. Cambridge, MA: Harvard University Press, 1984, 1987.

"The Boy Who Could Govern His Thoughts." *Youth's Companion* 13.37 (Jan. 24, 1840): 146.

Boynton, Henry Walcott. *Annals of American Bookselling, 1638–1850*. 1932. Reprint. New Castle, DE: Oaknoll Books, 1991.

Boys' Champion: An Instructive and Entertaining Journal for Young America. 1.1 (Oct. 1, 1881).

The Boys' Manual: Comprising a Summary View of the Studies, Accomplishments, and Principles of Conduct Best Suited for Promoting Respectability and Success in Life. New York: D. Appleton, 1837.

Briden, Earl F. "Kemble's 'Specialty' and the Pictorial Countertext of *Huckleberry Finn*." In *Adventures of Huckleberry Finn: A Case Study in Critical Controversy*. Ed. Gerald Graff and James Phelan, 383–406. New York: Bedford/St. Martin's, 1995.

Brodhead, Richard H. *Cultures of Letters: Scenes of Reading and Writing in Nineteenth-Century America*. Chicago: University of Chicago Press, 1993.

Brown, Gillian. *Domestic Individualism: Imagining Self in Nineteenth-Century America*. Berkeley: University of California Press, 1990.

Brown, John Mason. "Prigs Is Prigs." *Saturday Review* (Feb. 8, 1947): 20–22.

Butler, Judith. *Bodies That Matter: On the Discursive Limits of "Sex."* New York: Routledge, 1993.

———. *Gender Trouble: Feminism and the Subversion of Identity.* New York: Routledge, 1990.

Burgh. "Value of Spare Moments." *Young American's Magazine of Self-Improvement* (1847): 126.

Burnett, Frances Hodgson. *Little Lord Fauntleroy.* New York: The Century Co., 1886.

———. *Little Lord Fauntleroy.* New York: Charles Scribner's Sons, 1886.

———. *Little Lord Fauntleroy. St. Nicholas Magazine* 13 (Nov. 1885–Oct. 1886): 3–7; 82–92; 168–71; 252–57; 332–41; 408–16; 502–5; 564–70; 646–54; 734–38; 822–28; 884–90.

Burroughs, John. "British Fertility." *The Century Magazine* 28 (May–Oct. 1884): 42–49.

C., Bessie. "Letter-Box." *St. Nicholas* 13.2 (Sept. 1886): 877.

C., Clyde. "Letter-Box." *St. Nicholas* 13.1 (April 1886): 475.

Cadogan, Mary, and Patricia Craig. *You're a Brick, Angela!: A New Look at Girls' Fiction from 1839–1975.* London: Victor Gollancz, 1976.

Caldwell, Patricia. *The Puritan Conversion Narrative: The Beginnings of American Expression.* Cambridge: Cambridge University Press, 1983.

Cane, Aleta Feinsod, and Susan Alves, eds. *"The Only Efficient Instrument": American Women Writers and the Periodical, 1837–1916.* Iowa City: University of Iowa Press, 2001.

Carisford, John. "The Lost Express." *Boys' Life* 1.1 (March 11, 1911): 3–11.

Carnegie, Andrew. "Wealth." Rpt. in *The Industrial Revolution: Opposing Viewpoints.* Ed. William Dudley, 83–91. San Diego, CA: Greenhaven Press, 1998.

Carnes, Mark C., and Clyde Griffen. *Meanings for Manhood: Constructions of Masculinity in Victorian America.* Chicago: University of Chicago Press, 1990.

Carpenter, Humphrey, and Mari Prichard. *The Oxford Companion to Children's Literature.* Oxford: Oxford University Press, 1984.

Cary, Alice. "Plea for the Boys." *Our Young Folks* 3.12 (December 1867): 752–53.

Chamberlin, John Edgar. "The Foreign Elements in Our Population." *The Century Magazine* 28 (May–Oct. 1884): 761–70.

Channing, William Ellery. "Great Ideas Free to All Men." *Young American's Magazine of Self-Improvement* 1 (1847): 100–2.

Chapman, Mary, and Glenn Hendler, eds. *Sentimental Men: Masculinity and the Politics of Affect in American Culture.* Berkeley: University of California Press, 1999.

Cherny, Robert W. *American Politics in the Gilded Age.* Wheeling, IN: Harlan Davidson, 1997.

"The Cherries." *Youth's Companion* 13.20 (Sept. 27, 1839): 80.

Chodorow, Nancy. *Feminism and Psychoanalytic Theory.* New Haven, CT: Yale University Press, 1989.

———. *The Reproduction of Mothering: Psychoanalysis and the Sociology of Gender.* Berkeley: University of California Press, 1978.

Clark, Beverly Lyon. *Regendering the School Story: Sassy Sissies and Tattling Tomboys.* New York: Garland, 1996.

———, and Margaret R. Higonnet. *Girls, Boys, Books, Toys: Gender in Literature and Culture*. Baltimore: Johns Hopkins University Press, 1999.

Coats, Karen. *Looking Glasses and Neverlands: Lacan, Desire, and Subjectivity in Children's Literature*. Iowa City: University of Iowa Press, 2004.

Commons, John R. *Races and Immigrants in America*. New York: Augustus M. Kelly, 1967.

Connell, R. W. *Masculinities: Knowledge, Power, and Social Change*. Berkeley: University of California Press, 1995.

Cooper, James Fennimore. *The Last of the Mohicans*. 1826. Reprint. New York: Bantam, 1981.

Coultrap-McQuin, Susan. *Doing Literary Business: American Women in the Nineteenth Century*. Chapel Hill: University of North Carolina Press, 1990.

Crane, Stephen. *War Is Kind*. New York: Frederick A. Stokes, 1899.

"Dan Cohoon: *A = 1/f2*." *IPRC Newsletter* 2.1 (May 2001): 3.

Darling, Richard L. "Authors vs. Critics: Children's Books in the 1870's." *Publishers' Weekly* 192 (Oct. 16, 1967): 25–27.

Darwin, Charles. *On the Origin of Species by Means of Natural Selection*. 1859.

Davidson, Cathy N. *Revolution and the Word: The Rise of the Novel in America*. Oxford: Oxford University Press, 1986.

"Definition of Man." *Merry's Museum* 15.1 (Jan. 1848): 108.

Denning, Michael. *Mechanic Accents: Dime Novels and Working-Class Culture in America*. London: Verso, 1998.

Dick, Thomas. "Abridgement of the Hours of Business." *Young American's Magazine of Self-Improvement* 1 (1847): 122–24.

Diffley, Kathleen. "Home from the Theatre of War: The *Southern Magazine* and Recollections of the Civil War." *Periodical Literature in Nineteenth-Century America*. Eds. Kenneth M. Price and Susan Belasco Smith, 183–201. Charlottesville: University Press of Virginia, 1995.

Dizer, John T. "*Boys' Life*: The Real Beginnings." *Dime Novel Round-Up* 65.2 (1996): 39–48.

Donnegan, J. Abdon. "The Handiwork of Some Clever School-Boys." *St. Nicholas* 13 (May 1886): 547–51.

Donovan, Ellen Butler. "Reading for Profit *and* Pleasure: *Little Women* and *The Story of a Bad Boy*." *The Lion and the Unicorn* 18 (1994): 143–53.

Drotner, Kirsten. *English Children and Their Magazines, 1751–1945*. New Haven, CT: Yale University Press, 1988.

Dublin, Thomas. *Women at Work: The Transformation of Work and Community in Lowell, Massachusetts, 1826–1860*. New York: Columbia University Press, 1979.

DuBois, Ellen, Mari Jo Buhle, Temma Kaplan, Gerda Lerner, and Carroll Smith-Berg. "Politics and Culture in Women's History: A Symposium." *Feminist Studies* 6 (Spring 1980): 26–64.

Dudley, William, ed. *The Industrial Revolution: Opposing Viewpoints*. San Diego, CA: Greenhaven, 1998.

"Dull Boys." *Youth's Companion* 13.38 (Jan. 31, 1840): 152.

Dyhouse, Carol. *Girls Growing Up in Late Victorian and Edwardian England*. London: Routledge and Kegan Paul, 1981.

Eager, George. *Round-the-World Joe. Our Young Folks* (1867–1868).

———. *Round-the-World Joe*: "Head Hunters, Pirates, and Cannibals." *Our Young Folks* 4.3 (March 1868): 153–61.

———. *Round-the-World Joe*: "Poetry, Nonsense, and Useful Knowledge." *Our Young Folks* 3.9 (November 1867): 641–50.

———. *Round-the-World Joe*: "Tender and Tough." *Our Young Folks* 4.6 (June 1868): 321–29.

Eagleton, Terry. *The Idea of Culture*. Oxford: Blackwell, 2000.

Edgar, J. G. "Cressy and Poictiers; or, The Story of The Black Prince's Page." *Beeton's Boy's Own Magazine* 2 (1889): B1–B19 and following.

Eggleston, Edward. "The Colonists at Home." *The Century Magazine* 29 (Nov. 1884–Apr. 1885): 873–92.

———. *Hoosier School-Boy*. 1883.

Electronic Frontier Foundation. "Cracking DES." May 7, 2001. www.eff.org/des cracker.

Emerson, Ralph Waldo. "Self Reliance." 1841. *Selected Essays*. New York: Penguin, 1982.

———. "The Young American." *The Collected Works of Ralph Waldo Emerson*. Ed. Alfred R. Ferguson, Robert E. Spiller, Introductions and Notes, 217–44. Cambridge, MA: Belknap, 1971.

F., Rosy, Daisy, and Pansy. "Letter-Box." *St. Nicholas* 13.2 (Oct. 1886): 954.

"The Factory Boy." *Youth's Companion* 13.35 (Jan. 10, 1840): 137.

Faludi, Susan. *Stiffed: The Betrayal of the American Man*. New York: Morrow, 1999.

Featherstone, Mike. "Global and Local Cultures." *Mapping the Futures: Local Cultures, Global Change*, 169–87. New York: Routledge, 1993.

Feldberg, Michael. *The Turbulent Era: Riot and Disorder in Jacksonian America*. New York: Oxford University Press, 1980.

Feltes, N. N. *Modes of Production of Victorian Novels*. Chicago: University of Chicago Press, 1986.

Fenn, G. Manville. "Nic Revel or, A White Slave's Adventures in the Alligator Land." *Boy's Own Annual* 20 (1897–1898): 52 and following.

Fiedler, Leslie. *Love and Death in the American Novel*. New York: Clarion, 1960.

Fishkin, Shelley Fisher. *Lighting Out for the Territory: Reflections on Mark Twain and American Culture*. New York: Oxford University Press, 1997.

"Five Million Boys Have One Thing to Say." *Boys' Life*. Flier Advertisement.

Foner, Philip S., ed. *The Factory Girls*. Urbana: University of Illinois Press, 1977.

Forced Exposure Website. May 7, 2001. www.forcedexposure.com.

Forrest, Frank. "In the Secret Service; or, The Young Counterfeiters of the West." *Boys of London and Boys of New York* 10.479 (1886): 6.

Foucault, Michel. *Discipline and Punish: The Birth of the Prison*. Trans. Alan Sheridan. New York: Vintage, 1977.

———. *History of Sexuality, Volume 1: An Introduction*. New York: Pantheon, 1978.

———. *The Order of Things*. New York: Vintage, 1970.

Gabler-Hover, Janet. "The North South Reconciliation Theme and the 'Shadow of the Negro' in *Century Illustrated Magazine*." *Periodical Literature in Nineteenth-Century America*. Eds. Kenneth M. Price and Susan Belasco Smith, 239–56. Charlottesville: University Press of Virginia, 1995.

Gilber, William Schwenk. *The Mikado*. London: Routledge, 1885.

Gilmore, David D. *Manhood in the Making*. New Haven, CT: Yale University Press, 1990.

Gladden, Washington. "Three Dangers." *Century Magazine* 28 (1884): 620–27.

Gleason, Gene. "Whatever Happened to Oliver Optic?" *Wilson Library Bulletin* 49 (May 1975): 647–50.

Gorn, Elliott J., ed. *The McGuffey Readers: Selections from the 1879 Edition*. Boston: Bedford/St. Martin's, 1998.

Gramsci, Antonio. *Selections from the Prison Notebooks*. Ed. and trans. Quintin Hoare and Geoffrey Nowell Smith. New York: International Publishers, 1971.

Grant, Robert. *Jack Hall, or the School Days of an American Boy*. Boston: Jordan Marsh, 1888.

Greenslet, Ferris. *American Men of Letters: Thomas Bailey Aldrich*. Boston: Houghton Mifflin, 1928.

Greenwood, James. "The Adventures of Reuben Davidger, Seventeen Years and Four Months a Captive among the Dyaks of Borneo." *Beeton's Boy's Own Magazine* 3 (1889): c1–c12 and following issues.

Gurian, Michael. *The Wonder of Boys: What Parents, Mentors, and Educators Can Do to Shape Adolescent Boys into Exceptional Men*. New York: Tarcher-Penguin Putnam, 1996.

H., Effie. "Letter-Box." *St. Nicholas* 13.1 (Jan. 1886): 235.

halana. May 7, 2001. www.halana.com.

Halberstam, Judith. *Female Masculinity*. Durham, NC: Duke University Press, 1998.

Hall, David D. *Cultures of Print: Essays in the History of the Book*. Amherst: University of Massachusetts Press, 1996.

Harvey, David. "From Space to Place and Back Again: Reflections on the Condition of Postmodernity." *Mapping the Futures: Local Cultures, Global Change*. Ed. Jon Bird, et al., 3–29. New York: Routledge, 1993.

Hayes, Isaac I. "Cast Away in the Cold: An Old Man's Story of a Young Man's Adventures." *Our Young Folks* (1867–1868) (monthly serialization).

Hemingway, Ernest. *Green Hills of Africa*. New York: Charles Scribner's Sons, 1935.

Henty, G. A. "Nothing Derogatory about Labour." Editor's Table. *Beeton's Boy's Own Magazine* 6 (1890): c203–c204.

———. "The Subject of Strikes." Editor's Table. *Beeton's Boy's Own Magazine* 6 (1890): c459–c460.

———. "White-Faced Dick: A Story of Pine-Tree Gulch." *Beeton's Boy's Own Magazine* 2 (1889): B20–B27 and following.

Higham, John. "From Boundlessness to Consolidation: The Transformation of American Culture, 1848–1860." William L. Clements Library. 1969. Reprinted in *The Bobbs-Merrill Reprint Series in American History*, No. H-414.

Hilkey, Judy. *Character Is Capital: Success Manuals and Manhood in Gilded Age America*. Raleigh: University of North Carolina Press, 1997.

Hill, Hamlin. "Huck Finn's Humor Today." In *One Hundred Years of Huckleberry Finn: The Boy, His Book, and American Culture*. Ed. Robert Sattelmeyer, 297–311. Columbia: University of Missouri Press, 1985.

Horlick, Allan Stanley. *Country Boys and Merchant Princes*. Lewisburg, PA: Bucknell, 1975.

Howells, William Dean. *The Rise of Silas Lapham. The Century Magazine* 30 (1885).
Hunt, Peter. *An Introduction to Children's Literature*. Oxford: Oxford University Press, 1994.
———, ed. *Children's Literature: An Illustrated History*. Oxford: Oxford University Press, 1995.
———. *International Companion Encyclopedia of Children's Literature*. London: Routledge, 1996.
"I did It to Please a Mother." *Youth's Companion* 13.36 (Jan. 17, 1840): 144.
"The Independent Publishing Resource Center." May 7, 2001. www.iprc.org/index.html.
"Indy Unleashed." May 7, 2001. members.aol.com/vlorbik/tenpage/indy.html.
"Insound." Insound Zinestand. May 7, 2001. www.insound.com.
Jackson, James, ed. *Boys of London and Boys of New York* 10.44 (June 26, 1886).
Jacobson, Marcia. *Being a Boy Again: Autobiography and the American Boy Book*. Tuscaloosa: University of Alabama Press, 1994.
James, Henry. *The Bostonians. Century Magazine* 30 (1885).
Jeffords, Susan. *The Remasculinization of America*. Bloomington: Indiana University Press, 1989.
Jones, Anne Goodwyn, and Susan V. Donaldson, eds. *Haunted Bodies: Gender and Southern Texts*. Charlottesville: University Press of Virginia, 1997.
Jones, Dolores Blythe, compiler. *An "Oliver Optic" Checklist*. Westport, CT: Greenwood, 1985.
Jordan, Alice. *From Rollo to Tom Sawyer*. Boston: The Horn Book, 1948.
Jordan, Winthrop. *White over Black: American Attitudes toward the Negro, 1550–1812*. Baltimore: Penguin, 1969.
K., Etta. "Letter-Box." *St. Nicholas* 13 (1886): 634.
Kaestle, Carl F., et al. *Literacy in the United States: Readers and Reading since 1880*. New Haven, CT: Yale University Press, 1991.
Kaplan, Amy. "Manifest Domesticity." *American Literature* 70.3 (1998): 581–606.
Kellogg, Elijah. "Good Old Times: or, Grandfather's Struggle for a Homestead." *Our Young Folks* (1867) (monthly serialization).
———. "White Boy Chief! or, The Terror of the North Platte." *Boys of London and Boys of New York* 10.479 (July 10, 1886): 5.
Kelly, R. Gordon. *Children's Periodicals of the United States*. Westport, CT: Greenwood, 1984.
———. *Mother Was a Lady: Self and Society in Selected American Children's Periodicals*. Westport, CT: Greenwood, 1974.
Kerber, Linda. *Toward an Intellectual History of Women*. Chapel Hill: University of Chapel Hill Press, 1997.
———. *Women of the Republic: Intellect and Ideology in Revolutionary America*. Chapel Hill: University of North Carolina Press, 1980.
Kidd, Kenneth. "Boyology in the Twentieth Century." *Children's Literature* 28 (2000): 44–72.
———. "Farming for Boys: Boyology and the Professionalization of Boy Work." *Children's Literature Association Quarterly* 20.4 (Winter 1995–1996): 148–54.
———. *Making American Boys: Boyology and the Feral Tale*. Minneapolis: University of Minnesota Press, 2004.

Kimmel, Michael. *Manhood in America: A Cultural History*. New York: Free Press, 1996.

Kindlon, Dan, and Michael Thompson. *Raising Cain: Protecting the Emotional Life of Boys*. New York: Ballantine, 1999.

Knight, Arthur Lee. "Dicky Beaumont; His Perils and Adventures." *Beeton's Boy's Own Magazine* 4 (1890): A305 and following.

Knoepflmacher, U. C. "A Strobe-Light History of the MLA (II)." *PMLA* 115.7 (Dec. 2000): 1728–29.

Kolodny, Annette. *The Lay of the Land: Metaphor as Experience and History in American Life and Letters*. Chapel Hill: University of North Carolina Press, 1975.

Kringle, George. "Putting This and That Together." *St. Nicholas* 13 (Dec. 1886): 121–23.

Krüsi, Hermann. *Pestalozzi: His Life, Work, and Influence*. Cincinnati, Ohio: Wilson, Hinkle, [c. 1875].

Laqueur, Thomas. *Making Sex: Body and Gender from the Greeks to Freud*. Cambridge: Harvard University Press, 1990.

Leland, Emily H. "How a Little Boy Camped Out." *St. Nicholas* 15 (1888): 950–51.

Leonard, Ira M., and Robert D. Parmet. *American Nativism, 1830–1860*. New York: Van Nostrand Reinhold, 1971.

Lerner, Gerda. *The Creation of Patriarchy*. New York: Oxford University Press, 1986.

———. "The Lady and the Mill Girl: Changes in the Status of Women in the Age of Jackson." *Midcontinent American Studies Journal* 10 (Spring 1969): 5–15.

———. *The Woman in American History*. Menlo Park, CA: Addison Wesley, 1971.

"The Light." *Youth's Companion* 14.41 (Feb. 19, 1841): 161.

Light, George. "Editorials." *Young American's Magazine of Self-Improvement* (1847).

Lippman, Walter. Selections from *Drift and Mastery*. New York: Mitchell Kennerley, 1914. Rpt. in *The Industrial Revolution: Opposing Viewpoints*. Ed. William Dudley, 122–31. San Diego: Greenhaven, 1998.

Lowe, Lisa. *Immigrant Acts: On Asian American Cultural Politics*. Durham, NC: Duke University Press, 1996.

Lyon, Betty L. "A History of Children's Secular Magazines Published in the United States from 1789–1899." Diss. Baltimore: Johns Hopkins, 1942.

Lyotard, Jean François. *The Postmodern Condition*. Trans. Geoffrey Bennington and Brian Massumi. Minneapolis: Minnesota University Press, 1984.

MacLeod, Anne Scott. *American Childhood: Essays on Children's Literature of the Nineteenth and Twentieth Centuries*. Athens: University of Georgia Press, 1994.

———. "Children's Literature in America: From the Puritan Beginnings to 1870." *Children's Literature: An Illustrated History*, 102–29.

Manly, Marline. "Pandy Ellis, The Prairie Prince; or, The Shadow Scout of Red River." *Boys of London and Boys of New York* 10.481 (July 24, 1886): 2.

Marten, James. *The Children's Civil War*. Chapel Hill: University of North Carolina Press, 1998.

———, ed. *Lessons of War: The Civil War in Children's Magazines*. Wilmington, DE: Scholarly Resources, 1999.

Marx, Leo. *The Machine in the Garden: Technology and the Pastoral Ideal in America*. Oxford: Oxford University Press, 1964.

"Maxims for Scouts." *Boys' Life* 1.1 (March 11, 1911): 18, 23.

May, Larry, and Robert A. Strikwerda, eds. *Rethinking Masculinity: Philosophical Explorations in Light of Feminism*. Lanham, MD: Rowman & Littlefield, 1992.

McGill, Meredith L. *American Literature and the Culture of Reprinting, 1834–1853*. Philadelphia: University of Pennsylvania Press, 2003.

McGurgan, David, ed. *yak'uz'a*. May 7, 2001. www.yakuzamag.com.

McLaren, Angus. *The Trials of Masculinity: Policing Sexual Boundaries, 1870–1930*. Chicago: University of Chicago Press, 1997.

Meg and Jo. "The Letter-Box." *St. Nicholas* 13 (April 1886): 475.

Melville, Herman. "Paradise of Bachelors and the Tartarus of Maids." *Harper's* (1854). In *Billy Budd and Other* Stories, 261–86. New York: Penguin, 1986.

Meyers, Marvin. *The Jacksonian Persuasion: Politics and Belief*. Stanford: Stanford University Press, 1957.

Monroe, Will S. *History of the Pestalozzian Movement in the United States*. Syracuse: C. W. Bardeen, 1907. Facsimile. Ann Arbor, MI: University Microfilms, 1972.

Morrison, Toni. *Playing in the Dark: Whiteness and the Literary Imagination*. Cambridge, MA: Harvard University Press, 1992.

Mott, Frank Luther. *A History of American Magazines*. 5 vols. Cambridge: Harvard University Press, 1938–68.

Murray, Hugh. *The United States of America; Their History from the Earliest Period*. Edinburgh: Oliver and Boyd, 1844.

Musgrove, P. W. *From Brown to Bunter: The Life and Death of the School Story*. London: Routledge and Kegan Paul, 1985.

Myers, Mitzi. "Child's Play as Woman's Peace Work: Maria Edgeworth's 'The Cherry Orchard,' Historical Rebellion Narratives, and Contemporary Cultural Studies." *Girls, Boys, Books, Toys*. Ed. Beverly Lyon Clark and Margaret Higonnet, 25–39. Baltimore: Johns Hopkins University Press, 1999.

Nelson, Claudia. *Boys Will Be Girls: The Feminine Ethic and British Children's Fiction 1857–1917*. New Brunswick, NJ: Rutgers University Press, 1991.

———. *Invisible Men: Fatherhood in Victorian Periodicals, 1850–1911*. Athens: University of Georgia Press, 1995.

Nelson, Dana D. *National Manhood: Capitalist Citizenship and the Imagined Fraternity of White Men*. Durham, NC: Duke University Press, 1998.

New England and Her Institutions. Boston: John Allen, 1835.

"New Year's Gift. A Weekly Paper for Youth." 13.30 (Dec. 6, 1839): 120.

"Nicole Georges: *Invincible Summer*." *IPRC Newsletter* 2.1 (May 2001): 2.

Nodelman, Perry, ed. *Touchstones: Reflections on the Best in Children's Literature*. 3 vols. West Lafayette, IN: Children's Literature Association, 1985–1989.

Norris, Cecil Marryat. "Never Say Die." *Beeton's Boy's Own Magazine* 4 (1890): A177 and following.

"Notes on the Mechanic Apprentices Library Association." *Young American's Magazine of Self-Improvement* 1 (1847): 136.

Oates, Stephen B. *The Approaching Fury: Voices of the Storm, 1820–1861*. New York: HarperCollins, 1997.

"The Only Son." *Youth's Companion* 13.2 (Aug. 2, 1839): 45–46.

Page, Thomas Nelson. *Two Little Confederates. St. Nicholas* 15 (1888): 483–90 and following issues.

Petition to Save "Young Americans." April 12, 2001. www.petitiononline.com/SaveYA/petition.html.

Phillips, Angela. *The Trouble with Boys: A Wise and Sympathetic Guide to the Risky Business of Raising Sons*. New York: Harper Collins, 1994.

Phillips, Wendell. "Abolition Reasons for Disunion." *Young American's Magazine of Self-Improvement* 1 (1847): 113–20.

"Piety in a Wife." *Youth's Companion* 14.41 (Feb. 19, 1841): 162.

Pollack, William. *Real Boys: Rescuing Our Sons from the Myths of Boyhood*. New York: Random House, 1998.

Porter, Gene Stratton. *Freckles*. 1904.

———. *Girl of the Limberlost*. 1909.

Pratt, Mary Louise. *Imperial Eyes: Travel Writing and Transculturation*. London: Routledge, 1992.

Price, Kenneth M., and Susan Belasco Smith. *Periodical Literature in Nineteenth-Century America*. Charlottesville: University Press of Virginia, 1995.

"The Proud Boy." *Youth's Companion* 13.3 (May 31, 1839): 10.

Pugh, David G. *Sons of Liberty: The Masculine Mind in Nineteenth-Century America*. Westport, CT: Greenwood, 1983.

R., Harvey. "Letter-Box." *St. Nicholas* 14 (May 1887): 555.

R. C., Mary. "Letter-Box." *St. Nicholas* 13.1 (Jan. 1886): 235.

Rahn, Suzanne. *Rediscoveries in Children's Literature*. New York: Garland, 1995.

"A Reader's Guide to the Underground Press." May 7, 2001. www.undergroundpress.org.

Reck, Franklin M. *The American Boy Anthology*. New York: Thomas Y. Crowell, 1951.

Reed, David. *The Popular Magazine in Britain and the United States, 1880–1960*. Toronto: University of Toronto Press, 1997.

Roediger, David. *Towards the Abolition of Whiteness*. New York: Verso, 1994.

———. *The Wages of Whiteness: Race and the Making of the American Working Class*. New York: Verso, 1991.

Rogin, Michael Paul. *Fathers and Children: Andrew Jackson and the Subjugation of the American Indian*. New York: Knopf, 1975.

Roosevelt, Theodore. *The Strenuous Life: Essays and Addresses*. 1899. Reprint. New York: Century, 1903.

Rotundo, E. Anthony. *American Manhood: Transformations in Masculinity from the Revolution to the Modern Era*. New York: Basic, 1993.

Rowe, Chip. "Zine Resource." May 7, 2001. www.zinebook.com/main.html.

Ryan, Mary P. *The Cradle of the Middle Class: The Family in Oneida County, New York 1790–1865*. Cambridge: Cambridge University Press, 1981.

———. *The Empire of the Mother: American Writing about Domesticity, 1830–1860*. New York: Haworth Press, 1982.

Ryan, Susan M. "Charity Begins at Home: Stowe's Antislavery Novels and the Forms of Benevolent Citizenship." *American Literature* 72.4 (Dec. 2000): 751–82.

Savran, David. *Taking It Like a Man: White Masculinity, Masochism, and Contemporary American Culture*. Princeton, NJ: Princeton University Press, 1998.
Schlesinger, Arthur M. *The Age of Jackson*. Boston: Little, Brown, 1953.
Sedgwick [Catharine Maria?]. "Learning. What Is Education?" *Youth's Companion* 13.35 (Jan. 10, 1840): 137.
Sedgwick, Eve Kosofsky. *Between Men: English Literature and Male Homosocial Desire*. New York: Columbia University Press, 1985.
———. *Tendencies*. Durham, NC: Duke University Press, 1993.
———. *Epistemology of the Closet*. Berkeley: University of California Press, 1990.
Selden, Bernice. *The Mill Girls*. New York: Atheneum, 1983.
Shattock, Joanne, and Michael Wolff. *The Victorian Periodical Press: Samplings and Soundings*. Leicester and Toronto: Leicester University Press and University of Toronto Press, 1982.
Shavit, Zohar. *Poetics of Children's Literature*. Athens: University of Georgia Press, 1986.
Showalter, Elaine. *A Literature of Their Own*. Princeton, NJ: Princeton University Press, 1977.
Silber, Nina. *The Romance of Reunion: Northerners and the South, 1865–1900*. Chapel Hill: University of North Carolina Press, 1993.
Silverman, Kaja. *Male Subjectivity at the Margins*. New York: Routledge, 1992.
Smalley, Eugene V. "New Orleans Exposition." *Century Magazine* 30.1 (May 1885): 3–14.
Smith, Henry Nash. *Virgin Land: The American West as Symbol and Myth*. Cambridge: Harvard University Press, 1950.
———, and W. M. Gibson, eds. *Mark Twain-Howells Letters*. 2 Vols. Cambridge, MA: Harvard University Press, 1960.
Smith, Roger M. *Civic Ideals: Conflicting Visions of Citizenship in U.S. History*. New Haven, CT: Yale University Press, 1997.
Smith-Rosenberg, Carroll. *Disorderly Conduct: Visions of Gender in Victorian America*. New York: Oxford University Press, 1985.
Sommers, Christina Hoff. *The War against Boys: How Misguided Feminism is Harming Our Young Men*. New York: Simon & Schuster, 2000.
Spencer, Herbert. *System of Synthetic Philosophy*. 9 Vols. 1862–1893.
Spilka, Mark. "Victorian Keys to the Early Hemingway: Part II—Fauntleroy and Finn." 10: 1–2 (1983): 289–310.
Sprague, William C., ed. *American Boy Magazine*. 1899–1941.
Stalcup, Brenda. *Reconstruction: Opposing Viewpoints*. San Diego: Greenhaven, 1995.
"Stealing Pears." *Youth's Companion* 13.15 (Aug. 24, 1839): 59.
Steinbrink, Jeffrey. "Who Wrote *Huckleberry Finn*? Mark Twain's Control of the Early Manuscript." *One Hundred Years of Huckleberry Finn*, 85–105. Columbia: University of Missouri Press, 1985.
Stephens, John, ed. *Ways of Being Male: Representing Masculinities in Children's Literature and Film*. New York: Routledge, 2002.
Stephenson, George M. *A History of American Immigration: 1820–1924*. Boston: Ginn, 1926.
Stevens, D. W. "The Swamp Doctor or the Man Witch." *Boys of London and Boys of New York* 10.477 (June 26, 1886).

Stone, Albert E. *The Innocent Eye: Childhood in Mark Twain's Imagination*. New York: Archon Books, 1970.

"A Story for Boys." *Youth's Companion* 13.40 (Feb. 14, 1840): 159–60.

Streeby, Shelley. *American Sensations: Class, Empire, and the Production of Popular Culture*. Berkeley: University of California Press, 2002.

Sumner, William Graham. "The Absurd Effort to Make the World Over." *Forum* (March 1894). Rpt. in *The Industrial Revolution: Opposing Viewpoints*. Ed. William Dudley, 100–10. San Diego: Greenhaven, 1998.

Sutherland, John. *Stanford Companion to Victorian Fiction*. Stanford, CA: Stanford University Press, 1989.

Thomas, Calvin. *Male Matters: Masculinity, Anxiety, and the Male Body on the Line*. Urbana : University of Illinois Press, 1996.

Thwaite, Ann. *Waiting for the Party*. Boston: David R. Godine, 1991.

Tompkins, Jane. *Sensational Designs*. New York: Oxford University Press, 1985.

" 'Trench Coat Mafia' Not Liked by Students." *Detroit News Wire Service*. April 21, 1999. May 7, 2001. www.detnews.com/1999/nation/9904/21/04210219.htm.

"Trench Coat Mafia Website." May 7, 2001. www.everwonder.com/david/Rebldomakr.

Trowbridge, John Townsend. *The Adventures of Jack Hazard. Our Young Folks* 4 (1868).

———. *Half-Hours with Father Brighthopes. Our Young Folks* (1865) and following issues.

———. *My Own Story*. Boston: Houghton Mifflin, 1903.

———. "The Turning of the Leaf." *Our Young Folks* 1.6 (June 1865) 398–401.

Tucher, Andie. *Froth and Scum: Truth, Beauty, Goodness, and the Ax Murder in America's First Mass Medium*. Chapel Hill: University of North Carolina Press, 1994.

Turner, Victor. *Dramas, Fields and Metaphors: Symbolic Action in Human Society*. Ithaca, NY: Cornell University Press, 1974.

Twain, Mark. "An Adventure of Huckleberry Finn: With an Account of the Famous Granderford-Sheperdson Feud." *Century Magazine* 29.2 (1884–1885): 268–78.

———. *Adventures of Huckleberry Finn*. 1885. New York: Bedford, 1995.

———. *A Connecticut Yankee in King Arthur's Court*. 1889. Mark Twain Library Text. Berkeley: University of California Press, 1983.

———. "Jim's Investments and King Sollermun." *Century Magazine* 29.2 (1884–1885): 456–58.

———. *The Prince and the Pauper*. 1882.

———. *Pudd'nhead Wilson*. 1894. New York: Penguin, 1986.

———. "Royalty on the Mississippi: As Chronicled by Huckleberry Finn." *Century Magazine* 29.2 (1884–1885): 544–67.

Vann, J. Don, and Rosemary T. VanArsdel, eds. *Victorian Periodicals: A Guide to Research*. New York: MLA, 1978.

———. *Victorian Periodicals and Victorian Society*. Toronto: University of Toronto Press, 1994.

Virgil. *The Georgics, or the Art of Husbandry*. In *The Works of Virgil*, Vol. I. Trans. John Augustine Wilstach. Boston: Houghton Mifflin, 1884.

"Wade-Davis Bill." Excerpted in *Reconstruction: Opposing Viewpoints*. Ed. Brenda Stalcup. San Diego: Greenhaven, 1995.

Wadsworth, Sarah A. "Louisa May Alcott, William T. Adams, and the Rise of Gender-Specific Series Books." *Lion and the Unicorn* 25.1 (2001): 17–46.

Warner Brothers. *Young Americans*. Television Series. Summer 2000.

"Washington Loved His Mother." *Youth's Companion* 13.36 (Jan. 17, 1840): 142–43.

Waterman, Nixon. *"Boy Wanted": A Book of Cheerful Counsel*. Chicago: Forrest and Company, 1909.

Welter, Barbara. "The Cult of True Womanhood." *Dimity Convictions: The American Woman in the Nineteenth Century*, 21–41. Athens: Ohio University Press, 1976.

Welter, Rush. *The Mind of America*. New York: Columbia University Press, 1975.

Wharton, Edith. *The House of Mirth*. 1905. New York: Simon & Schuster, 1986.

Wheelock, Albert H. "An Appreciation of the Boy Scout Movement." *Boys' Life* 1.1 (March 11, 1911): 37.

White, George, ed. *Young American's Magazine of Self-Improvement* 1 (1847–1848).

Whitman, Walt. "Song of Myself." *Leaves of Grass*. Brooklyn: [Rome Brothers], 1855.

Wicke, Jennifer. *Advertising Fictions: Literature, Advertisement, and Social Reading*. New York: Columbia University Press, 1988.

Widmer, Edward L. *Young America: The Flowering of Democracy in New York City*. New York: Oxford University Press, 1999.

Wiebe, Robert H. *The Search for Order, 1877–1920*. New York: Hill & Wang, 1967.

Wilentz, Sean. *Chants Democratic: New York City and the Rise of the American Working Class, 1788–1850*. New York: Oxford University Press, 1984.

Wilkinson, Rupert. *The Pursuit of American Character*. New York: Harper & Row, 1988.

Williams, Raymond. *Keywords: A Vocabulary of Culture and Society*. New York: Oxford University Press, 1985.

Wilson, Anna. "Little Lord Fauntleroy: The Darling of Mothers and the Abomination of a Generation." *American Literary History* 8.2 (1996): 232–58.

Woodward, C. Vann. "Post-Reconstruction Periods Compared, 1890s and 1990s." *The Southern State of Mind*, 212–23. Columbia: University of South Carolina Press, 1999.

"You Are Making Yourself." *Youth's Companion* 13.43 (March 6, 1840): 170–71.

"The Young Man Away from Home." *Youth's Companion* 13.49 (April 17, 1840): 195.

Zboray, Ronald J. *A Fictive People: Antebellum Economic Development and the American Reading Public*. New York: Oxford University Press, 1993.

———, and Mary Saracino Zboray. "Books, Reading, and the World of Goods in Antebellum New England." *American Quarterly* 48.4 (1996): 587–622.

Zerbisias, Antonia. "*Young Americans* Made for Gay Crowd." *Toronto Star*. Online posting. Aug. 30, 2000. Fwd. by David Migicovsky. Google. May 6, 2001. groups.google.com/groups?q=YOung+Bfdmigicovihavenonamec%40216.206.190.2'.

Zinn, Howard. *A People's History of the United States*. 1980. New York: Harper, 1995.

Index

About the Author

Lorinda B. Cohoon is an assistant professor of English at the University of Memphis, where she teaches undergraduate and graduate courses in children's literature.